A City and Its Universities

The University of North Carolina Press

Chapel Hill

A City and Its Universities

Public Policy in Chicago, 1892–1919

STEVEN J. DINER

© 1980 The University of North Carolina Press
All rights reserved
Manufactured in the United States of America
ISBN 0-8078-1409-1
Library of Congress Catalog Card Number 79-16834

Library of Congress Cataloging in Publication Data

Diner, Steven J   1944–
A city and its universities.

Bibliography: p.
Includes index.
1. Community and college—Illinois—Chicago.
2. Universities and colleges—Illinois—Chicago.
3. Social reformers—Illinois—Chicago.   4. Chicago—
Social policy.   I. Title.
LC238.3.C46D56   378.1′03′0977311   79-16834
ISBN 0-8078-1409-1

From "Chicago" in CHICAGO POEMS by
Carl Sandburg, copyright 1916 by Holt,
Rinehart and Winston, Inc.; copyright 1944 by
Carl Sandburg. Reprinted by permission of
Harcourt Brace Jovanovich, Inc.

To my parents,
who had everything to do with this book

Contents

Illustrations

Acknowledgments

It is always a pleasure to acknowledge scholarly debts. For their critical reading of the manuscript, I am deeply grateful to Richard Angelo, Burton J. Bledstein, Ronald M. Johnson, Barry D. Karl, Richard King, Rachel Marks, and George Stocking. I wish to express special thanks to Morris Janowitz, for both his scholarly criticism and his continuing encouragement.

The archivists of the Chicago Historical Society and especially of the Department of Special Collections of the University of Chicago Libraries assisted me above and beyond the call of duty on innumerable occasions. A grant from the College-Supported Research Committee of the Federal City College (now the University of the District of Columbia) enabled me to be free from teaching responsibilities to devote an entire summer to this project.

This book began as a doctoral dissertation at the University of Chicago under the direction of Arthur Mann. There is no way that I can adequately express my appreciation to him. His extraordinary skill as an editor and teacher of the historian's craft, his constant encouragement and support, and his friendship made difficult tasks much easier.

Hasia Diner has lived with Chicago professors longer than either of us cares to admit. It is a delight to acknowledge her scholarly assistance at every stage of this project and her loving support.

A City and Its Universities

1

The New Professors and Public Policy

FEW AMERICAN INSTITUTIONS have been the subject of as much controversy in the last two decades as the university. It has been attacked by some as a bulwark of the status quo and by others as an agent of revolutionary social change. Its faculty has been accused alternately of irrelevance to social problems and of corruption because of its involvement in practical affairs. Underneath the controversy is a common recognition that the American university is of paramount importance both to the maintenance of social order and to the achievement of social change.

American language still contains terms like "ivory tower" and "academic" to describe the university's supposed qualities of aloofness and impracticality, but these words no longer reflect the realities of higher education. The stereotypes of the "absent-minded professor" befuddled by practical matters may die hard, but one need only look at the recent political appointments of governors, mayors, and the president to confirm that prominence in academia today makes one as much a candidate for high office as success in industry, public administration, or the practice of law.

The political influence of academicians like Henry Kissinger, Daniel Moynihan, Arthur Schlesinger, Jr., Edward H. Levi, and so many others can obscure the more profound influence of the academic enterprise on contemporary American society. Through the sum total of their scholarly research and their teaching, professors perform a task that is essential to the maintenance of modern society. Our government bureaucracies, public school systems, corporations, religious denominations, charitable foundations, and other large-scale institutions depend upon expert knowledge, and on functionaries who know how to perform particular tasks within a large system. We need people who can compile and manipulate statistical data to help deliver extensive health, housing, and welfare services. Local, state, and federal governments rely upon people trained in public administration and accounting to manage their bureaucracies and develop their budgets. In charitable foundations large staffs determine how money should be spent and assess the results of money expended. Our criminal justice system employs trained social workers, probation officers, and psychologists. For better or for worse, most public functions today depend upon these kinds of large organizations and institutions, and they in turn rely upon universities.

Indeed, bureaucracy is so much a part of everyday life that it is hard to imagine a time (not very long ago) when our society left many activities to families and informal groups. Before the 1930s, whatever government did about housing, public health, or social welfare was done by state and local agencies that in retrospect seem so tiny as to appear insignificant. Moreover, it was not so much government that concerned itself with these matters as it was political machines in city wards, religious groups, ethnic associations, or small groups of private individuals. More often than not, people relied only upon themselves and their families for their survival and well-being.

Several historians recently have depicted late-nineteenth- and early-twentieth-century America as undergoing a process of bureaucratic rationalization resulting in an "organizational society." Influenced by sociological theories of modernization, they have argued that the decentralized and informal social organization of earlier American history yielded to a nationally integrated, centralized, and bureaucratic social organization during this period, the inevitable accompaniment of industrialization and the creation of a unified national economy. This interest in the evolution of a nationally integrated social order has stimulated studies of the rise of nationally oriented professions and also several important reassessments of the personnel, ideologies, and motives of the reform movements of the progressive era.[1] The two phenomena are closely linked.

Professional scholars and modern universities arose through the complex social transformations of American society in the late nineteenth century. The American university and the academic professions first appeared in the 1870s and more or less assumed their present form by the time of America's entry into World War I. Until the 1870s higher education in the United States consisted of small, denominational colleges that inculcated mental discipline and morality in students through a fixed curriculum of classical languages and philosophy. Professors were typically ministers, and as members of faculties that numbered four or five, they taught many different subjects within the standard curriculum. Professional schools of medicine, law, ministry, and technology did not require college education for admission and were usually independent of these liberal arts colleges. The advancement of knowledge was a private endeavor of leisured individuals. People with the means and inclinations pursued scholarly or scientific interests, but they rarely belonged to a college or professional school faculty.

In the half century following the Civil War, both the pursuit of knowledge and the higher education of young people were captured and vastly expanded by a new type, the professional scholar, operating primarily out of the new American university. The new academic professionals of the late nineteenth century, unlike the older college teachers, viewed knowledge as ever expanding and engaged actively in the production of new knowledge through research.[2]

In modern societies, people engaged in specialized callings have sought to protect and enhance their positions in society by developing the structures and ideology of professionalism. Professions or aspiring professions claim expert knowledge of a discrete subject and skills different from those of any other profession. This, they claim, enables them to do things that no one outside the profession can do. Professions create institutions to pass on their collective knowledge and skills to new members. They then seek systems of certification giving them exclusive right to determine who is and is not a member of the profession. Professionals justify this claim to exclusive control over some activity and to high income and status on the grounds that such an arrangement serves the common good.[3]

The new academic professionals of the late nineteenth century behaved like members of other aspiring professions. Social science scholars, for example, used national organizations and a professional ideology of academic freedom to protect themselves from outsiders who challenged their right to teach and write as they saw fit. The development of graduate study leading to the doctorate and of associations for accrediting colleges and universities gave the new academic professionals a large measure of control over certification and admission to the academic disciplines. Through journals and scholarly books, membership in national scholarly associations and informal networks, economists, biochemists, or historians anywhere in the United States (and to a lesser extent anywhere in the Western world) shared the results of their professional work and developed a common set of professional norms and values.[4]

The new professors likewise embraced the ideology of service in the general good as their justification for seeking society's rewards. The antebellum colleges claimed to serve society by educating a social and intellectual elite for American democracy, but they fared poorly amid the anti-elitist impulses of Jacksonian democracy. In much of Europe, universities supplied personnel for civil service and diplomatic posts. In early-nineteenth-century America, however, most Americans scorned expertise gained through study and touted practical experience instead. Indeed, the absence of a direct relationship between higher education and employment, especially in government, retarded the development of the American university.[5]

The new academic professionals who emerged after the Civil War aspired to much higher prestige, material rewards, and influence than that bestowed upon their predecessors in the antebellum college. Merle Curti aptly described the "secularization of scholarship" that produced the twentieth-century scholar:

> The old-time scholar, dressing and behaving differently from most folk, whom more worldly friends regarded with the same pity and admiration that medieval knights and merchants must have shown the monks, gave way to a new type who dressed, talked, and acted very much as a man of the world. Like other men of affairs, he struggled for prestige and success in a highly competitive profession, fought for a greater measure of economic security, and increasingly immersed himself in the main stream of events.[6]

From the inception of the American university, its presidents and faculties recognized that their prosperity depended upon fashioning for themselves a role that society would think useful and, preferably, indispensable.

The manner in which the new academicians and their universities would serve society was not self-evident. Professors put forward a variety of responses to the question, Of what use is the advancement and dissemination of knowledge? The varied responses were not mutually exclusive, and no one of them has yet eclipsed the others.

The oldest answer, and the most characteristically American, asserted the Jeffersonian creed that an educated citizenry made democracy work. For some this meant simply that institutions of higher education should educate liberally an elite leadership class. This, of course, was the major self-justification put forward by the defenders of the old-time college. Jacksonian America's unwillingness to defer to the leadership of a liberally educated elite and the consequent low status afforded colleges, however, made this view seem unpromising to the young academic professionals seeking public esteem and support.

Others argued that the university, as the pinnacle of a democratic nation's educational system, must move beyond the education of an elite and concern itself with the education of all persons in all subjects on all levels. From the perspective of the late nineteenth century, such a view suggested a more promising way of exerting national influence, one that many academicians worked vigorously to implement.

A third response insisted that simply by advancing the frontiers of knowledge the university served society, since all knowledge eventually served practical ends. Scholars were inherently comfortable with the idea that the advancement of knowledge was useful in its own right. Nevertheless, this view provided a shaky foundation upon which to seek support. It required that Americans support work they could not understand on the faith that one day it might contribute to social progress.

Like most successful professionals, academic people proved highly eclectic. Many professors at the new universities pursued knowledge for its own sake, while others offered education for various gainful occupations through professional schools of medicine, law, agriculture, teaching, business, social work, and the like. The enormous success of the American university in no small part stems from the manner in which it linked itself irrevocably to the nation's occupational structure. Academic professionals from the late nineteenth century on also provided expertise to solve various practical problems. Modern university faculties devote much of their time to research applied to national or local needs and to collaboration with people engaged in worldly pursuits.

Academic professionals could forge a practical role for themselves in still another way: they could advocate social change and try to advance worthy causes. Unpopular social advocacy and activism were fraught with dangers. Universities might withstand negative reverberations from the unpopular views and activities of individual faculty members, but they could not survive as permanent centers of extreme dissent. On the other hand, if the activism and advocacy of professors won support from those upon whom the university depended, it would greatly enhance the university's position. To win such support, professors had to forge a style of activism and advocacy consistent with their professional aspirations.

The formative years of the American university provided the new academic professionals with an extraordinary opportunity to advocate and work for the kind of social change that would enhance their own status and rewards and, thereby, stimulate the growth of academic professions and the university. This was accomplished in part by forging an alliance with those social groups whose support the university needed. American universities thrived in these years not only because they provided education for a democratic society and for specialized occupations, not only because they advanced knowledge of all kinds and contributed to the solution of specific problems, but also because they worked actively with political groups, business elites, and members of other professions to create a bureaucratically rationalized social order in which the influence of all of these groups was greatly enhanced.

The professionalization of academia occurred at the very moment that older professions such as law and medicine were expanding their training, specialization, and certification standards. About the same time, endeavors like social work, city planning, engineering, and public school teaching were also seeking the trappings of professionalism. University-based professional schools soon became the indispensable agency for establishing professional standards and transmitting professional expertise. Products of social change, the new professors became agents of change as well.

Recent writing on the progressive era has stressed the role of educated professionals in reform movements and public affairs. The first generation of academic professionals lived in a world that did not yet depend upon their expertise. However, their faith in knowledge as the key to social progress and their commitment to public service stimulated many of these new professors to set about actively remaking society along lines they believed most rational. The changes they sought grew out of their perspective as professionals and thus relied upon knowledge, training, and expertise as the cornerstones of public policy.

This study seeks to illustrate the process by which our modern mechanisms of public policy evolved, by focusing on the public activities of Chicago's first generation of academic professionals in the last decade of the nineteenth century and the first two decades of the twentieth century. These were years in which many of the nation's leaders became acutely aware of the problems and requirements of an urban society. Prior to World War I, social policy most directly affecting urban life was made almost entirely on the local level, and reform battles were fought city by city and state by state. Only in the war and postwar years and especially in the New Deal did the federal government become substantially involved with the social problems of American urban areas. When this involvement did occur, federal officials drew heavily upon the experience of cities and states. Therefore, any attempt to assess the impact of the new academic professionals on urban social policy must begin at the local level.

Of course, many areas of public policy that had nothing to do with urban problems were also greatly affected by the professionalization of academia and the rise of an organizational society. Modern agricultural policy, the management of the national economy through fiscal and monetary policy, the regulation of railroads and corporations, the conduct of foreign affairs, and the use of science and technology by the military also stem in large part from the emergence of the academic professions. This study is limited to those aspects of policy that grew out of urban reform.

Chicago is an ideal setting for a case study of professors' impact on urban policy in these years. The nation's second largest city, it attracted national attention for the magnitude of its social ills but also for the dynamism of its reform movement. Many of the nation's most important reform leaders lived in the city of Jane Addams, and what happened in Chicago had ramifications for the rest of the nation. The University of Chicago was founded at the very beginning of a period of nationwide reform. From the start, it was a full-fledged graduate university, emphasizing scholarly research and graduate teaching. The university brought to Chicago many of the nation's leading scholars and produced several major intellectual movements. The Chicago area also housed an older undergraduate college, Northwestern University, which became a modern professional university during this period, and two Catholic colleges—Loyola and DePaul universities—which were only minimally influenced by academic professionalization. These institutions demonstrate by contrast how important the role of the professors as academic professionals really was in motivating their interest in Chicago affairs.

Of course, because Chicago had such an active reform movement and such an extraordinary university, it was hardly a "typical" American city, whatever that might be. Its reform movement and the role of professors within that movement were shaped by the local milieu as well as by the larger forces of modernization and professionalization. Insofar as possible, this study compares the activities of Chicago's professors with those in other big cities. The particular circumstances varied from city to city, but professors in Baltimore, New York, Philadelphia, Boston, and Chicago acted in strikingly similar ways. In any case, local activities of the sort portrayed in the following pages had long-term consequences far beyond city and state boundaries.

This book provides no extended analysis of the internal development of professional structures and ideologies within the academic disciplines. Rather, I focus on the consequences of academic professionalization for urban social policy. The following chapters describe the behavior of academic professionals in Chicago and its consequences and explain that behavior as an outgrowth of the values and needs of new academic professionals. I seek neither to extol nor to condemn the subjects of this book. The new professors, like most people, thought and acted within a world view conditioned by their experiences. The society that they envisioned and worked to bring about was one that would depend heavily upon people like themselves. As such, their behavior was self-serving, although they did not see it that way. Today we recognize the deficiencies of bureaucratic centralization and look with greater tolerance at the informal and decentralized systems of an earlier day. The new professors honestly believed that their public service activities were selfless and in the general interest. I believe that was a reasonable self-perception for people with their experiences.

I have considered not only what professors did and why they did it, but how. Historians have paid insufficient attention to the informal networks and local institutions that enabled upper-strata reformers in a particular place to unite and press their demands on a variety of fronts. Professors in Chicago were a force with which to be reckoned because they united effectively with other groups. This study illuminates the manner in which Chicago's reform coalition functioned and the relationship of its various components to each other.

The main story begins with the arrival of Chicago's first academic professionals upon the opening of the University of Chicago in 1892 and ends in 1919 with the final defeat of political science professor Charles E. Merriam in his bid to become mayor. In these twenty-eight years, an extraordinary university and a pervasive and dynamic reform movement arose to demand control of a city whose machine politics, violence, and social ills attracted notice even from Americans who had come to expect such things in their cities. In these years, Chicago displayed in microcosm the raw confrontation between the old and the new social orders.

2

The Uses of the University

OCTOBER 1, 1892. In an uncompleted building on Chicago's south side, William Rainey Harper led a simple convocation and declared the University of Chicago officially open. The event had a touch of the bizarre and more than its share of pretension. After all, the infant institution appeared in a lusty and vulgar city noted for its size, its money, and its corruption, a city whose contribution to American letters and to science had heretofore been negligible, a city that proudly eschewed gentility. Yet within a decade the skeptical detractors of the new university—and there were plenty in the established intellectual circles of the East—had to concede that something of academic importance was happening in Chicago. Many of the nation's outstanding professional scholars now lived and worked in this crude boom town of the West, and through their new university they were reshaping American higher education. Within the same decade, Chicago witnessed the emergence of an aggressive coalition of highly educated and prosperous citizens demanding that city affairs and social problems be subjected to the best expertise and the most advanced scientific methods available. These two developments had everything to do with each other.

American higher education had changed dramatically in the preceding decades. The passage of the Morrill Act in 1862 granted federal aid to states for college instruction in agriculture and mechanics. In 1868 Cornell University challenged the curriculum of the traditional colleges by dedicating itself to Ezra Cornell's aspiration to "found an institution where any person can find instruction in any study." The following year, Charles W. Eliot was elected president of Harvard. Eliot led Harvard from a college to a university, encouraging graduate study and abandoning the traditional fixed classical curriculum in favor of a system of free student electives.

In 1876 Johns Hopkins University opened its doors, the first institution in the United States dedicated primarily to graduate study and advanced scientific research. The founding and success of Hopkins stimulated older institutions to offer graduate study. In 1881 Columbia began advanced academic work by establishing its faculty of political science. In the same year the University of Pennsylvania trustees approved formation of a faculty of philosophy for graduate studies and established a new school for business and finance named after Joseph Wharton, its original benefactor. Eight years later, Clark University became the first higher educational institution in the United States limited exclusively to graduate study and dedicated single-mindedly to the advancement of science. These and similar developments elsewhere demonstrated widespread interest in reform of higher education, but also great diversity with regard to the direction such reform should take. Cornell and Clark universities, for example, espoused such contradictory ideals that they shared only their revolt against the old liberal arts college.

Simultaneously, the emergence of national academic professions also threatened the hegemony of the antebellum college. Specialized professional associations, scholarly journals, and other forms of publication constituted outward evidence of profound change. The American Historical Association was begun in 1884, the American Economic Association in 1885, and the American Psychological Association in 1892, for example. In 1882, Herbert Baxter Adams began editing the Johns Hopkins University *Studies in Historical and Political Science*, followed quickly thereafter by Columbia University's *Political Science Quarterly*, Harvard's *Quarterly Journal of Economics*, and the American Economic Association's *Publications* in 1886. G. Stanley Hall's *American Journal of Psychology* appeared the next year, the *American Anthropologist* the year after that, and the *Annals of the American Academy of Political and Social Science* published by the University of Pennsylvania in 1890.

It was still unclear exactly where all of these developments would lead when the University of Chicago opened in 1892, but there was no longer any doubt that industrial society was radically altering the pursuit and dissemination of knowledge. Industrialization allowed successful capitalists to amass great personal fortunes, and those huge surpluses of wealth could endow the new universities on a scale hitherto unknown. Industrialization demanded people with new kinds of

knowledge or skills—mechanical skill to build better railroads or agricultural machines, chemical knowledge to refine petroleum, economic
knowledge to determine the proper treatment of industrial workers. In
1870 everyone did not agree that colleges or universities constituted the
best potential vehicles for providing the education and training needed
by an industrial society, but a strong case could be made for them, as
Senator Morrill had proved. Furthermore, dramatic improvements in
transportation and communications technology made nationally
oriented academic professions feasible. Railroads could carry people
and correspondence quickly, and the telegraph and other communications advances enabled people throughout the country engaged in a particular academic pursuit to remain in touch with each other.

These developments constituted necessary but not sufficient causes
for the educational ferment of the postwar decades. The modern university and the academic professions arose because advocates of a new
kind of higher learning sold their ideas to persons of wealth, social prestige, or political influence. The higher education reformers of the late
nineteenth century understood that the failures of the antebellum college stemmed in large measure from its reputation as elitist, aloof, and
detached from practical affairs in a period of expanding democratic
ideology. Whatever their version of reform, university advocates argued
for it on the grounds of its usefulness to society. Those who were most
convincing built the most successful institutions.

Cornell University and land grant colleges in western states like the
University of Michigan vied for support by offering practical courses
in agriculture, mechanics, and the like without imposing rigorous
academic prerequisites to study. However, the early experience of Johns
Hopkins University demonstrated that the elitist Germanic conception
of the university as a center of advanced study and scientific research
could also be reconciled with the utilitarian imperative facing American
university advocates in the late nineteenth century. Daniel C. Gilman,
the founding president of Johns Hopkins, originally toyed with the idea
of limiting the new institution to graduate study. He was dissuaded
from this course by community criticism and by trustees who warned of
the danger of public alienation from so elitist an institution.[1]

Gilman understood the importance of fashioning a public service
role for his new university to guarantee the financial support that would
allow it to foster scientific research and advanced study. In the late
1870s and the 1880s, Gilman organized the Baltimore Charity Organization Society and arranged for lectures on charity methods at the university. He worked actively to reform Baltimore's public schools, and

the university offered its first courses for public school techers only a few years after it opened. Hopkins also offered extension courses for railroad workers and others who would not usually receive advanced formal education. Members of the Hopkins faculty served on city and state commissions and undertook research on practical problems such as the purity of Baltimore's water supply. Faculty at Hopkins's pioneer medical school, which revolutionized medical education in America, exhibited deep interest in social reform from the start; indeed, a recent history asserts that the opening of the Hopkins Medical School "marks the real beginning of the age of social medical reform in America."[2]

Gilman believed deeply that the advancement of knowledge in and of itself held out prospects of solving society's problems and establishing a more humane, efficient, and democratic social order. However, he also marshaled the resources of the university and its faculty to the task of providing concrete services. This service orientation in no small measure accounted for the early success of Johns Hopkins. President Eliot at Harvard and many of the young faculty in the vanguard of the movement for graduate study and research elsewhere in the 1880s acted similarly.

Of the various institutions of the 1880s with pretensions to university stature, only Clark University eschewed any extension and service functions in favor of pure scholarship and graduate teaching. Lacking even an undergraduate college, Clark University depended almost entirely on its temperamental founder and benefactor, Jonas Clark. When Clark became disillusioned with his university, President G. Stanley Hall had no community ties upon which to call. Clark University foundered in the early 1890s, just as other private and public institutions made major strides in the promotion of both pure research and public service.[3] The problems of Clark University grew partly out of the idiosyncratic behavior of Hall and Clark; but in a larger sense, its problems demonstrated the dangers in forging an American university devoted exclusively to advanced research and graduate training, however much such work might ultimately benefit humanity. The lesson was not lost on other university builders.

HIGHER EDUCATION IN CHICAGO

William Rainy Harper, the founding president of the University of Chicago, drew upon the experiences of university reformers of the 1870s and 1880s in fashioning his own institution. Unlike Johns Hopkins, Clark, Cornell, and Leland Stanford University, the University of Chicago began as a denominational institution, a project of the Baptists.

Chicago Baptists had started a college in 1857, called the University of Chicago, but the school closed its doors when its trustees declared bankruptcy in 1886.[4] Almost immediately thereafter, Thomas W. Goodspeed, an active supporter of the defunct college, sought to interest others in a new, soundly financed Baptist college in Chicago.

Frederick Gates, corresponding secretary of the American Baptist Education Society, backed Goodspeed's plan. His support was cautious, however, because wealthy Chicago Baptists had thus far been reluctant to support another college unless its financial success could be guaranteed. When a committee of the Baptist Education Society voted in 1889 to back the project, Gates announced that he had received a pledge of $600,000 from John D. Rockefeller for the project, provided the committee could raise $400,000.[5] Chicago Baptists proved unwilling to pledge the full $400,000, so the committee turned to non-Baptist Chicagoans. Wealthy philanthropist Charles L. Hutchinson agreed to support the new college and brought the matter before the city's Commercial Club. Department store magnate Marshall Field gave both money and the land on which the university was to be built, and Eli Felsenthal, a prominent Jewish lawyer, encouraged support among wealthy Chicago Jews. The sum was raised and the university incorporated in 1890.[6] The turn to non-Baptist Chicagoans proved fortuitous, however expedient. The "Baptist" university owed as much to Chicago's elite as to the denomination, and its continued alliance with this elite guaranteed its ongoing support and expansion.

It did not take the trustees very long to decide whom they wanted to head the new institution. William Rainey Harper, a member of the board and an active participant in the early discussions, was perhaps the most prominent Baptist educator in the country, a man of rare achievements and dynamism.[7] Harper has been aptly characterized as a "young man in a hurry."[8] The son of an Ohio drygoods shopowner, he was an intellectual prodigy, graduating from Muskingum College at the age of thirteen and receiving a Ph.D. in philosophy from Yale at the age of nineteen. Harper served one year as principal of Masonic College in Tennessee, then taught Greek and Latin at Denison University, a small Ohio Baptist institution, and later Hebrew at Union Theological Seminary in Morgan Park, just outside of Chicago. In addition to his regular duties at Morgan Park, he established special classes in Hebrew during Christmas and summer vacations.[9]

Harper's talents as a teacher soon led him in 1883 to Chautauqua, an innovative educational institution for adults in southwestern New York state. Founded in 1874 as a summer institute for Sunday school teachers, it proved so successful that its founders added secular educational programs. Harper taught Hebrew at Chautauqua during the summers and by correspondence the rest of the year, became principal of the Chautauqua School of Hebrew in 1885, and the Chautauqua College of Liberal Arts in 1887.[10] In 1889, Harper helped to initiate an extension program whereby university professors traveled to a town, presented lectures, and provided a bibliography. Those who passed an examination received credit toward a college degree.[11]

At Chautauqua, Harper met many of the young scholars who were forging the modern academic professions and the new universities. In the 1880s, Chautauqua provided an important vehicle for their efforts to wed scholarly endeavors to public service. By the turn of the century, their own universities had preempted much of this extension work, and Chautauqua declined as a major academic institution. Indeed, the Chautauqua experience encouraged Harper to start his own correspondence courses at Morgan Park. In 1886, when he moved to Yale as professor of Semitic languages in the Divinity School, he brought his correspondence program with him.[12]

The man whom the trustees nominated for the presidency of their new college was thus a prominent scholar and teacher committed to carrying intellectual work beyond the walls of the university through innovative programs. Harper weighed the Chicago offer for six months before accepting in 1891. Asserting that he would not head merely an undergraduate college, he convinced Rockefeller to donate an extra million dollars to be used for graduate and divinity instruction.[13]

Harper's design for the University of Chicago drew heavily upon the experiments in higher education of the preceding two decades and his own experiences at Chautauqua, Morgan Park, and Yale. In the first issue of the university's *Official Bulletin*, Harper announced that, in addition to the traditional college for undergraduate instruction and the graduate and professional schools, secondary schools and undergraduate colleges could affiliate with the university, if they met prescribed academic standards, and then could use university staff and facilities in improving instruction. In this way, Harper hoped to elevate the standards of secondary schools and small undergraduate colleges.

Furthermore, classes for credit would be conducted at various locations in and around Chicago and even at points distant from the city. The university would also offer correspondence courses. The University

Publication Department was to publish journals and books to promote teaching and scholarship. In addition, Harper divided the regular academic year into four quarters of about three months each, thereby making full use of the summer.[14]

As president, Harper also engaged personally in a wide variety of public activities. Shortly after the university opened in 1892, he got himself appointed to the Chicago Board of Education, chaired the education committee of the Civic Federation, and most important, headed a special city education commission to study and propose means of modernizing the Chicago public schools. As a member of the Union League Club, Harper arranged the club's civic education program for students, and he also served on the Merchants' Club educational committee.[15] He chaired the advisory board of Cook County Hospital from 1903 until his death in 1906, participated actively in the Chicago Association of Commerce, organized the Industrial Art League of Chicago, and was a trustee of the Chicago Symphony Orchestra.[16] Nor did Harper sever his connection with Chautauqua when he came to Chicago. He remained principal of instruction until 1899, resigning only when the institution's trustees rejected his plans to move the bulk of their activities to the campus of the University of Chicago.[17]

Extensive public activities of this kind were quite common for university presidents in the late nineteenth century. Cornell's president, Andrew White, held a variety of diplomatic posts and was active in the civil service reform movement. Charles W. Eliot, like Harper, took a lively interest in public education, chairing important committees of the National Education Association and working closely with the Cambridge and Boston public schools. He was also the first president of the American Social Hygiene Association. James B. Angell, president of the University of Michigan from 1871 to 1909, served on diplomatic missions to Turkey and China and on several commissions appointed by President Grover Cleveland. Daniel C. Gilman at Johns Hopkins founded and served as president of the Charity Organization Society of Baltimore, held a seat on the Baltimore School Board, headed the National Civil Service Reform League in 1904, and served on the United States commission that investigated the Venezuela–British Guiana boundary dispute in the 1890s.[18] Such activities bestowed prestige upon the president's institutions and thereby undermined the popular notion that university professors inhabited isolated ivory towers.

Like his colleagues elsewhere, Harper looked favorably upon scholars who engaged in public service that benefited the university. On occasion, he even informed public officials of the talents of particular faculty members. He wrote to Mayor George B. Swift, for example, calling to his attention the experience of Professor Edwin O. Jordan, a bacteriologist, in public health work. Similarly, he wrote Herman H. Kohlsaat, editor of the *Record Herald*, about the desire of Professor E. R. L. Gould, a statistician, "to do some particular work in connection with municipal affairs in Chicago." In 1897, he told an inquirer that Albion W. Small and George Vincent, both sociologists, could be of assistance in "deciding how to furnish relief for Chicago's unemployed citizens." [19]

Chicago's commitment to public service went beyond that of most other universities in the 1890s both because Harper was more skilled and more aggressive than many of his colleagues elsewhere and because local circumstances were particularly fortuitous. However, prominent leaders in the movement for university development everywhere, with the exception of G. Stanley Hall, shared Harper's public service spirit. Gilman had already shown that public service and pure scholarship could live comfortably under one roof in America. Harper simply carried on both kinds of activities on a far grander scale.

Harper justified the extensive involvement of the university in civic affairs with the familiar argument that democratic society demanded an educated citizenry and that social progress depended upon wide dissemination of knowledge. "The progress of the last century has been the result of the work of millions, not hundreds," he wrote in 1905, "and the immensity of this progress, as compared with that of preceding centuries, is in proportion to the number of individuals whose minds have been awakened." [20] He termed the university "the state's chief agent for its proper guidance," insisting that it must be "a potent factor in its public life." He explicitly acknowledged, however, that public service also aided the growth of the university, since it made the university indispensable to society. "If humanity . . . counts as its ally a power by which, one by one, the problems of that civilization are resolved," he wrote in 1905, "humanity and this allied power must in due time come to have interests and aspirations which bind them irrevocably together." [21]

Harper's successor, Harry Pratt Judson, in many ways seemed the antithesis of Harper. Cautious, conservative, business-minded, he achieved a feat Harper had never accomplished—a balanced budget. [22] Judson was a manager, not an innovator, and he eliminated some of Harper's experiments. However, like Harper, he acknowledged that public service was indispensable to the university.

Son of a small-town New York minister, Judson taught history in high school and then at the University of Minnesota before coming to the University of Chicago in 1892 as head professor of political science. Although not an important scholar, he showed talent for administration and became dean of faculties in 1894. On Harper's death, he assumed the presidency, a position he held until his retirement in 1923.[23]

Judson's style contrasted sharply with Harper's ambitious empire building, and he avoided undertaking reform activities that would consume significant amounts of his time. He held strong political views, more so than Harper, and supported a variety of political movements in Chicago and nationally. Judson was a business-oriented progressive Republican who voted for Taft in the 1912 presidential election. He believed that "special interests" were the nation's most serious threat, argued that municipal government ought to be nonpartisan and run along business lines, and strictly interpreted the powers granted to the federal government in the United States Constitution.[24] He staunchly opposed labor unions and was lukewarm about woman suffrage.[25] Like his predecessor, however, he argued that education provided the key to social progress and that universities must use their resources in the service of the general good. He endorsed numerous reform proposals in his years as president and remained a member of many civic and political associations.[26]

Harper and Judson, like the leaders of other universities in large cities, made a virtue of their urban locations. Harper insisted that "urban universities are in the truest sense national universities" because "the great cities represent the national life in its fulness and its variety."[27] Judson went further, insisting that the service responsibilities of the urban university should be applied primarily to the city itself:

> In a great city with its crowded population the limits of the university duties are to be conceived as coterminous with the limits of the city itself. In other words, the university should not be content with the discovery only of scientific truth, which may have most direct bearing upon the city life, but should be especially industrious in the investigation and dissemination of such forms of truth as are directly related to the city.[28]

Elsewhere, other urban university leaders echoed these sentiments. Nicholas Murray Butler, in one of his earliest reports as president of Columbia University, stated that "there is no doubt whatever as to the superiority of the city's opportunities and environment as a place of graduate, professional and technical study" and astutely observed that, although the university was a national institution, "it will be dependent in large measure . . . upon the support of the city in which it is." Professor John W. Burgess, who led the transformation of Columbia from a college to a university, taught at Amherst College before coming to Columbia in 1876. "I had . . . come slowly, gradually, even unwillingly, to see that Amherst was not the place for a university such as I had in mind, especially in the branches of historical, political, economic, sociological and juristic research," he later recalled, "but that the city with its libraries, museums, laboratories . . . and its large wealth was the natural home for such an institution." Herbert Baxter Adams, who introduced advanced study in history and the social sciences to Johns Hopkins University, suggested in his history of the College of William and Mary that that institution would have done better had it located in Alexandria or Richmond because a city provided the best climate for the development of a strong university.[29] Clearly, an urban location enabled institutions such as the University of Chicago to win financial support from a prosperous local elite. To do so, however, the university had to confront in concrete ways the problems of the city so as to win support from these elites.

Nontraditional extension teaching afforded one opportunity for a new university to serve the community and the nation. The university extension movement in the United States began modestly in the late 1870s, inspired by similar activities initiated earlier in the decade by students at Cambridge University in England. In the early 1880s, while Chautauqua grew, faculty at Johns Hopkins established a workingman's institute in an industrial suburb of Baltimore, and the biology department initiated a special course for Baltimore and Ohio Railroad laborers. Herbert Baxter Adams became a major advocate of university extension work in the late 1880s.[30] Under the leadership of Nicholas Murray Butler, Teachers College in New York offered general extension work beginning in the 1890s.[31] Edmund J. James, the major faculty advocate of university development and graduate study at the University of Pennsylvania, helped establish a Philadelphia society for university extension in 1890. The following year, this local association became the American Society for the Extension of University Teaching, a national group headed by James.[32]

No institution remained more thoroughly associated with extension in the 1890s than the University of Chicago. Under Harper's leadership, Chicago sought to provide university education to all who wanted and might profit from it. The university thereby substantially insulated itself from accusations of elitism, while it imposed rigorous academic standards on its regular undergraduates and graduate students in a variety of esoteric fields. Extension courses at various locations around the city, in towns distant from Chicago, and by correspondence received high priority in Harper's university, and even senior faculty commonly offered extension and correspondence courses. Although Judson continued many of these programs, he lacked his predecessor's enthusiasm for extension. Still, by 1920, 3,880 students were enrolled in the "home-study" division, which offered correspondence work, and many more participated in classroom programs.[33]

Most extension students were moderately educated and able to pay university fees. The university also tried to reach the working class. In conjunction with the board of education, it offered free lectures in public school auditoriums so as to bring university faculty to "those districts in the city which owing to their general economic character, are least able to afford or to provide for their own lecturers."[34] Furthermore, in 1904 and 1905, Harper induced several railroads to donate funds for special instruction for railroad employees. Each contributing railroad was to send twenty workers for two evenings a week for six months. The program was not very successful. The Chicago Transfer Railroad Company could induce only thirteen of its employees to join classes, of whom six were "advised to discontinue, because of their apparent want of either ability or application."[35] Harper's correspondence institute for Bible study, which moved to Chicago from Yale, was still another part of the extension program. Ostensibly independent until 1905, it became a regular part of the university in that year.[36]

The new universities took a special interest in extension work for public school teachers. Chicago's Department of Philosophy, Psychology, and Pedagogy educated many teachers and administrators who went on to play a major role in modernizing Chicago's public schools. University College, begun in 1898, provided courses for Chicago school teachers, conducted by regular instructors at convenient times and places.

Other university departments also provided practical service-oriented teaching. The Department of Household Administration argued that specialized education for housewives enhanced the health and welfare of the modern family. The Divinity School offered extensive courses in social problems and social welfare, so that trained ministers could work directly for the betterment of society. In 1904 an undergraduate College of Religious and Social Service was begun to train students for social work in religious agencies. A training school for social workers began in the extension division of the University of Chicago. The School of Commerce and Administration (now the School of Business) and its Law School offered practical professional education. Even some academic social science disciplines had strong practical orientations in those years. Chicago's sociology department, for example, the first such department in the United States, claimed to use the findings of the other social and natural sciences to formulate the laws of society, with the ultimate purpose of mitigating social ills; many sociology graduates pursued full-time careers in reform or social service.[37] In short, Chicago, like other privately endowed urban universities, fashioned visible public service teaching programs that won support from potential benefactors in the same way that agricultural and mechanical programs won political support for land grant state universities. At the same time, Chicago, Hopkins, Columbia, Pennsylvania, Harvard, and other private universities developed pure scholarship and advanced teaching in the strictly scientific fields.

If the University of Chicago epitomized the expansive aspirations of new universities, Northwestern University, located just outside of Chicago, typified the limits of the old-time college and the process by which some of those colleges became modern universities. A group of Chicago and midwestern members of the Methodist Episcopal Church founded Northwestern in 1850.[38] By 1890, it still offered only the traditional undergraduate curriculum of classical languages, philosophy, and mathematics. There was no graduate work, but like other institutions Northwestern offered the master's degree to graduates of three years standing on the condition of "the maintenance of good moral standing." Only three of its sixteen faculty in 1890 held the Ph.D. Quasi-autonomous professional schools of medicine, law, pharmacy, dentistry, and ministry were affiliated with Northwestern, but with the exception of the latter, they were located in Chicago and had no real relationship to each other or to the undergraduate college in Evanston. Typically, none of the professional schools required an undergraduate degree for admission.[39]

In three decades after 1890, Northwestern transformed itself into a modern university under the leadership of four different presidents. The first, Henry Wade Rogers, pioneered in the professionalization of legal practice and in the development of university-based law schools.[40] Thirty-seven years old upon assuming Northwestern's presidency, Rogers began the process of making Northwestern a university. He brought the professional schools under a single university administration, although they remained physically separate. He rearranged some of the work in liberal arts to reflect better the contemporary trends in the

development of academic professions. For example, he divided natural philosophy into the departments of geology and biology, separated mathematics from philosophy, and divided history from political
economy. His additions to the faculty were almost entirely young men
trained in the new disciplines, and many of them were engaged in research. Six of the faculty appointments made by Rogers held Ph.D.'s
from Johns Hopkins.[41] He did not initiate substantial graduate study in
the liberal arts and scientific disciplines, however.

Like other university presidents, Rogers felt compelled to participate in civic affairs. He served on the executive committee of the Civic
Federation of Chicago, and as a trustee of the Chicago Bureau of
Charities. He also helped set up the Northwestern University settlement
near downtown Chicago and worked actively in 1899 to establish a
state commission on minimum professional standards for the public
schools.[42] On the other hand, however, Rogers moved slowly on university extension work.

Edmund J. James succeeded Rogers. A pioneer in the development
of professional social science in the United States, James had received
a Ph.D. from the University of Halle in 1877. At the University of
Pennsylvania and later the University of Chicago, James had worked
vigorously to develop graduate study and to forge a public service mission for the American university and for professional social scientists.[43]
James's presidency lasted only two years; in 1904 he resigned to become president of the University of Illinois. In that time, however, he
attempted to bring full university status to Northwestern. Unlike Rogers, who placed greatest emphasis on the professional schools, James insisted that the prime goal must be the development of graduate study in
the academic disciplines. In a memorandum to the trustees in April
1902 on the needs of Northwestern, he indicated that he regarded "as
the most important and fundamental need of all, a GRADUATE SCHOOL"
based upon "a strong, well-developed, college such as the College of
Liberal Arts in Northwestern University may be easily made. . . . In my
opinion," he added, "no institution will be entitled within a very few
years to the name of University which does not include as its CENTRAL
feature a graduate school." James also vastly expanded Northwestern's
extension work.[44]

Abram W. Harris, who held only an undergraduate degree and had
occupied a wide variety of positions in secondary and higher education
and government, succeeded James. Since Harris was active in Methodist
affairs,[45] his appointment seemed to be something of a setback for uni-

versity advocates. Yet by 1904, the trend toward university development nationally was so strong, especially in large cities, that Northwestern almost inevitably moved in that direction.

In 1908, the efforts of several Northwestern professors in political economy and members of the Chicago Association of Commerce, the Industrial Club, and the Illinois Society of Certified Public Accountants produced the Northwestern School of Commerce. Initially, the school's core faculty consisted of several young scholars with Ph.D.'s, who taught political economy at the Evanston campus.[46] Under Harris, Northwestern also began offering courses for primary and secondary school teachers in downtown Chicago, and in 1908 it opened its College of Engineering.[47] Harris also helped further modernize the liberal arts college. A graduate school was established in 1910, although graduate study remained relatively modest.[48] In 1915, a political science department was established. Through steady changes in its faculty and programs, Northwestern in 1918 resembled a modern university much more than an old-time college, and in that year it was admitted to the Association of American Universities.[49]

Chicago's two Catholic institutions—St. Ignatius College, renamed Loyola University in 1909, and St. Vincent's College, renamed DePaul University in 1907—were largely unaffected by the changes occurring in mainstream American higher education in these years. Catholic institutions of higher learning, in these years, aspired to status only within the Catholic church and held no pretense of national stature. This parochial stance stemmed from the ostracism of American Catholics by the nation's Protestant majority. Most of the urban immigrants in cities like Chicago after 1885 were Catholic, and Protestants viewed the conservative Catholic church as an alien institution. Some American Catholics opposed the church's rigid conservatism and sought to make Catholicism compatible with American ideals and to harmonize its teachings with scientific advances. A group of these liberal Catholics founded the Catholic University of America in Washington, D.C., in 1889. By the early twentieth century, however, the liberals had lost.[50]

It is, therefore, not surprising that the faculties of Loyola and De-Paul included very few academic professionals. Most faculty were assigned to these institutions by the Jesuit order in the case of Loyola and the Archdiocese of Chicago in the case of DePaul. Loyola had seven different presidents between 1891 and 1921, all Jesuit fathers. Its undergraduate curriculum derived from the order's original mission as an intellectual arm of the Counter-Reformation. The first faculty member to hold the doctorate came in 1915 to teach chemistry; four years later,

Loyola still had only one Ph.D. on its faculty. DePaul was equally insulated from national academic trends.[51] In 1908, DePaul's president summed up the tension between the Catholic and the mainstream institutions. The University of Chicago and Northwestern were not "ample to satisfy all the demands of higher education" in the city, he insisted, because many people "recognize the consistency, the stability and the conservatism of Catholic teaching, especially in matters of political, moral and social import."[52]

The growing professionalization of such fields as law, medicine, engineering, and business, however, forced the Catholic institutions to develop professional schools, lest potential Catholic lawyers or businessmen be attracted to the Protestant universities instead. The only program in either institution that genuinely mirrored the movement toward academic professionalization, however, was the Loyola School of Sociology, a professional school for social workers, which began in 1912 as the University Lecture Bureau "to give extension lectures of a popular character on social subjects." Many of its lecturers were non-Catholics. The Loyola School of Sociology, the first school of social work at a Catholic University in the United States, was the brainchild of its first dean, Father Frederic Siedenburg, a Jesuit who had studied social economics in Berlin and Vienna and became a leading national figure in Catholic social welfare work.[53]

SCHOLARS, TEACHERS, AND DOERS

University presidents, then, instituted public service programs to enhance the power and prestige of their institutions. Individual faculty members, however, advanced professionally by gaining esteem from others in their disciplines throughout the nation as well as from administrators and colleagues within their own institutions. At Chicago and other new universities, significant numbers of professors engaged directly in civic affairs, knowing that these efforts could enhance their national professional stature and their standing within their own university.

The kinds of extra-university activities in which scholars in different disciplines might be engaged varied enormously. Even within a single discipline, members vigorously debated the propriety of various kinds of extramural activities and the proper relationship of such activities to scholarship and teaching, debates that are by no means settled today. Yet from the 1890s to the end of World War I, new academic professionals developed a fairly broad consensus that, whatever the appropriate means, scholars should exert a profound influence on what we now call social policy.

To be sure, some professors, especially in the humanities, opposed the national trends toward specialization, fragmentation of the undergraduate curriculum, and vocationalism in American higher education. Centered primarily at Yale, Princeton, and several small-town or rural northeastern colleges, this group insisted that the liberal education of an intellectual elite for leadership in a democratic society constituted the only appropriate public service that professors as professors should perform.[54] In universities like Chicago, which had not undergone a metamorphosis from the old-time college, open critics of specialization, utilitarianism, and public service appeared only rarely.

Thorstein Veblen, Chicago's brilliant radical economist, criticized university and professorial involvement in civic affairs more thoroughly than any advocate of liberal culture, but on entirely different grounds. Veblen started a book attacking the university's ties with business elites and civic affairs just after he left Chicago in 1906, but he did not publish it until 1918. Still, his observations derived largely from Chicago. *The Higher Learning in America*, which announced its author's viewpoint in the subtitle, *A Memorandum on the Conduct of Universities by Business Men*, presents an extraordinarily accurate description of the ties between the University of Chicago and local elites fostered by the service activities of the university and its faculty. American universities, he argued, had adopted business values and thereby abandoned the "disinterested pursuit of idle knowledge" for which they existed. Thus, they invested their efforts instead in practical matters like the development of good citizens.

> Citizenship is a larger and more substantial category than scholarship; and the furtherance of civilized life is a larger and more serious interest than the pursuit of knowledge for its own idle sake. . . . These are too serious a range of duties to be taken care of as a side-issue, by a seminary of learning, the members of whose faculty, if they are fit for their own special work, are not men of affairs or adepts in worldly wisdom.[55]

Similarly, Veblen asserted that extension work and education "for proficiency in some gainful occupation . . . has no connection with the higher learning." His illustrations read like the blueprint for Harper's university.

> Educational enterprise of this kind has, somewhat incontinently, extended the scope of the corporation of learning by creating, "annex-

ing," or "affiliating" many establishments that properly lie outside
the academic field and deal with matters foreign to the academic
interest,—fitting schools, high-schools, technological, manual and
other training schools for mechanical, engineering and other industrial pursuits, professional schools of divers kinds, music schools, art
schools, summer schools, schools of "domestic science," "domestic
economy," "home economics" (in short, housekeeping), schools for
special training of secondary school teachers, and even schools that
are avowedly of primary grade; while a variety of "university extension" bureaux have been installed, to comfort and edify the unlearned
with lyceum lectures, to dispense erudition by mailorder, and to
maintain some putative contact with amateur scholars and dilettanti
beyond the pale.[56]

Finally, Veblen attacked the university for encouraging individual faculty to participate in community projects. Professors, he noted cynically,
were expected to

expend time and means in such polite observances, spectacles and
quasi-learned exhibitions as are presumed to enhance the prestige of
the university. They are so induced to divert their time and energy to
spreading abroad the university's good repute by creditable exhibitions of a quasi-scholarly character, which have no substantial bearing on a university man's legitimate interests.[57]

Few of Veblen's contemporaries shared these doubts. They exhibited instead the boundless optimism of pioneers convinced that in
science lay the key to social progress. Even Veblen readily acknowledged that faith in science had become the arbiter of the problems of
western civilization. "On any large question which is to be disposed
of for good and all," he observed in 1906, "the final appeal is by
common consent taken to the scientist. The solution offered in the
name of science is decisive so long as it is not set aside by a still more
searching scientific inquiry." Veblen was quick to add that "this state
of things may not be altogether fortunate, but such is the fact."[58]

Sociologist Albion W. Small, for instance, warmly greeted the
scientific age. In 1894, in "The New Humanity," Small predicted that
"the brightest page in history ought to fill the blank reserved for the
next generation's record." His optimism stemmed from "the growing
popular and scientific belief that the elements of human welfare are
knowable and controllable." Nearly twenty years later, Small's faith
remained unshaken. "In no period of history," he wrote, "has it been
possible for social scientists to perform more fundamentally constructive public service than present conditions throughout the world de-

mand." [59] James Hayden Tufts of Chicago's philosophy department echoed Small's sentiments in a classic statement of twentieth-century liberalism:

> We are in the mere beginnings of possible control over human associ-
> ation, of politics, and of economic life. But if there is any maxim that
> we may cast to the rubbish heap it is the dictum, "You cannot change
> human nature." Human nature is in certain respects at least the
> most changeable thing, the most flexible and adaptive thing in the
> universe, so far as we know. It apparently would not survive at all
> were it not flexible and adaptive. Why should we not assume that
> science can do more intelligently and directly what has thus far taken
> place so largely by the method of trial and error? [60]

Similarly, Willard Eugene Hotchkiss, dean of the Northwestern School of Commerce, asserted in 1918 in a discussion of business education, "We are now coming to understand that scientific method is the only sure approach to all problems; it is a thing of universal application." Charles E. Merriam believed that one reason for the rise of interest in social legislation and policy was "the advance of science, whether in the form of public sanitation or of social science." [61]

Along with this enormous faith in the potential of natural and so-cial science went an extraordinary faith in expertise. In 1895, Small explained to the readers of the *American Journal of Sociology* that the Civic Federation of Chicago had been so successful largely because of the "unusual degree to which the aggressive work of the Federation was assigned to people who might be called experts." "The work of the Federation was conducted as a business man would manage his com-mercial enterprises, viz., by securing specialists for special work, and by depending upon them to know their business," Small boasted, and it succeeded because it was "superintended by people fitted by talent and experience to carry on for themselves work requiring similar qualifica-tions." [62] Decrying the poor quality of legislation in the United States, Ernst Freund, a lawyer and political scientist, told members of the American Political Science Association in 1908 that "the patient and slowly maturing labors of the student [of government] are required to aid the legislative expert who will always have to perform his task under considerable stress." [63] Bacteriologist Edwin O. Jordan more bluntly insisted, "It ought to be possible for a large city to place its water supply under expert and specialized control, thus averting from the ig-norant and careless members of the community the consequences that would otherwise follow their ignorance and neglect." [64]

Science not only enabled society to solve technical problems; it determined what ought to be done as well as the best way to do it. "It is the duty of the scholar to place and keep before the public the supreme criterion of social conduct, the common welfare," wrote sociologist Charles R. Henderson in 1896. "The scholar's duty is to aid in forming a judicial public opinion, as distinguished from the public opinion of a class and its special pleaders." [65] According to Tufts, the university existed not simply to advance science, but "to use science for human advancement, rather than for private ends." The task of the university was "not only to professionalize a part of society but to socialize the professions." [66] George Herbert Mead, like Tufts a member of Chicago's philosophy department, rejected any limited technocratic view of the university as "an office of experts to which the problems of the community are sent to be solved. . . ." Instead he argued,

> it is a part of the community within which the community problems appear as its own. It is the community organized to find out what culture is as well as to give it; to determine what is proper professional training as well as to inculcate it; to find out what is right and what is wrong as well as to teach them; to state and formulate research problems as well as to solve them; in general to fix from moment to moment the changing meaning of life and the fitting tools for appropriating it. . . . [67]

The antebellum colleges had also asserted that their classical curriculum inculcated moral behavior. Many of the new university scholars, however, believed that moral questions could be answered inductively through the scientific method. Herein lies the critical intellectual transformation of the late nineteenth century.

From these assumptions, activist scholars readily fused the ideals of research and service. In the first issue of the *American Journal of Sociology*, Small urged American scholars to "repeal the law of custom which bars marriage of thought with action" and "become more profoundly and sympathetically scholarly by enriching the wisdom which comes from knowing with the larger wisdom which comes from doing." [68] "By the simple strength of his knowledge of past resources and his forecast of future powers," wrote Tufts in 1914, "the scholar will more and more enter into the promise by becoming servant of all." [69] Scholarship must be "freed from mediaevalism and dialectics," thought Henderson, and come to mean "social service." [70] Even practioners of "pure" research in the natural sciences, like Chicago biologist John M. Coulter, argued that their work ultimately produced practical results. "Training in the foundation principles of Botany is a necessary prerequisite to any intelligent work in the economic directions," Coulter wrote to a colleague. "I should say, therefore, that all of our courses have a very direct bearing upon the practical things of life, in that they bring that knowledge which is necessary as a background for rational technical training." [71]

This broad consensus regarding the usefulness of scholarship in solving practical problems had different consequences for scholars in different fields. A majority of Chicago's new academic professionals partook personally in programs for social betterment only to the extent that their teaching (including extension work) or their research had long-range social importance. A more aggressive minority of scholars primarily in the social sciences, philosophy, law, and social work, however, devoted major efforts to social reform and politics. As modern scholars seeking status within their disciplines, these men and women had to devise professionally acceptable ways to connect their extensive public activities with the customary academic work of teaching and research.

In the social sciences, a tension had long existed between the objectives of study and improvement of society. Many of the young social scientists of the late nineteenth century actively sought to improve society through political advocacy and action; they embraced careers in social science as much from their desire to change society as from intellectual curiosity about social phenomena. As the social science disciplines emerged, beginning in the 1880s, members of aspiring professions like economics recognized that their acceptance as bona fide experts in a discrete subject area demanded that they adopt a detached, scientific posture and treat social questions with specialized analysis to distinguish themselves from mere politicians and polemicists. Without such public acceptance, they could anticipate neither material rewards, social prestige, nor even job security.

On the other hand, the utilitarian imperative that made public service such a large concern of the new universities likewise demanded that the social science disciplines be put to practical use in resolving the social problems of late-nineteenth-century industrial society. Here, in short, was the dilemma of the new social science scholars: advocacy and political action in the traditional political forums undermined the claim to scientific expertise, but public acceptance of their professions demanded that they demonstrate the utility of their work.

Social scientists resolved this dilemma in part by writing primarily for scholarly books and journals read mostly by others in the profession, by examining specialized problems, and by developing methods, jargon, and theoretical constructs distinctive to their disciplines. Over time, members of the various social science professions developed also a rough consensus as to the appropriate ways to apply the discipline's knowledge and skills to social needs.

Nationally, the social science professions quickly developed a consensus as to the kinds of advocacy and public activities that were consistent with the professional status to which they aspired.[72] However, local conditions and opportunities also held enormous sway over the new professional social scientists. If in the long run a professor's career depended upon favorable recognition from the national profession, in the short run it hinged upon recognition within one's own institution. In the 1890s, advocacy of the gold standard in western Populist-dominated state universities proved as dangerous as support for bimetalism and attacks on corporate power in private eastern institutions. In the heyday of LaFollette progressivism and the "Wisconsin idea," leading social scientists at the University of Wisconsin advanced professionally through close association with the governor's policies. At the University of Chicago, as at Johns Hopkins University, Columbia, and, to a lesser extent, the University of Pennsylvania and Harvard, many social scientists successfully combined scholarly research and teaching with the kind of public service that won support from both the elites of wealth upon whom their universities depended and from their professions. The intellectual biographies of a few of Chicago's activist professors show a symbiotic relationship between public service in an urban setting and intellectual or professional success.

The development of sociology at Chicago illustrates well one successful linkage between scholarship and activism. The Department of Sociology at Chicago, the first such department in the country, began with the university in 1892, the creation of Albion W. Small. Small, a Baptist minister who had studied history and political economy at Johns Hopkins, sought to establish a discipline of sociology that would coordinate the knowledge of more "specialized" disciplines so as to discover the laws of society and use them to solve social problems. Small himself, although primarily a social theorist, participated in the formation of the Civic Federation of Chicago in the 1890s and in other reform activities.[73] Charles R. Henderson, another Baptist minister who had been active in social reform work in the 1870s and 1880s, developed extensive connections between sociology and local social welfare agencies. Henderson wrote numerous books and articles on methods of charity organization, "dependent, defective and delinquent classes," labor problems and social insurance; taught courses on all of these subjects; and worked in numerous local organizations and commissions. Henderson's method was consistent and uncomplicated. He examined a problem of social policy by looking at its causes and treatment in other countries and other parts of the United States, past and present. From all of these data, he extrapolated commonsense guidelines for present policy.

Henderson, like many early American sociologists, came to reform and social science through deep religious convictions. University chaplain throughout his academic career at Chicago, Henderson once wrote that "to assist us in the difficult task of adjustment to new situations God has providentially wrought out for us the social sciences and placed them at our disposal." His moralism did not sit well with some of his younger, secularly oriented students. One of them later described his teaching as "stilted, almost antagonistic, as if afraid some one would impose upon him or penetrate his outer defenses of assumed omnipotence." [74] A man of few doubts and little introspection, he worked at a feverish pace, collecting data, churning out books and reports, attending meetings, and presenting lectures with the same fervor with which a revivalist minister saved souls. His death in 1915 at the age of sixty-seven occurred largely from exhaustion brought on by intensive work on an unemployment crisis in Chicago.

Henderson was not alone in undertaking this kind of empirical study of social welfare problems. Across the country, amateur social scientists and reformers in settlement houses and charitable agencies collected and analyzed social data to gain immediate insight into urban problems. The work done by Charles Booth on London a decade earlier was more elaborate and sophisticated than anything Henderson produced. But Henderson had the influence that came from a major university position. Many of Henderson's students and faculty successors took his crude empiricism and developed it into the Chicago tradition of meticulous observation of the city. Nor did later, more sophisticated sociologists eschew service in government commissions and local organizations. Robert E. Park, one of the most important American sociologists of race, ethnicity, and urban life, for example, served as president of the Chicago Urban League and worked closely with a local commission on race relations partly to gather data on social questions that interested him, as Henderson had earlier. William F. Ogburn produced a major study of social change after working on President Hoover's Commission on Recent Social Trends; and Louis Wirth wrote his seminal essay, "Urbanism as a Way of Life" after serving on the National Resources Planning Board's committee on urbanism during the New Deal.

Henderson became a leading figure in his discipline, if not a lasting one, largely through the opportunities provided by a university position and public service in the city of Chicago. In 1892, Henderson had been a minister with interests in reform. (He obtained a Ph.D. in Germany during a leave of absence in 1895 and 1896.) In 1915, he died a nationally prominent sociologist who had also won wide recognition for his social service in Chicago and throughout the nation. Highly regarded by local businessmen and other prominent Chicagoans for his "scientific" and meticulous approach to social problems, his obituary appeared on the front pages of several local newspapers. One article dubbed him a "citizen saint."[75]

Like Henderson, political scientist Charles E. Merriam exhibited an extraordinary capacity for work and a deep commitment to combining scholarship and action. Like sociology and economics, political science began in the United States with high aspirations for public influence. Many early political scientists expected that their courses would eventually become the prerequisite for entrance into the civil service. John Burgess justified his proposed School of Political Science at Columbia partly on the grounds that the training offered should become the "indispensable condition of appointment to government office"; the curriculum of the school stated that it was "designed to prepare young men for public life whether in the Civil Service at home or abroad, or in the legislatures of the States or of the nation."[76]

Unlike Henderson, Merriam, the son of a small-town Iowa Republican politician, began his academic career with doctoral study early in life. After graduate study at Columbia University, the preeminent center of scholarship in government and politics in the 1880s and 1890s, Merriam came to Chicago in 1900 as a very junior member of the Department of Political Science. The smallest and weakest of Chicago's social science departments, it was headed by Harry Pratt Judson, who retained the head professorship even after his elevation to the presidency. Early political science was closely linked to constitutional history, and Judson, a man of limited intellectual vision, preferred to concentrate the department's work on traditional constitutional analysis.

Merriam's doctoral dissertation had examined the history of the theory of sovereignty since Rousseau, and shortly after coming to Chicago he published *A History of American Political Theories*. The complexities of city politics soon captured Merriam's imagination, however. Like other young political scientists, he sought to study the actual processes of government and politics; as such he departed substantially from the intellectual tradition of his mentor, William A. Dunning.

This young and extremely aggressive political scientist quickly perceived the possibilities of obtaining financial and civic support for studies of urban government from local reform-oriented elites. In 1905, Merriam studied municipal revenues and expenditures for the City Club of Chicago and obtained appointment to a City Charter Commission, in which he chaired the committee on revenue and taxation. Therein began Merriam's career as an academic entrepreneur, uniquely talented at winning private philanthropic support of social research for social policy.[77] (The culminating achievement of his entrepreneurial skills would come in the 1920s, when he organized the Social Science Research Council to exert scholarly influence on national policy.)

Judson did not approve of Merriam's new kind of political science or of his writings on political parties, primary elections, urban planning, and what soon became known as public administration. Expert service to Chicago's charitable and welfare agencies, such as Henderson performed, appeared dignified and politically neutral (which, in fact, it was not). Direct participation in partisan political issues, however, raised potential problems for the university. But Merriam understood, as Judson did not, that political activity of the right sort could actually enhance the university's position in the community. As Merriam's biographer has asserted, "Whatever the university administrators chose to think now of Merriam's role in the university, he was in the process of making himself visible to—and indispensable to—the same wealthy leadership to which the university looked for its sustenance."[78] Indeed, Merriam's position in the university and the community became so strong by 1909 that he ran successfully for the city council, and two years later nearly won election as mayor, without jeopardizing his professorship. Before and after World War I, Merriam suffered severe political defeats that ended his career in electoral politics, but his extensive relationships with wealthy elites who shared his interest in scientific approaches to public administration and policy endured and enabled him to make the Chicago department a nationally renowned center of political science research.[79]

Such close ties between local elites and the development of social science departments occurred elsewhere also, especially at Columbia, Chicago's closest rival for national preeminence in the social sciences until the 1940s. John Burgess, who built Columbia's social science faculty, commented in his autobiography that economist E. R. A. Seligman proved particularly useful to him because of his local connections. "I found his wide relationships and acquaintance with men in the business and financial circles of New York a very great help in the work of the development of the institution," Burgess recalled in 1934.[80]

Academic philosophy in twentieth-century America has not profited from the kind of entrepreneurship that characterizes successful social scientists, but in the first three decades of the University of Chicago's growth, three philosophers under John Dewey's intellectual leadership established extensive relations with Chicago elites similar to those forged by Henderson and Merriam and other social scientists. Dewey came to Chicago in 1894 from the University of Michigan to head a combined department of philosophy, psychology, and pedagogy, bringing with him his colleague George Herbert Mead. James Hayden Tufts, who came to Chicago upon its opening in 1892 from Dewey's department at Michigan, originally proposed Dewey's appointment to Harper. The Chicago department soon gained national repute as the intellectual center of pragmatic philosophy. The Chicago philosophers rejected the traditional philosophical premise that the world constituted a fixed external reality and the mind a different internal reality. Instead, the pragmatists argued that both mind and matter were part of a dynamic, changing process. This philosophical view encouraged the development of inductive scientific inquiry and held up practical experience as the indispensable test of social theory.[81]

Pragmatism had implications for numerous social activities, and Chicago philosophers needed to test their formulations in practical settings. At the Laboratory School that Dewey established at the University of Chicago, he developed his enormously influential theories of progressive education. Dewey has always been described as shy, retiring, and personally awkward, qualities alien to aggressive civic activists like Henderson and Merriam. Yet, like these colleagues, Dewey established extensive connections with local civic elites of wealth or influence who provided financial support for his Laboratory School. The same elites later supported his student and protégé, Ella Flagg Young, who as superintendent of Chicago's public schools fought to implement many of Dewey's ideas. And Dewey also worked closely with Jane Addams and Hull House, whose innovative kindergarten program greatly influenced his educational theory.[82]

Dewey left Chicago in 1904 as a result of personal and professional disputes with Harper, but his colleagues continued to elaborate pragmatic philosophy and remained profoundly linked to local elites. George Herbert Mead shared Dewey's shyness to an extreme, so much so that he thought unduly little of his own work and published sparsely throughout his career. (His four "books" were compiled posthumously by former students from unpublished papers and students' own classroom notes.) One former student related that Mead rarely appeared in class until all his students had been seated for several minutes. Then, he would

> stride to the front of the room, sit down, take up a piece of chalk or other object, fix his eyes on a corner of the ceiling, and begin talking without any sign of awareness that there was anyone else present. He would cogitate aloud without interruption for the duration of the hour; then just before the time was up, without stopping his lecture, he would walk to the back of the room, stop talking precisely at the end of the hour, dart out the door, shutting it behind him.

One student remarked that "Professor Mead conversed with God and allowed the students to listen in." [83]

Those who knew Mead found it hard to believe that he was a leading figure in Chicago progressivism, president of the City Club, a major protagonist in several heated political battles over the public schools, a labor arbitrator, and the initiator of social surveys and a city bureau of social research. Mead's reputation as a philosopher in his own day was negligible, but after his death his work profoundly influenced the development of social psychology within the discipline of sociology; particularly lasting were his concepts of the "generalized other" and the "self." Mead's thought was fundamentally influenced by his social reform activities, which provided a basis in experience for his view of social behavior. Likewise, his pragmatic social psychology formed the foundation for his vigorous reform career. "In the social world we must recognize the working hypothesis as the form into which all theories must be cast as completely as in the natural sciences," he wrote in 1899. "The highest criterion that we can present is that the hypothesis shall *work* in the complex forces into which we introduce it." [84]

James Hayden Tufts shared none of the shyness and social awkwardness of his close friends Mead and Dewey. Unlike Mead, he published regularly, edited the *School Review* and the *International Journal of Ethics*, headed the department after Dewey's departure, and held various high administrative posts within the university. He was also alone among the trio in attending church regularly. Tufts specialized in ethics and jointly authored a book on the subject with Dewey. A prominent advocate of housing reform in Illinois and agitator for labor and social welfare legislation, he taught and wrote largely on moral and ethical dimensions of contemporary social problems and legislation. Perhaps

*View of the University of Chicago from the Ferris Wheel at the Columbian
Exposition on the Midway, 1893. Courtesy of* Cap and Gown, *1896.*

*William Rainey Harper. Courtesy of The Department of Special Collections,
The University of Chicago Library.*

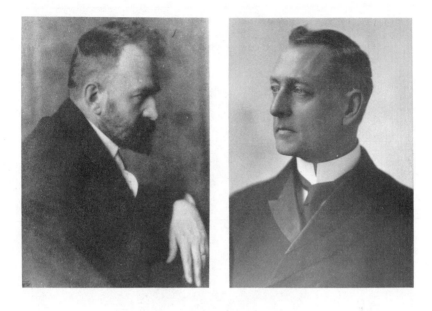

(left) *George Herbert Mead. Courtesy of The Department of Special Collections, The University of Chicago Library.*

(right) *Charles Richmond Henderson. Courtesy of The Department of Special Collections, The University of Chicago Library.*

PLATFORM

ALD. CHARLES E. MERRIAM
✕CANDIDATE
REPUBLICAN NOMINATION
FOR
MAYOR

"HE DOES NOT HAVE A PLATFORM BE-
CAUSE HE IS A CANDIDATE; HE IS A CAN-
DIDATE BECAUSE HE HAS A PLATFORM."

PRIMARY ELECTION, FEBRUARY 28

Charles E. Merriam Campaign Pamphlet, 1911. Courtesy of The Department of Special Collections, The University of Chicago Library, from the Merriam Papers, Box 75, folder 3.

(left) *Ernst Freund. Courtesy of The Department of Special Collections, The University of Chicago Library.*

(right) *James Hayden Tufts. Courtesy of The Department of Special Collections, The University of Chicago Library.*

(left) *Sophonisba P. Breckinridge. Courtesy of The Department of Special Collections, The University of Chicago Library.*

(right) *Edith Abbott. Courtesy of The Department of Special Collections, The University of Chicago Library.*

for this reason, he had little lasting impact on pragmatic philosophy; his importance lay in the application of pragmatism to contemporary affairs.[85]

Civic activism in the city of Chicago thus provided Mead and Tufts with an indispensable laboratory for philosophical inquiry, but unlike their colleagues in political science, sociology, or economics, they did not use their close association with local elites of wealth to win material support for their discipline and thereby advance themselves professionally. Dewey, of course, raised a great deal of money for his educational experiments through his local connections. Scholars in the field of education, which soon separated from philosophy, still profit richly today by linking their scholarship to public needs. The extensive civic activism of Tufts and Mead enhanced the prestige of the university generally, but it had limited impact on the development of academic philosophy.

The symbiotic relationship between civic reform and scholarship established by men like Henderson, Merriam, Dewey, Tufts, and Mead grew even more readily in the professional schools, particularly in law and social work. Since university professional schools educated people to perform particular social tasks and to advance the knowledge needed to do these tasks, civic involvement seemed only natural. The career of Ernst Freund best exemplifies the mutually supportive influences of activism and scholarship on the law and jurisprudence.

Freund, a German Jew who moved to the United States after completing advanced study in canon and civil law at Berlin and Heidelberg, did further work at Columbia University and taught public law there. In 1894, he came to Chicago to teach political science, and he played a major role in establishing the Chicago Law School in 1902. Freund, an active member of both the political science and the law professions, rebelled against the view, then prevalent, that the law is a coherent set of principles derived from judicial interpretation of the constitution. Freund belonged to the group of young legal thinkers in the early twentieth century who believed that the state must intervene in the economy to guarantee the social welfare of citizens in an industrial society. Thus he examined the actual process of law enforcement and legislative drafting so as to develop sound principles of legislation and administrative law, subjects hitherto minimized or ignored by legal scholars.

The Chicago setting clearly stimulated Freund's interest in these subjects. Confronted with the raw evidence of social misery all around him and with the aggressive efforts of reformers at Hull House and elsewhere to win legislative protection for children, women, immigrants, or factory workers, Freund became the major legal expert of

Chicago reform. Through a variety of local and national organizations and as a member of a city charter revision commission and a state constitutional convention, Freund wrote or reviewed literally hundreds of proposed laws, always looking for the best administrative remedy for a particular problem and avoiding the pitfalls of imprecise legal language. Freund's extensive writings grew largely from his attempts to systematize this experience; his close relationship with reformers gave him the opportunity to affect concretely the writing of the law, which enhanced his professional reputation. Soft-spoken and erudite, Freund was highly regarded and personally well-liked in reform circles. He, too, worked at a phenomenal pace.[86] "I don't think I ever met anybody in the academic world who more justly merited the characterization of a scholar and a gentleman than did Ernst Freund," observed his close friend, Mr. Justice Frankfurter.[87]

In no field did scholars advance their reputations through connections with local reform more completely than in social work. At the turn of the century, leaders in charitable and settlement work started organizing training courses for workers in their growing field. At Chicago, these courses were first offered through the extension division of the University of Chicago, primarily by Graham Taylor, who taught Christian sociology at Chicago Theological Seminary and headed the Chicago Commons settlement house, and Charles R. Henderson. In 1908, the Russell Sage Foundation granted substantial sums to five social work training schools for social research work. The Chicago school, which had separated from the university after Harper's death because Judson withdrew financial support, placed its research department under the leadership of Julia C. Lathrop of Hull House. She in turn recruited two dynamic young economists who had recently completed doctorates at the University of Chicago, Sophonisba P. Breckinridge and Edith Abbott.

Both women came from activist political families and arrived in Chicago thoroughly imbued with intense fervor for social service. Breckinridge's ancestors had held high political office in Kentucky and the nation since the earliest days of the Republic; Abbott's paternal grandfather vigorously opposed slavery, but her father had to run away from home to fight in the Civil War because his father was a pacifist as well as an abolitionist. He later became the first lieutenant governor of Nebraska. Both women combined their activist heritage with a profound scholarly inclination. Their search in life was for a way to advance social reform through scholarship.

Breckinridge arrived at the university in 1897 and received her

Ph.D. in 1901, after which she attended the university's new Law School. The social science departments in which she studied had been sufficiently liberal to admit women to graduate study, but were not quite ready to offer major academic appointments to promising young females; so Breckinridge taught courses on family life and social welfare instead on a part-time basis until 1920 in the Department of Household Administration, the precursor of what is now called home economics. Abbott came to the university in 1901 and, after completing her doctorate, studied for a year with Beatrice Webb at the London School of Economics. Much to the surprise of many colleagues, she left a secure position teaching economics at Wellesley after one year to join her friends Julia Lathrop and Sophonisba P. Breckinridge at the new and financially unstable Chicago School of Civics and Philanthropy. She later also accepted a part-time position in the Chicago sociology department teaching methods of social investigation.

Lathrop left Chicago in 1913 to head the new United States Children's Bureau, leaving Breckinridge, Abbott, and Taylor as the leading figures at the school. Taylor, like many early social work educators, lacked intellectual sophistication and rigor and favored a highly practical education for social work. Breckinridge and Abbott, nearly alone among the founders of academic social work, urged rigorous academic training, preferably on the graduate level, to enable social workers to conduct research on social problems and contribute to their remedy as well as to provide direct services to the needy. In short, they thought social work should become the science of social policy, which applied the most advanced knowledge and research to concrete human problems by combining academic work and fieldwork. Such an ideal, they believed, could best be realized within a university and not, as almost everyone else in the field insisted, in an independent, vocationally-oriented school.[88]

The years through the end of World War I proved frustrating for Breckinridge and perhaps even more so for Abbott. Breckinridge, by all accounts, was mild in manner, extremely proper in bearing, and not terribly forceful. Abbott, ten years her junior, was tough, even blunt, and extremely aggressive. A colleague who knew both women intimately described how "their minds were cast in different molds." Abbott's she called "direct" but capable of seeing nuances and relationships; Breckinridge's thoughts, however, were "ever active, amazingly fluid," and "seemed to dart now here, now there, so that the more pedestrian-minded had difficulty in following and were wont sometimes to believe that her thoughts were disconnected."[89]

Both women, but for the handicap of gender, had the potential for great academic achievement and professional recognition in the social sciences. Abbott, however, also had the qualities of an academic entrepreneur that would certainly match those of Charles E. Merriam. The established social science disciplines presented too many obstacles to professional achievement to satisfy the ambition of an Edith Abbott. Her best hope and that of Breckinridge, perhaps their only one, lay in a separate field of social work fashioned to their own scholarly temperaments and distinct from the other social sciences.

In the years between 1908 and the end of World War I, Breckinridge and Abbott laid the groundwork for their new discipline by undertaking with their students numerous studies of housing, child welfare, juvenile delinquency, and other urban problems. They also established extensive relationships with Chicago elites. Both women had been Hull House residents since their graduate student days and were charter members of the circle of women reformers and philanthropists who orbited around Jane Addams. Breckinridge, for example, developed a close rapport with Anita McCormick Blaine, a leading Chicago philanthropist, and with Julius Rosenwald, the extraordinary benefactor of hundreds of social welfare enterprises in the first three decades of the twentieth century. Both women also remained intimate with Julia Lathrop at the Children's Bureau and her successor, Edith's sister Grace. Indeed, the Children's Bureau connection provided both funding for much of the research conducted by their students for several decades and a focal point for political influence in Washington in the 1920s and 1930s.

None of these connections compensated for the absence of adequate financial resources and the intellectual support of other social science disciplines, which location within a university provided. In the late 1910s, after Russell Sage terminated its grant, the Chicago school suffered continual financial crisis, which drained the energies of everyone involved with the project. Toward the end of the decade, Breckinridge successfully maneuvered to bring the school into the University of Chicago, ostensibly for financial reasons. In this she won the wholehearted support of Julius Rosenwald and the reluctant support of other board members, who feared that practical training would be dwarfed in an excessively academic environment. Graham Taylor felt betrayed by Breckinridge and Edith Abbott and never really forgave them.

In 1920, Breckinridge and Abbott moved back to the University of Chicago as the core faculty of the new School of Social Service Administration, and in 1924 Abbott officially became dean. The school prospered, and Breckinridge and Abbott exerted wide influence in social work and social policy generally through their students, their journal, monographs, and textbooks published by the university press, and the continued close association between their academic program and local and national social welfare agencies and officials. If Charles Merriam secured his place at the university through civic activism, Breckinridge and Abbott practically imposed their places upon the university through the strength of their local influence and the quality of their scholarship.[90]

THE LIMITS OF FACULTY ACTIVISM

Faculty activism, then, proved a major source of professional stimulation and advancement for scholars like Henderson, Merriam, Dewey, Mead, Tufts, Freund, Breckinridge, and Abbott. All of their civic activities had an aura of scientific expertise about them, and all of these scholars worked closely with sympathetic elites in the city. Successful activist academicians, Merriam included, argued that their civic work was nonpartisan and politically neutral, as befitted people of science. They sought changes in social policy to serve the common good, and they had no special self-interest in them; or so they believed.

Later generations would question their supposed neutrality and objectivity. Even in their own day the acid test of successful activism unquestionably was its acceptability to those upon whom the university depended for support. Conversely, activism might be unacceptable not so much for its unscientific qualities as for its unfavorable reception among the university's potential supporters.

In the first three decades of the University of Chicago's existence, the form of activism potentially most damaging to the institution was *public* advocacy of radical political ideas, especially attacks on businessmen and corporations. Harper appreciated the importance of freedom of inquiry for the academic enterprise. Indeed, he recognized that his own "modernist" scholarship on the Old Testament aroused passionate criticism in some circles, and before accepting the Chicago presidency he sought assurances from Rockefeller (never given) of freedom to teach his views.[91] Judson proved less tolerant personally. Both men, however, expelled professors who espoused ideas in public forums unpopular with university benefactors.

The most celebrated instance came in the case of Edward Bemis, a former student of economist Richard T. Ely and an aggressive exponent of the new "institutional economics," which attacked rigidly deductive laissez-faire economics and supported trade unions and government intervention in the economy. Harper hired Bemis to teach primarily in the extension division because the conservative head professor of economics, J. Laurence Laughlin, vigorously opposed him from the start. The precise circumstances of Bemis's dismissal remain in dispute even today.[92] Harper claimed that Bemis proved unsuccessful in extension teaching, but Bemis's widely publicized attack on the railroads during the Pullman strike probably proved decisive. "Your speech . . . has caused me a great deal of annoyance," scolded Harper in a letter to Bemis, adding, "It is hardly safe for me to venture into any of the Chicago clubs. I am pounced upon from all sides." Harper then proposed to Bemis "that during the remainder of your connection with the University you exercise very great care in public utterance about questions that are agitating the minds of the people."[93]

A spate of similar attacks on faculty advocacy occurred at other American universities in the 1890s. In Wisconsin, Ely was tried by the regents for favoring labor unions, but the case ended in dismissal of the charges and an affirmation by the regents of the right of academic freedom. In 1900 E. A. Ross was dismissed from Stanford University because of his opinions on free silver and immigration.[94] The University of Pennsylvania fired Edmund James in 1895 because his views proved unpopular. Professor John Henry Gray, who held Northwestern's position in political and social science from 1892 to 1907 claimed that "at Northwestern . . . I was under constant fire for my economic, social, and political views." He asserted that "the Records of the Board show a motion made by a sitting judge to dismiss me 'for criticizing the United States Constitution'—not carried."[95]

Significantly, however, colleagues around the country who shared Bemis's views did not rally publicly to his defense, as they did in some other cases, with the exception of Ely, who supported him mildly. In part, they too feared for their positions, but the manner of Bemis's advocacy also proved embarrassing. Concerned with establishing prestige and influence for their profession, other economists recognized the practical disadvantages of popular agitation. The need for acceptance by people of influence and wealth proved no less important to the social science professions nationally than to university presidents.[96]

Fourteen years after the Bemis case, Judson, like his predecessor, acted to end dysfunctional public advocacy. When Charles Zueblin, a sociologist who had taught at Chicago since 1893, delivered a stinging attack on businessmen in a public speech, Judson reprimanded him for his remarks:

> I have felt that as a member of our faculty it is not expedient for the lecturer on the public platform to attack individuals unless the University has been informed in advance and is willing to put itself in the position of supporting such policy. It is impossible to differentiate the lecturer on the public platform who bears the name of the University from the University itself . . . as members of the university faculty we all of us represent the University.[97]

Zueblin resigned his position that year, although no one publicly accused Judson of suppressing unpopular advocates and the circumstances of his resignation may not have been widely known at the time.

A faculty member's personal activities could also provoke dismissal if they embarrassed the university, even if they had no political implications. In 1917, the brilliant sociologist W. I. Thomas was arrested in violation of the Mann Act, prohibiting white slavery, after registering with a woman under a false name in a Chicago hotel. The university quickly moved to dismiss him, despite Small's protests, even though the charges were dropped.[98]

On the other hand, activism in forums that semed inappropriate for scholars did not necessarily meet with condemnation, if they served the interests of the university sufficiently. Merriam's career in electoral politics (as distinct from his activities in reform organizations and government commissions) is an obvious case in point.

In 1901, economics professor William Hill, in a public address, "The Ward Boss as an Educational Factor," declared that Honroe Palmer, son of Chicago's hotel baron, would be a tool of the bosses if elected alderman because he was nominated by Mayor Carter Harrison alone and not by the electorate. Palmer's mother, Mrs. Potter Palmer, angrily protested to Harper this slur against her son. Harper responded that "the University is not to be held responsible for utterances made by the Professors . . . our friends must understand that each and every Professor is a law unto himself and that he must be dealt with individually, just as any other citizen is dealt with."[99] Had Harper criticized Hill, he would have risked antagonizing many wealthy reformers, most of whom were Republicans and who in any event opposed "boss rule." Harper's staunch defense of faculty freedom in this instance must be understood in light of his action in the Bemis case, when local business elites were united in their anger.

To cite another example: J. Laurence Laughlin, the conservative head of the economics department, who vigorously opposed the use of silver as a monetary standard, undertook popular agitation for this cause in almost an identical way as Bemis. Laughlin attacked the popular silver crusader William H. (Coin) Harvey in newspaper articles and even debated him on the same platform in 1896. Such popular means of influencing public policy hardly diminished Laughlin's position at Chicago, because his views received wide approval from the business community. Nationally, however, they undermined his credibility among other economists and government officials and limited his influence over monetary policy in the early twentieth century.[100] The message soon got across to faculty members. Respectably "scientific" means of influencing social policy in an acceptable direction could pave a path to academic success; and advocacy of unpopular ideas through seemingly "unscientific" means could result in dismissal.

Later generations shared some of Veblen's anxieties that either individual or institutional involvement in public affairs might compromise the university and turn its energies away from the pursuit of knowledge for its own sake. Few person's of Harper's generation shared these fears. Why this self-assurance that scholarship, teaching, and public service were fully compatible? For one thing, little in these professors' experiences revealed the dangers. From Puritan times on, colleges had concerned themselves with developing good citizens, and few people questioned Jefferson's conviction that education had to be the foundation of a democratic society. From the vantage point of the early twentieth century, the college's concern with citizenship had been necessary and good.

More important, when the University of Chicago opened in 1892, universities were still quite new and were just beginning to explore the possibilities of service to their society. This was not a time for introspection or self-criticism, but an era of growth and experimentation. Nothing in the experience of American universities thus far indicated that public service might harm the university; but the experience of the antebellum college suggested the shortcomings of a remote seminary of learning for its own sake. Its detachment from public service had resulted in neither solid scholarship, sound teaching, nor popular support. Indeed, most university presidents of the early twentieth century concluded that service was the only way to win support for the advancement and dissemination of knowledge on the highest level.

Finally, the new academic professionals of the late nineteenth century were immensely self-confident. They had discovered science— natural and social—and were convinced that in knowledge lay the answer to all problems. There was a common good, they believed, and science would reveal it. Progress was inevitable and human beings malleable. The failures of progressive reform, the disillusionment of two world wars, a major economic depression, and the disappointments of a war on poverty shook national self-confidence and led people to wonder whether science really had all the answers.

Indeed, as the twentieth century progressed, the service function of the university came under ever greater, if contradictory, attack. The role of natural scientists in the development of nuclear weaponry and in other forms of advanced technological and biological warfare troubled many faculty and students, as did involvement of the United States Central Intelligence Agency with universities and individual professors. On the other hand, many of these same persons called upon the university to end its complacency in the face of social injustice and demanded that scholars make their research and teaching "relevant." Minority groups and women demanded that universities compensate for society's past discrimination. The Vietnam War once again raised the issue of the propriety of popular agitation and advocacy for faculty members.

Although an occasional voice called consistently for the university's withdrawal from all public service activities, the majority of the critics advocated withdrawal from some and entrance into others. Herein lies the old dilemma of the university. Service remains essential for social support of higher education, but unpopular advocacy or activities can harm the university's reputation among those upon whom it depends for support. Indeed, in the late 1960s, militant student protests, sometimes supported by faculty members, caused a significant decrease in contributions to private universities and appropriations for public ones.

Ironically, the very faculty who attacked the university for its corrupting relations with government and other major institutions in the 1960s and 1970s benefited from the prosperity and prestige that academia had acquired largely as an outgrowth of a service mission carefully forged by earlier university generations. A major part of that mission in the three decades before World War I was an assault on the problems of the city through an alliance with other municipal reformers.

3

The Anatomy of a Reform Movement

WHAT MANNER OF PLACE was this city called Chicago? The question still evokes a myriad of responses from those who know it and those who do not. Heterogeneity is a defining quality of cities, but few of the world's great cities have evoked so many distinct images as did the metropolis on Lake Michigan in the three decades before the end of World War I.

Chicago, first of all, was big and getting bigger. The nation's second largest city doubled its population between 1880 and 1890 from 503,185 to 1,099,850. Of the ten largest cities in the nation, none grew faster in the 1890s than Chicago. Ten years later its population stood at 1,698,575. It doubled its 1890 mark again by 1910. In 1920, 2,701,705 people lived in Chicago. Altogether, during these forty years, the city's population increased a little more than fourfold.[1] The physical city expanded with the population. In 1889, it more than doubled through annexation of adjacent areas, and several smaller annexations followed.[2] This growth in size and population took place in a city that had to be substantially rebuilt after the great fire of 1871.

Chicago also evoked the image of ethnic diversity. From 1900 to 1910, roughly 35 percent of its people were foreign-born. New immigration largely ceased when war broke out in Europe in 1914, but in 1920 foreigners still accounted for 30 percent of the population. Moreover, in 1900, 36 percent of the city's people were children of foreigners, and that figure dropped only slightly in the next two decades. More than thirty-five different nationalities were represented.[3]

Chicago's reputation as a center of industry and rail transport spread throughout the world long before Carl Sandburg indelibly etched the image with his lines, "Hog Butcher for the World, / Tool Maker, Stacker of Wheat, / Player with Railroads and the Nation's Freight Handler." The stockyards, the steel mills of South Chicago, the railroads, the garment factories, and the McCormick agricultural works employed numerous Chicagoans, as did George Pullman's sleeping-car plant in his "model" suburban town. Such extensive industrialization inevitably brought widespread poverty and the social ills that accompany it. In *Hull House Maps and Papers* (1895), residents of the famous settlement on Halstead Street revealed desperate economic conditions in the neighborhood just east of the settlement. The average wage rate, said Julia Lathrop, was "so low as to render thrift, even if it existed, an ineffective insurance against emergencies."[4] The sweating system, in which workers sewed garments in their own homes, resulted in "grinding poverty, ending only in death or escape to some more hopeful occupation," concluded Florence Kelley. "Within the trade there has been and can be no improvement in wages while tenement-house manufacture is tolerated."[5] As for child labor, Kelley and Alzina Stevens concluded that it was an "unmitigated injury to . . . [the children], to the community upon which they will later be burdens, and to the trade which they demoralize."[6] Two decades later, the situation was not much better. The average wage of men supporting a family in the stockyards was $503 per year, an economist concluded in 1915, even though the minimum sum needed to support a family of five efficiently was $800 per year. The same study found that unskilled workers in the steel mills earned less than eighteen cents an hour.[7] Upton Sinclair's graphic descriptions of living and working conditions in his widely read novel, *The Jungle* (1905), popularized this side of Chicago's image more thoroughly than the meticulous studies of social workers and social scientists.

The results of inadequate wages were writ large in Chicago's poorest neighborhoods. The worst slums included the Hull House district east and west of Halstead Street, the stockyards district further south on Halstead Street, the steel mills in the far southeastern section of the city, the First Ward running along Clark Street from the Loop south past Roosevelt Road, the southwest section of the near north side west of Wells Street and south of Chicago Avenue, and the largely black district along the lake between Twentieth and Fortieth streets. In these areas, six and seven people commonly lived in one or two rooms. The disease rate was frighteningly high. Professional criminals operated freely. The First Ward and the "black belt" contained most of the city's prostitution. Animal waste polluted the stockyards district, as did steel mill smoke in South Chicago.

Small wonder that Chicago also acquired an unenviable reputation for violence. In 1877, a year of nationwide depression and labor unrest throughout the nation, a large number of Chicago workers went on strike. The riots that followed were subdued by police, federal troops, and private guards. Nine years later, in the midst of a campaign for the eight-hour day in Chicago, someone threw a bomb just as the police began to break up a meeting sponsored by Chicago's Anarchists. Seven policemen died. On flimsy evidence, a jury convicted nine radicals of conspiring to throw the bomb in a trial that received considerable national attention. In 1894, workers at Pullman struck and precipitated a nationwide railroad stoppage, and once again federal troops subdued the strike.

Chicago was also known as a city of crime long before the heyday of gangsters like Al Capone in the 1920s and 1930s. In 1901 a writer for *McClure's* interviewed hundreds of criminals and found that the people in that business agreed "that Chicago was the best stopping-place for tramps and thieves in the United States."[8] Six years later, another writer in the same journal observed that Chicago, "perhaps the most typically American of our cities," had the reputation of being "preeminently notorious for violent crime."[9]

In recent years, Chicago's reputation for machine politics has been unrivaled; yet as early as 1894, the British journalist William Stead noted in his widely read book, *If Christ Came to Chicago*, that "leading citizens of Chicago have repeatedly assured me that there is no hope and no future for the city of Chicago under the system of popular government."[10] Between the opening of the University of Chicago in 1892 and the end of World War I, Chicagoans witnessed endless factional struggles within the Republican and Democratic parties. Political power was highly decentralized, and seldom did a mayor have a firm grip on the city council. In the poorest districts, ward bosses financed their organizations by extorting operators of prostitution or gambling establishments, by demanding kickbacks from the salaries of patronage appointees, and by accepting bribes from companies seeking city council franchises. Among the Democrats, Johnny Powers controlled the Nineteenth Ward, in which Hull House was located, and "Hinky Dink" Kenna and "Bathhouse John" Coughlin jointly ruled over the First Ward, commonly known as the Levee.

Hinky Dink and Bathhouse ruled by methods that appalled respectable citizens. These bosses organized a legal defense fund for brothel keepers, gamblers, and hoodlums who were occasionally arrested. Prostitutes suffering from tuberculosis were sent by the organization to sanitariums in Denver. In the depression winter of 1893, thousands of tramps were housed and fed by the organization, and a few years later Kenna established his "Workingmen's Exchange," a flophouse on Clark Street where tramps and vagrants could come for a free meal and a place to sleep. Grateful to their benefactors, thousands of tramps would vote the Kenna-Coughlin ticket on election day.[11]

Ward bosses and aldermen saw politics from the perspective of their district and were generally uninterested in citywide matters unless the issues affected their home districts or might be profitable. The mayor, on the other hand, confronted broader problems. Among Chicago's most popular mayors were Carter Henry Harrison, who began his fifth term in 1893 and died at the hands of an assassin several months later, and his son, Carter Henry Harrison II, who served five terms of his own, not all consecutive, between 1897 and 1915. The younger Harrison was well educated, socially polished, and independently wealthy. Like his father, he was an able politician, relatively honest, but a believer in the art of the possible. He was lax in enforcing laws against prostitution, gambling, and Sunday closing, a popular policy among the city's large German population. He undertook a campaign against Charles Yerkes, the traction magnate who systematically bribed the city council, but remained closely aligned with Hinky Dink and Bathhouse upon whose support he depended. In exchange, the Levee was not bothered by the police.[12]

The Republican who eventually defeated Harrison, William Hale (Big Bill) Thompson, grew up in equally advantageous circumstances. A loud and aggressive politician, Thompson skillfully played upon people's prejudices. First elected mayor in 1915, Thompson successfully developed a centralized party organization. He freely fired city civil service employees and appointed "temporary" replacements loyal to himself. He accepted money from leaders in the criminal underworld and allowed their prostitution and gambling establishments to flourish. Like Harrison, Thompson appealed to immigrant groups, and he also won strong support from Chicago's black voters.[13]

Other dimensions of Chicago life also evoked vivid images. The literary achievements of men like Dreiser, Anderson, Fuller, Norris, Herrick, Wright, and Sandburg created a distinctively midwestern literary tradition centered in Chicago. The bold and innovative architecture of Daniel Burnham at the World's Columbian Exposition and later in the development of a "Chicago Plan" helped establish the Chicago School of Architecture.[14] And, of course, the various "Chicago Schools" of sociology, theology, philosophy, political science, social welfare, and economics emanating from the University of Chicago advanced the city's reputation as a center of learning.

Closely tied to these various dimensions of life in the midwestern metropolis was Chicago's reputation as a center of aggressive reform in the late nineteenth and early twentieth centuries. An incredibly diverse set of organizations worked for change in virtually every area of local government and public policy, from city charters to public health, from urban planning to labor legislation, from crime control to public education. The roster of prominent progressives from Chicago is by itself impressive—Jane Addams, Julia Lathrop, Florence Kelley, Alice Hamilton, Harold Ickes, Julius Rosenwald, Sidney Hillman, Clarence Darrow, Grace and Edith Abbott, Sophonisba Breckinridge, Charles Merriam, Graham Taylor, Raymond and Margaret Dreier Robins, to name a few. Lincoln Steffens pointed to Chicago as an example of a city that "should be celebrated . . . for reform, real reform, not moral fits and political uprisings . . . but reform that reforms, slow, sure, political, democratic reform, by the people, for the people."[15] Similar activities went on elsewhere at the same time, but Chicago provided much of the initiative and leadership for what historians have dubbed "urban progressivism."

No single agency or set of leaders directed Chicago's widely diverse campaigns; nor was there a single platform to which all elite reformers subscribed. Yet a network of interlocking directorates and personal ties among their leaders welded these diverse crusades into a distinct movement. Around a relatively small group of leaders, constantly interacting with each other, orbited a wide variety of political and social movements. These men and women constituted a reform community.

Who belonged to this community? Over 2,500 men and women participated in the work of at least one of some seventy reform groups and agencies in the city between 1892 and 1919. Only 215, however, were involved in three or more organizations. Most of the latter were fairly prominent, and it was not difficult to obtain basic biographical data for nearly all of the 169 men and more than half of the 46 women and to trace the connections among them.[16]

The most prominent members of the reform community commonly held leadership positions in a dozen or more different reform organizations. A variety of informal ties supplemented formal organizational connections through the interlocking directorates. Not the least of these were ties through blood or marriage. The McCormick family provides a case in point. Anita Blaine was the benefactor of numerous reform projects. Her first cousins, Robert Rutherford McCormick (president of the *Chicago Tribune* and alderman) and Joseph Medill McCormick (congressman) were both active in the movement for cleaner and more efficient city government and greater local home rule. Joseph's wife participated in organizations committed to child welfare, labor legislation, and woman suffrage.[17]

Similarly, both Charles R. Crane of construction fame and his brother, Richard, Jr., held important positions in government reform organizations and social welfare agencies. Julius Rosenwald and his brother Lessing, Edith Abbott and her sister Grace, social worker Raymond Robins and his wife, Margaret Dreier Robins, all held important positions in local reform associations, as did numerous others related by blood or marriage. In fact, 20 of the 215 reform leaders had spouses who held office in one or more reform associations.

Social ties also bound the reformers into a community. Most of them lived in the same parts of the city. Excluding those who resided among the poor in social settlements, 32 percent of the reform leaders lived in the area from Fortieth Street on the north to Sixtieth Street on the south (about three miles) and from Drexel Boulevard on the west to Lake Michigan on the east (about one mile). Within this three-square-mile rectangle lay the University of Chicago. An additional 21 percent lived in the wealthy area just north of the Loop along the lake, bounded by East Lake Street on the south and North Avenue on the north (just under two miles) and the lake on the east and Dearborn Avenue on the west (a little more than half a mile at its widest point), which included the section later known as the "Gold Coast."[18]

Reformers also attended the same churches and synagogues and joined the same clubs. Of the 169 men, 113 were members of the City Club, 55 belonged to the Union League Club, 45 to the Chicago Club, and 36 to the Commercial Club. Of the 46 women, 35 belonged to the Woman's City Club, and 22 were members of the Chicago Woman's Club.[19]

What were these people like? Of the 215 members of the reform community, all of the men and nearly half of the women were in business or the professions, and all of the nonemployed women were married to businessmen or professionals. Of 161 men, 34 were lawyers and 5 were judges, 53 were in commerce, industry, or banking, 8 were physicians, 23 were university professors, 13 were social workers, and 6 were clergymen. Of the 21 working women, 14 were social workers, 2 were university professors, 2 were lawyers, 1 was a physician.[20] These people were exceptionally well educated. Three-quarters of them had some higher education, including more than half the women. Forty-four percent of the group went on to graduate or professional schools after college.[21]

In other ways, the data support familiar characterizations of urban reform leadership in this period. Religion could be determined for only approximately half of the total group, but of these, 81 percent were Protestants—in a city with a majority Catholic population. Only 5 percent were Catholics, but 14 percent were Jewish. Jews were only about 8 percent of the population of Chicago by 1920, and the vast majority of them were immigrants from Eastern Europe and their children.[22] Almost all of the Jewish reform leaders were of Western European origin, however. These "German" Jews, as they were popularly called, traveled freely in old-stock Protestant circles, unlike the recent Jewish immigrants from Russia, Poland, Lithuania, and elsewhere.

Only sixty-seven of the men and almost none of the women listed party affiliation in Who's Who questionnaires. Fifty-three of these sixty-seven men called themselves Republicans in 1917, as compared to twelve Democrats and two Independents. A good number had joined the Progressive party in 1912. These national party affiliations did not necessarily extend to municipal politics, however. Indeed, many of the reformers favored nonpartisan municipal elections.

Only 16 percent of these reformers were born in Chicago; the rest came to the city at various times between the 1850s and the beginning of the twentieth century. They migrated primarily from New England, the Middle Atlantic States, and the Midwest. Eighteen (10 percent) were born abroad; seven of these came from English-speaking countries, two were sons of American citizens living abroad, and all but one of the others were born in Western Europe.[23] The leaders of reform in Chicago were not predominantly old local elites, then, but migrants from the East and Midwest.

THE SIGNIFICANCE OF THE PROFESSIONS

The most significant fact about this group is that most of its members were either businessmen or professionals and, therefore, affected by the rapidly changing occupational structure of the United States in the late nineteenth and early twentieth centuries. Role, status, and training changed as drastically in these years for businessmen, lawyers, and physicians as it did for professors. Furthermore, new professions like social work, urban planning, and public administration also emerged to perform tasks hitherto either relegated to amateurs or not performed at all. This emergence of new occupational roles helps explain why so many seemingly comfortable and prosperous upper-strata people fought so vigorously in the reform crusades of the progressive era and, more importantly, why they came up with the kinds of proposals that they did.

Each of these occupational groups organized local and national societies to look after the interests of the profession and to exchange information. Each started schools to train new members of the profession, claimed exclusive expertise over a limited subject, and argued that its members were dedicated to serving the common good.

Most of these men and women worked in large-scale enterprises. After the Civil War, the successful businessman increasingly became a manager of hundreds, perhaps thousands, of employees. Likewise, lawyers in private practice declined in importance next to specialized lawyers in firms or partnerships, which handled much of the legal work for the large corporations. Even social workers, who began in relatively small charities or settlement houses, by the second decade of the twentieth century found themselves in large welfare agencies like the United Charities of Chicago.[24]

The proliferation of organizations and the growth of large-scale enterprises fostered the development of specialization within each profession, which demanded the evolution of more elaborate means of formal training. The rise of large corporations demanded people with training in engineering, economics, finance, accounting, and management.[25] Like the new universities, the new law partnerships and firms encouraged specialization in a limited area.

As a result, more rigorous formal education for businessmen, lawyers, physicians, and other professionals increasingly became a prerequisite for entrance into these callings. The old apprentice system of "reading law" in a law office gave way to formal legal training in law schools. The Wharton School of Finance and Economy at the University of Pennsylvania opened in 1881, and the modern university business school became commonplace in the early twentieth century. In the early and middle nineteenth century, colleges of medicine were staffed by practicing physicians in a particular locale, who passed on to the students in the classic manner of apprenticeship the skills they had gained in practice over the years, without much understanding of the causes of illness and of why particular treatments did or did not work. Johns Hopkins was the first university in the United States to establish a medical school, and as time went on, the example set by Hopkins was followed elsewhere. The affiliation of medical colleges with universities enabled the medical schools to provide much sounder training in the theoretical sciences and to become centers of medical research as well as clinical centers.[26] As professions became more specialized, they asserted claims to exclusive expertise in their special areas even more vigorously. Lawyers and physicians obtained laws licensing practitioners of their crafts through certification processes that they themselves controlled.

It is not surprising that these men and women also asserted their superior qualifications to determine social policy. They depicted their interest in social policy as a selfless manifestation of a commitment to service in the common good. Henry Baird Favill, a physician and prominent Chicago reformer, insisted that in the prevention, treatment, and cure of industrial diseases "nobody so directly . . . knows all about it" as "the doctors."[27] Another Chicago reformer, businessman David Forgan, similarly asserted that "any good work, whether it is charitable, civic, religious, or anything else that is well done," or any "institution that is well run" contains "a few, good, successful business men" who are "not only supplying the funds, but have their hands on the management."[28]

Today, such claims of selfless service are usually greeted with considerable skepticism by people who recognize that professionals and businessmen, like other groups in a pluralistic society, compete to influence public policy in ways that will enhance or protect their material rewards, social status, or political power. Persons outside the professional and managerial occupations in the late nineteenth and early twentieth century were often skeptical about this claim of disinterestedness, but the newness of the professions and the still-untarnished faith in science made the claim of selfless, expert service in the common good somewhat believable. Even so sharp a critic of business practices as Louis Brandeis, a professional lawyer and reformer, suggested in 1912 that business was becoming a profession, which meant in part that it would be pursued "largely for others and not merely for one's self," and that it would measure achievement by criteria other than financial success. "As the profession of business develops," he predicted, "the great industrial and social problems expressed in the present social unrest will one by one find solution."[29]

Activist professors thus found striking compatibility of ideology and social experience with the businessmen, lawyers, social workers, physicians, and other professionals engaged in reform. All groups claimed expertise in special areas, experienced specialization and initiated advanced training programs, worked primarily in large and bureaucratic institutions, and believed that professionals should serve the common good. It is not surprising, therefore, that they joined together so readily to form a highly organized and unified reform community.

The shared experiences and values of activist professors and other professionals in the Chicago reform community generally characterized the University of Chicago's trustees and benefactors as well. Almost all of the Chicago trustees worked in business or the professions. Only 21 percent of the men reformers and 25 percent of the trustees had no higher education. Eighty-eight percent of the men reformers and 84 percent of the trustees were native Americans, and the seven trustees born abroad all came from English-speaking countries.[30] All of the non-Baptist trustees who listed their religion on *Who's Who* questionnaires were either Protestants or Western European Jews. Finally, seventeen (45 percent) of the thirty-eight Chicago-based trustees whose addresses could be determined resided in the three-square-mile rectangle on the south side that included the University of Chicago.[31]

Chicago's trustees typified the men who supported the new privately endowed universities in major cities. Whereas the trustees of the old-time college were frequently ministers, those of the new universities were mostly wealthy men of affairs. The twelve men named by Johns Hopkins in his will as trustees for his university included seven businessmen, four lawyers (two of whom were judges), and one physician. Between 1900 and 1922, the years in which Columbia University became a full-fledged university, twenty of the fifty-nine men who served as trustees were businessmen. The group included also twenty-one lawyers, eight ministers, six physicians, three engineers, and one educator. In the late 1870s and early 1880s, when John Burgess struggled to gain support for university work in the social sciences, he received little help from the college faculty but a great deal from trustee Samuel Ruggles, a banker and businessman who was a leading champion of continued improvement of the Erie Canal and a builder of the Erie Railroad. The appointment of another businessman and reform politician, Seth Low, to the Columbia presidency in 1890 proved a victory for advocates of university development.[32]

Northwestern's trustees more closely resembled those of the antebellum college than of the new universities. The various midwestern Methodist conferences appointed many of them, and these trustees frequently lived outside of Chicago. Of 139 Northwestern trustees between 1892 and 1919, 43 were non-Chicagoans, as compared with 6 of 50 Chicago trustees. Furthermore, Methodist clergymen account for

41 of the 98 trustees in this period whose occupations could be determined, the largest single group.[33] Significantly, only 2 Northwestern trustees were prominent in local reform.

Two other groups of reformers did not share all of the characteristics of the businessmen and professionals—ministers and club women. Protestant ministers were conspicuously underrepresented in the reform leadership. Only six of the reform leaders were clergymen, and of these only three were Protestant ministers. Their sparse numbers or complete absence from the boards of the new universities reflects the disinclination of wealthy benefactors to entrust management of large enterprises to clergymen. Indeed, the founders of the University of Chicago, vividly recalling the financial failure of the old ministerial-run Baptist college by the same name less than a decade earlier, placed only one minister on the original board of trustees, and he was the last one named![34]

The absence of Protestant clergymen in the reform movement cannot be explained so simply. Traditionally, Protestant ministers had been leading figures in almost all the major reform movements in American history. In the late nineteenth century, American Protestantism experienced another social awakening, and many Protestant ministers argued that Christianity demanded that they work to end social injustice. The resulting secularization of Protestantism became known as the "Social Gospel." Why, then, were Protestant ministers so underrepresented in Chicago reform?

For many Protestant ministers the Social Gospel proved so powerful that they left the ministry for full-time, activist careers. Several important reform leaders in Chicago, including Small, Henderson, and Graham Taylor, began their professional lives as ministers but shifted to professional social work or social science. Younger men like sociologist Charles Zeublin abandoned the ministry after a few years of theological study. Even those Social Gospel ministers who continued to work as clergymen often undertook other major activities. One of the three practicing ministers in the reform group, Jenkin Lloyd Jones, established and headed a settlement house, the Abraham Lincoln Center, in addition to his ministerial duties.[35] Besides the three practicing ministers, seven of the social workers and professors in the reform leadership were either ordained Protestant ministers or graduates of Protestant seminaries. In short, in Chicago as elsewhere the Social Gospel movement expressed itself more through the entry of ministers into new, service-oriented professions than through the more traditional activities of the clergy.

Club women, the contemporary term used to describe women who were not employed but who engaged in a variety of social and cultural activities usually centered around women's clubs, also proved important in reform. Although they did not share all of the experiences of the professional men and women, even some women's clubs had become large and quasi-bureaucratic. Federations of clubs enabled women to exchange ideas and work cooperatively on civic projects.[36] Furthermore, almost all of the club women were married to men in business or the professions.

The women's clubs began as cultural and literary groups, but after the 1890s, they participated in numerous social welfare and educational activities. Some of the women spent so much time in reform work that it became difficult to distinguish them from professional social workers, even though they lacked salary or formal positions. Louise deKoven Bowen first discovered social work through Jane Addams at Hull House and later became the head of the Juvenile Protective Association and one of the leading figures in juvenile reform in Chicago. Looking back on her activities years laters, Bowen recalled that at Hull House, "in certain measure, I received there from Miss Addams the training and education in social work which is now given at the School of Civics and Philanthropy."[37] Independently wealthy women like Ethel F. Dummer or Anita Blaine became quasi-professional philanthropists.[38] Most club women, however, deferred to the leadership and expertise of the professional women like Jane Addams or Sophonisba Breckinridge who made club women a major force in Chicago affairs.

The rapid growth of specialized professionals and their desire to determine social policy, along with the changing status of women and the Social Gospel movement in American Protestantism help to explain why so many comfortably middle-class people entered the crusades for municipal and social reforms after 1890. Of course, none of these elements was entirely unique to the late nineteenth century. Professionalization in law, medicine, and the ministry started well before the Civil War, the status of women changed significantly in the early nineteenth century (with important consequences for the history of reform), and Protestantism had fostered social activism before. The clean-government crusades associated with men like William F. Havemeyer, mayor of New York in the 1870s or Buffalo's Grover Cleveland and Brooklyn's Seth Low in the 1880s owed their temporary successes to the efforts of businessmen and lawyers who were disgusted with the corruption, inefficiency, and high taxes fostered by immigrant political machines.

The reform movement that gripped Chicago and other cities after

1890 differed from these earlier crusades in significant ways, however. For one thing, it united the traditional social reform concerns of women with the political and administrative interests of businessmen and lawyers. For another, the movement that began in the 1890s included the first generation of *professional* women in the United States, the first social workers, and the first academic professionals. Most important, the new urban reform movement replaced an older faith in the morality of "the best men" with a new faith in "scientific" systems and specialized expertise.

ASSUMPTIONS AND PROGRAMS

If interlocking directorates, shared experiences, and personal inter-relationships united the personnel of the reform community, a common ideology and reform agenda defined its purposes. In almost everything they wrote, these men and women exhibited their belief in progress. Although society was getting better, they insisted that progress was achieved only by conscious human effort. Progress could be measured by the extent to which individuals in a society worked in harmony for the common good, since it was achieved collectively, not individually. Individual fulfillment came only through society.

Science, reformers insisted, determined the common good. To establish "scientific" social policy, society must first collect as much data as possible on a particular problem. Before one could formulate intelligent programs to cope with poverty, for instance, one had to know who the poor were, where they lived, how many of them there were, what caused their poverty, and so on. One had to know how other United States cities and other countries dealt with poverty and which approaches worked best. Reformers generally thought muckraking unscientific and counterproductive. The authors of *Hull House Maps and Papers*, for example, insisted that "The determination to turn on the searchlight of inquiry must be steady and persistent to accomplish definite results, and all spasmodic and sensational throbs of curious interest are ineffectual as well as unjustifiable."[39] Armed with hard data, experts could devise scientific solutions for the common good, which would be readily obvious from the data. Those who pursued their own special interests in opposition to the needs of society constituted the enemies of progress—political bosses, radical demagogues, or dishonest businessmen. It never occurred to this generation of reformers that the common good might consist of a balance among the competing interests of different social groups or that the reformers themselves had a vested interest in this "scientific" approach to public policy.

Because American society was democratic, social progress demanded that every member of society be socialized to place collective interests ahead of personal impulses. Therefore, education became the indispensable key to social control in a democratic society. Educated individuals would understand society's needs and support those programs that the evidence indicated served the common good. Thus, reformers used the old Jeffersonian faith in education to reconcile their elitist assumptions with American democratic ideology.

Reformers shared assumptions, but they commonly split on specific issues. Sometimes they simply disagreed over tactics, but they also had substantive differences, such as their opinions on labor unions. For example, businessmen who saw trade unionists on picket lines concluded that they were selfish revolutionaries intent on limiting management's proper prerogatives, but social workers, who lived among the poor and understood the human consequences of inadequate wages or unhealthy working conditions, thought the demands of trade unionists reasonable.

Still, these differences of opinion did not create distrust among reformers or keep them from uniting behind the majority of programs on which they agreed. During Chicago's 1911 garment strike, Julius Rosenwald and Grace Abbott were attending a meeting of the Immigrants' Protective League. At the close of the meeting, Abbott hurried to leave and, according to Rosenwald's biographer, Rosenwald stopped her. " 'You're going to that strike meeting, aren't you?' She said that she was, and Rosenwald said that he probably would not agree with a single statement she made there, but that he was going to see that she did not catch cold on the way. He took her down to the street, put her in his automobile and sent her to the strike meeting." [40]

Even though all reform leaders did not agree on everything, a broad general program still united them. Just about everyone wanted to expand the city's educational opportunities by upgrading and reorganizing the public schools, expanding adult extension programs, and supporting libraries, museums, art galleries, orchestras, and other cultural institutions. [41] Virtually everyone in the group sought to rescue municipal government from those whom they considered corrupt and self-serving and place it in the hands of experts like themselves who would serve, they believed, only the public interest. They tried to accomplish this change by exposing graft and organizing systematically to elect honest candidates, by making local elections nonpartisan, and by introducing devices of direct democracy like primary elections, initiative, and referendum. They agreed that city government needed modernization to give it the authority and ability to meet the growing needs of its diverse population. But adequate authority was only a start. To be effective, government must conform to modern principles of scientific management and efficiency. Furthermore, reformers insisted that systematic city planning replace haphazard growth.

Reformers also united in a war against urban crime, including such moral offenses as prostitution and gambling as well as theft and violent crime. They exposed corruption and complacency within the police force, attempted to eliminate the sources of crime, and tried to turn prisons into agencies of rehabilitation rather than punishment. All of the elite reformers agreed on the desirability of voluntary agencies for social and economic improvement of the poor—charity organizations, settlements, homes for orphans, and the like. Most also maintained that government must assume a larger role in guaranteeing the social well-being of the population. The crusade for a separate juvenile court won wide support, for example, as did the campaign for adequate protection of the public's health.

This broad program had nearly unanimous *support*, but not everyone *worked* on every issue. Most of the businessmen and lawyers entered reform to work for honesty, efficiency, economy, and planning. The social workers began in the slums, and their first concern was the immediate welfare of the poor. Professors and social workers showed special interest in expansion of educational opportunities. This division of reform labor along occupational lines remained flexible, however. Charles Hutchinson maintained a keen interest in education and supported the Art Institute and other museums as well as the University of Chicago. Jane Addams tried to oust Johnny Powers as alderman of the Nineteenth Ward. Rosenwald, a businessman, played an active role in the deliberations of settlements and welfare agencies. No occupational group monopolized any cause to the exclusion of everyone else.

Several issues and programs won support from only a portion of the reform leadership, however. Some of the men opposed woman suffrage, and the women reformers themselves led the struggle for their right to vote. Social workers and many professors urged laws regulating hours, wages, and conditions of workers over the opposition of some reform businessmen. Many reformers favored temperance or prohibition, while others saw the saloon as a basic social institution for the poor. A small group of reformers confronted the problems of Chicago's black people, but most were indifferent. Some reformers favored immigration restriction, others opposed it. Still, these differences did not keep them apart.

If reformers genuinely believed that they were serving the common good, hindsight enables the historian to see clearly that their behavior was nonetheless self-serving. Samuel Hays has argued that the urban world against which such reformers reacted had decentralized political power to a considerable degree.[42] Ward politicians answered to local constituencies and pursued particularistic interests. By urging consolidation and centralization—whether in the schools, in charity, in city planning, or in budgeting—reformers increased the likelihood that they would control those areas. The agencies created by social work women produced a demand for people with the skills and techniques of social work. When professors sought to upgrade the academic preparation of schoolteachers, they demanded, in effect, that teachers come to them for their education. When businessmen demanded comprehensive city planning, they wanted to make sure that citywide improvements important to business and commerce—streets, harbors, and terminals— took precedence over the needs of local neighborhoods. The political machines that opposed the reformers depended upon graft for the money they needed to win elections. By fighting dishonesty, reformers who represented the well-to-do in effect denied adequate financing to politicians who represented the poor.

This was not hypocrisy. People seldom see themselves as self-serving or sinister, and it is only natural that human beings see issues through the perspective conditioned by their experiences. These men and women were genuinely disturbed by corruption and waste, by poverty and social misery. They sincerely believed that they, more than any other group, exercised power in the interests of everyone, just as the emerging professions insisted that their monopoly over entrance into and standards of their occupations served society. But then Hinky Dink and Bathhouse also believed that they performed important services for the poor. Reformers, despite their self-image, had considerable political and economic stake in the battles over public policy.

PREREQUISITES FOR ACTION

How did reformers go about developing and implementing their programs? First, behind every reform program stood some organization. Reformers employed many kinds of organizations. When an immediate problem required an immediate solution, an ad hoc committee was formed. Thus, to bring about a settlement of a strike in 1911, a group of men and women formed the Citizens' Committee on the Garment Workers' Strike. More often, they founded permanent associations to advance a single cause. Many such organizations performed a dual function: they worked for legislation to advance their cause and also monitored laws or programs already in existence.

Some reform agencies provided services directly to particular groups and, at the same time, urged government to assume responsibility for these services. Such agencies provided legal aid for the poor (founded in 1905), protected youth (founded in 1907), coordinated charity work (founded in 1908), aided immigrants (founded in 1909), protected infants (founded in 1911), protected women travelers (founded in 1914), and aided blacks (founded in 1916). Similarly, many of the city's social settlements, while primarily serving neighborhood residents, also attempted to change laws or improve their administration.

Reformers commonly recruited support for their causes at certain Protestant churches and Reform Jewish synagogues, usually those located in the wealthier sections of the city. Some clergymen devoted much time to reform and delivered sermons on social issues from the pulpit. A worshiper at the Hyde Park Baptist Church, Temple Sinai, or All Souls Unitarian Church, for example, was likely to hear the case for some worthy reform presented by his clergyman. Similarly, reformers worked effectively through committees of social and professional clubs. The Union League Club maintained its political action committee, and the Chicago Woman's Club had divisions devoted to philanthropy, reform, and education. The Commercial Club of Chicago sponsored Daniel H. Burnham's now-famous *Plan of Chicago*, first published in 1909.[43]

The apparatus of the two major political parties rarely provided vehicles for reformers, although some reform leaders were influential Republicans. However, reformers initiated and controlled the Progressive party of Illinois during its short life from 1912 to 1917 and won a number of local and statewide contests. Nonpartisan groups like the Municipal Voters' League of Chicago and the Legislative Voters' League of Illinois, which publicized the records and endorsed candidates for alderman and the state legislature, respectively, scored some spectacular victories. Reformers worked successfully through certain government agencies, particularly investigating or recommending commissions. They only briefly controlled the Chicago Board of Education, the Chicago Civil Service Commission, and the Chicago Municipal Department of Public Welfare.

Finally, these men and women created umbrella organizations to unify many different concerns. The Civic Federation was organized in 1893 as a "voluntary association of citizens for the mutual counsel, support and combined action of all forces for good." The federation, headed by banker Lyman Gage, included many of the most prominent Chicagoans—businessmen, professors, clergymen, lawyers, settlement workers, and women socialites. With a central council and branches in each city ward, the federation developed major programs in six areas: philanthropy, industry, municipal affairs, education, morals, and politics. The federation helped pass the city's first civil service law, organized relief during the depression winter of 1893–94, attacked gambling, exposed corruption in the city administration, and cleaned the streets.[44]

At the City Club, founded in 1903, men reformers discussed and debated civic issues. Through its committees, the club promoted projects in virtually every area of municipal concern. In 1911, Chicago women founded a similar group, the Woman's City Club. The Illinois Society for Social Legislation, launched that same year, coordinated the efforts of several dozen reform agencies to get bills through the Illinois legislature by employing a common lobbyist.[45]

Social or political action through voluntary association of this kind dated back to the earliest American settlements. Alexis de Tocqueville's observations on this point have been frequently quoted: "Americans of all ages, all conditions, and all dispositions constantly form associations. . . . Wherever at the head of some new undertaking, you see the government in France, or a man of rank in England, in the United States you will be sure to find an association." In aristocratic societies, explained Tocqueville, a small number of powerful men forced their designs upon the multitude. In a democratic society, however, individuals were powerful only when they combined forces with large numbers of other individuals for a common purpose.[46]

This observation applied even more strongly to Chicagoans of the 1890s and 1900s than it did to the predominantly rural Americans whom Tocqueville observed in the 1830s. City people lived closer together, and this physical proximity, along with technological improvements in transportation and communication, made it much easier for individuals to meet. Sociologist Louis Wirth, who began his graduate studies at the University of Chicago in the final years of this period, observed in his seminal essay, "Urbanism as a Way of Life," (1938), "Reduced to a stage of virtual impotence as an individual, the urbanite is bound to exert himself by joining with others of similar interest into groups organized to obtain his ends." This results, he suggested, "in the enormous multiplication of voluntary organizations directed toward as great a variety of objectives as there are human needs and interests." [47]

For Chicago's reform community, the voluntary association represented not only the necessary means of accomplishing something in a democratic society and urban environment; it was virtually an end in itself, an embodiment of the very *method* that reformers were seeking to impose on all activities. The voluntary associations had clearly defined purposes and constitutions laying out procedures for governance. They employed professional staffs who became expert in the matter at hand, they kept detailed records of their operations, they were audited by a public accountant, and they published annual reports to inform the public of their work. In short, voluntary associations of this sort showed that intelligent people could do things efficiently, honestly, and systematically. The means here was almost as important as the end itself.

Behind this elaborate network of organizations and leaders lay a constituency that approved at least tacitly of this work. It is extremely difficult to identify the constituency of reform, but several crude indicators reveal its nature and extent. In terms of numbers alone, approximately 2,500 men and women held office or directorships in at least one Chicago reform organization between 1892 and 1919. Furthermore, while only a few of those who belonged to clubs participated actively in their civic activities, the others apparently sympathized sufficiently to allow the use of the club's name, facilities, and money for such programs. Thus, the approximately 2,500 members of the City Club, the 2,900 members of the Woman's City Club, the 2,600 members of the Chicago Woman's Club, and the 200 members of the Commercial Club can reasonably be counted among the reformers' constituents. [48] These are trifling numbers, however, in a city of millions.

Electoral success of reform candidates provides another crude indicator of reform support. The graft exposés of the Voters' Leagues regularly took their toll of politicians in many city wards, suggesting that large numbers of Chicagoans were not unsympathetic to this phase of reform. When Merriam ran for mayor in 1911, he polled 34,000 votes in the Republican primary, defeating the organization candidate, and

161,000 votes in the general election despite efforts by regular Republicans to defeat him; he lost by only 17,000.[49] Obviously, under the right circumstances, political reform could attract significant support. In the end, however, what mattered most was not how many people supported reform but what kinds of people. The wealth and power of its supporters and members proved of much greater importance to the reform community than the size of its constituency.

The wealth of the reformers and their constituents insured reform's financial solvency. Several reform leaders and constituents were millionaires, and many others were well off. Julius Rosenwald, Anita Blaine, members of the great meat-packing families—the Armours and the Swifts, and Marshall Field all donated money to various enterprises. Those not sufficiently wealthy to finance a movement—the social workers, professors, and many lawyers—could nevertheless afford to devote much of their time to reform without financial remuneration. Jane Addams, for instance, was independently wealthy and did not rely upon a salary. George E. Cole devoted almost no time to his stationery business during the month or so before elections and headed the work of the Municipal Voters' League instead.[50] On the other side of the tracks, political machines depended upon graft and patronage positions in government to staff their precincts and get out the vote. Few local residents of these wards could afford to engage in politics.

A reform group that included judges, congressmen, aldermen, professors, and millionaires, figures like Jane Addams and Julius Rosenwald, had no difficulty winning a hearing. The publishers of three major Chicago daily newspapers, Colonel Robert Rutherford McCormick of the *Tribune*, Victor Lawson of the *Daily News* and Herman Kohlsaat of the *Record Herald* appeared in the leadership group.[51] Several Chicago reformers held high government positions in Washington. Franklin McVeagh served as President Taft's secretary of the Treasury from 1909 to 1913. Walter L. Fisher, a prominent Chicago lawyer active in government reform and civil service organizations, held the post of interior secretary under Taft. Louis F. Post, a Democrat active in several reform groups, became assistant secretary and then secretary of labor in the Wilson administration. Wilson appointed another Chicago reformer, Frederick A. Delano, to the Federal Reserve Board in 1914. Julia Lathrop, Hull House resident, directed the Children's Bureau of the Department of Labor from its inception in 1912.[52]

The men and women who constituted the reform community believed that they had the right and responsibility to direct their city.

But wishing did not make it so. They were a force with which to contend in the years between 1890 and 1919 because, in addition to the will to rule, they marshaled their money and prestige through elaborate reform organizations.

THE CHICAGO MILIEU

To a greater or lesser extent, virtually every American city of consequence witnessed this kind of upper-strata reform movement in the early twentieth century. Chicago's reform movement shared a reputation for extraordinary aggressiveness with those of Boston and New York. In one regard, at least, Chicago was unique. An economic rival to the large eastern cities, it had no serious competitors in the Midwest. Chicago's population, and especially its elite, exhibited a unique combination of defensiveness and city boosterism and this attitude profoundly influenced its cultural life and its reform movement. Chicago's local milieu combined with the larger forces of professionalization and the growth of large-scale enterprises to produce its own peculiar brand of reform.

As midwesterners by birth or by choice, Chicago's reformers were inspired by the legacy of Lincoln. "Abraham Lincoln for four years served his country as a great president," wrote Ray Ginger, "for a much longer period he served it as a great symbol. Nowhere was this more true than in the Midwest, and in his home state of Illinois." [53] In Boston, old-stock elites pointed with pride to Emerson, Thoreau, or Garrison, themselves members of old New England families. For Chicago's reformers, a majority of whom were not even born in Chicago and many of whom made their own fortunes, however, Lincoln proved more inspiring because of his humble origins and his dedication to public service. In young Chicago, where achievement counted for more than birth, Lincoln symbolized for reformers the duty of the talented and successful to serve society. [54]

Chicago, second in size only to New York, was self-conscious about its newness. It was western and fully aware that easterners saw it as the frontier—wild, uncivilized, and lacking in social grace. "Chicago seemed like a very wild and woolly place to my friends," wrote Bostonian Marion Talbot regarding her departure in 1892 for the University of Chicago, "and they were almost horrified at the idea of my leaving Boston. Many of them expressed the hope that I would soon return, and some were quite certain that I would get enough of the west pretty soon." [55] In the same year, a member of the Spanish nobility visiting the Columbian Exposition declined to be the guest of honor at a reception held by the acknowledged first lady of Chicago society, Mrs. Potter Palmer, because this Spanish aristocrat did not care to meet the wife of an innkeeper.[56] As late as 1915, the editors of the progressive *New Republic*, published in New York, condescendingly mocked Chicago:

> Chicago has once more consulted an expert on the problem of washing its dirty face. . . . But the whole inquiry is fundamentally disloyal and insincere. Everybody knows that in its secret heart Chicago has not the slightest desire to change its appearance. It is not merely inured to dirt. It would feel naked and indecent without it. It is all very well for effeminate travelers to return with emulous tales of New York's smartness. But Chicago knows better. It has taken years for it to generate a particular tone and flavor. Such things are not lightly parted with. As it is now, the entire Middle West revels in the effluvia of Chicago. It scents it joyously from afar, and young visitors still dream and rapture of walking on the face of the Chicago river.[57]

Chicagoans turned the stereotype on its head, asserting that they represented the real America, democratic, simple, unsnobbish, and unpretentious. In 1895, Albion Small, who like Marion Talbot had left New England, told students that municipal reform in Chicago was "in advance of New York." Chicago, he argued, "has developed among its people a deep civic sentiment which New York has yet to develop."[58] In 1905, William Kent, wealthy Chicago businessman and reformer, called New York "the center of things most despicable" and the "home of extravagance." "We have not surrendered our democracy in Chicago," he asserted.[59]

In the same year, the editors of a Chicago journal of current affairs stated that "American does not mean Anglo-Saxon. . . . Provincialism in any arrogant sense of the term you will not find outside of the thirteen original states of the union." "The West," the editorial continued, is "a synonym for democracy. Not the democracy of the doctrinaire who worships the Declaration of Independence and keeps 'servants,' but that democracy of practice which sees a partner in every man and woman who is accomplishing something."[60]

Thomas F. Holgate, a dean at Northwestern University, believed western universities were more democratic than those of the East. In eastern universities, he wrote in a Chicago newspaper in 1908, "some of the most valuable sides of college life are open only to those of wealth and position," whereas "in the Western college every valuable department is open to the masses." In the East, Holgate continued, "the question is asked, 'What are your family connections?' or 'What is your father's income?' [but] the only question asked of the student in the West is 'What can you do?'"[61] Similarly, William Rainey Harper suggested once that western schools were more serious than eastern ones.[62]

Even an outsider like H. L. Mencken thought Chicago "the most civilized city in America, . . . and the most thoroughly American." Calling Boston the home of the "fourth rate colonial snob," New York a city in which a "ludicrous horde of social climbers . . . infest the town, wildly trying to buy their way into a codfish aristocracy through opera houses, picture galleries, and various pecksniffian philanthropies," and Philadelphia "a Sunday school with a family entrance up the alley," Mencken praised Chicago as a place where "originality still appears to be above conformity." What easterners, he asked, could equal Mark Twain, Bret Harte, Theodore Dreiser, Sherwood Anderson, Henry Fuller, Frank Norris, or Robert Herrick? "The sharp winds from the lake seem to be a perpetual antidote to the Puritan mugginess of soul which wars with civilization in all American cities."[63]

Perhaps Carl Sandburg summed up the Chicago milieu best in his famous poem:

> They tell me you are wicked and I believe them, for
>   I have seen your painted women under the gas
>   lamps luring the farm boys.
> And they tell me you are crooked and I answer: Yes,
>   it is true I have seen the gunmen kill and go free
>   to kill again.
> And they tell me you are brutal and my reply is: On
>   the faces of women and children I have seen the
>   marks of wanton hunger.
> And having answered so I turn once more to those who
>   sneer at this my city, and I give them back the
>   sneer and say to them:
> Come and show me another city with lifted head
>   singing so proud to be alive and coarse and
>   strong and cunning.
> Flinging magnetic curses amid the toil of piling job
>   on job, here is a tall bold slugger set vivid
>   against the little soft cities.[64]

All cities had boosters. For Chicago's elite reformers, however, the "debate" was not idle. Easterners held the Midwest metropolises in special disdain. Since Chicago was the capital of the West and the West the heart of democratic America, Chicago elites determined to keep their city more democratic than the East. At the same time, they wanted to challenge the East in that which the East claimed ultimate superiority—culture and learning. The same impulse that led prominent Chicagoans to welcome the infant University of Chicago also led them to undertake numerous reform crusades.

Chicago's reform movement was shaped by major forces transforming American society—professionalization, the emergence of career women, the Social Gospel, and the rise of large-scale enterprises. Nonetheless, it displayed a peculiarly local flavor and style. The new professors who were such an important part of the reform movement were likewise products of both the larger forces and the local conditions.

4

The Control of Public Education

"IT MATTERS NOT how many truths about society are brought to the light of scholars' eyes by research, if they are withheld from the light of the people's eyes in the darkness of those scholars' libraries," wrote Albion W. Small in 1889. "The educators who grasp the situation and adapt their work to its demands will be the helmsmen of future civilizations."[1] Small's candid advice did not fall on deaf ears. Indeed, by 1889 it need hardly have been given at all. The leaders of the new American universities, determined to steer the ship of American civilization, had already identified public education as an extraordinarily promising route to conspicuous and profitable public service.

Involvement in primary and secondary education seemed the obvious extension of the university's commitment to advancement and dissemination of knowledge. Furthermore, it posed fewer hazards than economic issues like the conditions of factory workers or the rates charged by public utilities, where activist professors could readily step on the toes of potential university benefactors. Almost everyone in America favored education. Elites boasted that public education provided equality of opportunity, and at the same time they looked to the schools to socialize the large immigrant population flooding American cities. Workers looked to it as the key to their children's mobility. Beginning in the late nineteenth century, university presidents and professors, closely aligned with businessmen, social workers, and other aspiring helmsmen, fought vigorously to reform and control public education in American cities.

Reformers of urban education pursued a number of closely related objectives. They sought to "professionalize" public school teaching by encouraging teachers to broaden their knowledge of child development, the learning process, and academic subjects, and by securing tenure and promotion for teachers on the basis of "objective" professional criteria. "The time has come when preparation for teaching, even in the grades, requires a proficiency equal to that demanded by any other profession," argued William Rainey Harper in 1904.[2]

At the same time, reformers sought to apply new scientific knowledge to the task of mass education through standardized tests and other means of collecting social and educational data. These tools enabled them to differentiate students and classify them according to ability, thereby adjusting instruction and curriculum to individual needs. Deeply influenced by their understanding of John Dewey's ideas on education, many reformers also sought to introduce whole new subjects and innovative methods into the curriculum at all levels, so as to relate education to "real life" more effectively.

Educational reform also had a political and administrative side. Reformers generally fought to wrest control of big-city school systems from ward politicians, immigrants, and local neighborhood residents and vest it in persons like themselves. To accomplish this, they fought a vigorous battle everywhere against the highly decentralized system of school administration of the late-nineteenth-century American city, in which either ward-level boards exercised effective control over the schools, or a large central school board consisting of ward representatives ran their schools by placating the various local interests.

Such a diffuse system, reformers argued, encouraged political manipulation of the schools for special interests or private gain and made professionalization and educational innovation within the schools extremely difficult. "To a large extent the educational policy of most of our large cities has represented a fluctuating compromise between forces that have been by no means all educational forces," wrote George Herbert Mead in 1913.[3] Reformers believed that people like themselves, with citywide orientation and educational expertise, could more easily control smaller boards of education elected or appointed on a citywide basis. They alone would operate the schools scientifically in the common interests of all children.

In the late nineteenth century, in almost every city the campaign for change in public education included among its leaders businessmen, club women, and settlement workers. Concern for honest and efficient management in all matters of urban government normally motivated the businessmen, whereas a humanitarian interest in the social welfare of children sparked the educational work of most club women and settlement house workers. University-based programs in education, with their professorial experts in learning, child development, and school administration, infused the movement with a powerful ideology. These self-assured academicians were certain that science had shown them how to administer public schools efficiently so as to educate children of all social origins creatively and successfully.

Almost from the beginning, private urban universities forged a special relationship with the public schools. At Johns Hopkins, a physiology professor organized a class for Baltimore schoolteachers in the fall of 1877, one year after the university began, and similar courses were offered in succeeding years. The University of Pennsylvania likewise offered occasional courses for teachers, and in 1894 organized these courses into a special extension program.[4] The most successful efforts of this kind in a city occurred in New York and Chicago, although in rather different ways. Both experiences are instructive.

In New York, Teachers College of Columbia University originated in the Kitchen Garden Association, a philanthropic group founded by the daughter of a wealthy New York merchant in 1880 to educate poor girls in proper household management. Four years later, the association broadened its scope to all forms of industrial education for women and changed its name to the Industrial Education Association. Three years after that, Nicholas Murray Butler became president of the association and quickly moved to transform it into a college for training teachers. Chartered as Teachers College in 1892, it affiliated with Columbia University the following year, becoming essentially the pedagogy department of the university. Butler had long been interested in educational questions but had previously failed to win support for a chair of pedagogy at Columbia; he thus accomplished his goal of a university school of education through a circuitous route. In the process, he successfully tapped the philanthropic and humanitarian interests in educational reform in New York and channeled them into the university he would soon head.[5]

For several years before the opening of the University of Chicago, Chicago citizens interested in professionalizing teacher education had rallied behind Colonel Francis Parker, head of the Cook County Normal School, whose experimental and controversial work in individualized instruction of children attracted national attention. Parker and his allies in Chicago engaged in annual fights with the Cook County Board of Education over the school's budget, and not long after the University of Chicago opened, prominent Chicagoans including Jane Addams, John

Dewey, James Hayden Tufts, and several other professors convinced the Chicago Board of Education to take over Parker's school. The Chicago board proved no more generous to Parker, and shortly thereafter, Anita Blaine endowed a private school for his work. William Rainey Harper soon convinced Parker and Blaine to incorporate Parker's new Chicago Institute into the University of Chicago, endowment and all![6] This, of course, was in addition to the pedagogy department headed by John Dewey and the Laboratory School associated with it. In 1902, with Parker's death, these various schools and programs combined to form the University of Chicago School of Education. Furthermore, Harper obtained in 1898 another large sum from Anita Blaine to establish University College in downtown Chicago, where regular University of Chicago instructors offered their courses to public school teachers.[7] Like Butler, then, Harper proved quite successful at exploiting local educational reform sentiment in building the university.

Harvard also initiated a program in teacher education in 1891, hardly surprising since President Eliot played a key role in the National Education Association's efforts to upgrade and standardize secondary school education. Yet the Harvard program remained modest and lagged far behind those at Columbia, Chicago, and elsewhere, largely because it failed to tap the resources of Boston school reformers. One historian of education at Harvard concluded that its program "was oriented toward academic teacher education from its inception in 1891," and since "it never existed apart from the University, no Boston group could look upon it as its own." Harvard professor of pedagogy, Paul H. Hanus, received little support from the university. "Lacking the reform base which enabled Teachers College [in New York] to prosper in the eighties and nineties, Harvard's program foundered." Between 1907 and 1912, however, Hanus began developing strong ties to Boston social reform, and after that point "the benefactions of the philanthropists poured in and the curriculum exploded."[8] In Baltimore, President Gilman and several Johns Hopkins faculty had close ties to local school reformers; yet despite some extension courses in the early years, not until 1909 did Hopkins develop a full program for teachers. There resistance to coeducation apparently retarded the growth of a school of education. Hopkins lacked either an independent school of education like Teachers College, which could affiliate with the university, or its own women's college like Radcliffe, where much of Harvard's work in pedagogy developed. When Hopkins finally established its teacher education program, it did so jointly with Goucher College, an independent women's institution.[9] Chicago, like most midwestern schools, educated men and women together; therefore, coeducation was not an issue there.

Harper and Butler proved more adept than any other university men of their generation at capitalizing upon local educational reform sentiment, but academicians everywhere saw the importance of the public schools to their professional success. Establishing schools of education, studying the learning process, devising new methods of teaching or new forms of administration could lead nowhere, however, unless professors and their reform allies succeeded in gaining influence in the large public school systems. Private schools like Parker's Chicago Institute or Dewey's Laboratory School provided fine experimental centers, but schools of pedagogy could not grow unless a wide demand for their expertise and for the services of their graduates developed. The large parochial school systems naturally were closed to them, so the public schools provided university professors and their allies with their only chance for widespread influence on American education.

The early experience of Chicago's University College illustrates the problem that university schools of education confronted. University college competed with the Chicago Normal College, administered by the Chicago Board of Education, which offered extension classes to prepare teachers for promotional examinations. Harper publicly accused the Chicago school system in 1903 of pressing teachers to enroll in the Normal College classes instead of those at University College, and he attacked the quality of the work at the Normal College. His criticisms brought an angry denial and protest from School Superintendent Edwin Cooley. Despite Cooley's denial, Harper had to work hard to keep the board of education from designating the Normal College as the only place teachers could do extension work. Harper succeeded and University College grew.[10]

Other groups had an equally strong need for control over the schools; however, ward politicians depended upon the patronage that a ward school committee or a seat on the citywide board could provide: Teachers and administrators sought to improve their job security, working conditions, and livelihood. Both organized labor and businessmen also sought power over educational policy and curriculum, particularly with regard to vocational education. These and other groups vied for power over the schools. In Chicago as elsewhere, different coalitions formed over different issues.

Most of the presidents of the new urban universities considered expertise in primary and secondary schooling merely an extension of expertise in higher education. Nicholas Murray Butler remained the major figure in the struggle to establish a centralized school system in New York until that goal was fully realized in 1917.[11] Daniel C. Gilman and his two successors in the Johns Hopkins University presidency, Ira Remsen and Frank Goodnow, all served on the Baltimore Board of Education, and Gilman played a major role in replacing a twenty-two-member school board composed of representatives from each ward with a nine-member board appointed by the mayor.[12] In 1896, Butler lobbied vigorously for Gilman's appointment as superintenent of schools in New York and might have succeeded but for Gilman's last-minute withdrawal from consideration. Eliot, Butler, and President David Starr Jordan of Stanford all headed the National Education Association, and Eliot chaired the National Education Association's Committee of Ten (established by a resolution put forth by Butler), which studied secondary education and encouraged the creation of the Board of College Entrance Examinations.[13] His successor at Harvard, Abbott Lawrence Lowell, served on the Boston School Board. Andrew Draper left the superintendency of the Cleveland public schools to become president of the University of Illinois, and E. Benjamin Andrews became superintendent of schools in Chicago after leaving the presidency of Brown University.[14]

THE STRUGGLE FOR CONTROL OF PUBLIC EDUCATION

Throughout his presidency, William Rainey Harper led the group of Chicago reformers who sought political control of the schools and administrative reform in the interests of higher professional standards. A twenty-one-member board of education, appointed by the mayor, dominated the school system that reformers confronted beginning in the 1890s. (Chicago lacked the ward school committees that held power in many other cities.) Many Chicago board members held office because of their ties to political bosses in the various wards, however, or to the mayor himself. The board fought continually with the superintendent of schools, who usually sought greater independence from the board. The superintendent had no statutory authority, and the board preferred to exercise directly its authority to hire and fire teachers, select textbooks, and determine curriculum.[15]

Harper used three agencies in his attempt to gain power over the Chicago school system: his seat on the board of education, to which he was appointed in 1896, the education committee of the Civic Federation, which Harper headed, and a special Education Commission appointed by Mayor Harrison in 1897, chaired by Harper. Even before the university opened its doors, Harper initiated discussions with Chicago's school superintendent regarding the coordination of the high school curriculum with that of the university.[16] By April 1894, Harper's friends were urging Mayor Harrison to nominate him to the board of education but discovered that he was not yet eligible because he had not lived in Chicago for five years.[17] Two years later, when he had fulfilled the residency requirement, Harper's friends again pressed for his appointment. Two of the university's trustees tried to discourage Harper from accepting. "While you might be able after two or three years of distasteful work, to succeed in carrying out your wishes as to a closer contact between the university and the Public Schools," wrote D. G. Hamilton to Harper prophetically in 1896, "yet it seems the game would not be worth the powder. . . . You cannot handle dirt without soiling your hands. . . ."[18]

Harper remained as undeterred by such pleas as by sensational newspaper claims that he wished to affiliate the public high schools with the university, or by the jealousy of Northwestern.[19] "I should have thought that the general results gained by the presence of a University man in the Board would have been of a character to please all institutions," Harper wrote to the school superintendent, "but I suppose the world is yet narrow."[20]

In his first year on the board Harper studied teachers' salaries and helped to defeat a law that would have required all schools in Illinois to use the same textbooks. He also served on a committee that granted use of schoolrooms for free public lectures by institutions, like the University of Chicago, involved in extension work.[21] Furthermore, Harper was instrumental in getting the school board to appoint Brown University president E. Benjamin Andrews as superintendent of schools.[22] Harper used his position as chairman of the education committee of the Civic Federation to bolster his position on the board. The committee undertook activities supplementary to Harper's work on the board, especially collecting data on public education, which Harper eventually used to formulate a new education law.[23]

The Education Commission, appointed by Mayor Carter Harrison on resolution of the city council in December 1897, became Harper's most powerful instrument. Established to recommend changes "in regard to educational and business conduct of the school system," the commission consisted of eleven members, including three city council members and two school board members.[24] Harrison not only named Harper to the commission but asked his advice on other appointments.[25] At one of its early meetings, the commission elected Harper its chairman.

The commission spent almost a year in research and deliberation before submitting its report. It solicited testimony from the close-knit group of university experts that included Draper, Eliot, Butler, Gilman, Jordan, and others. A proposed new school law embodied its detailed recommendations. The superintendent would be given legal recognition, his duties vastly enlarged to include direct responsibility for hiring and promoting teachers, determining curriculum, choosing textbooks and apparatus, and all other purely educational matters. A business manager "capable of formulating sound business methods in his department" would be appointed and "left free in the application of these to the executive work which is assigned him," declared the final report of the commission. Thus, Harper sought to remove control over the schools from a politically sensitive board and place it in the hands of professionals like himself.

The commission also urged that the board be reduced from twenty-one to eleven members, a favorite device of reformers in these years. (In cities with a population of 100,000 or more, the average size of the school board dropped from 21.5 members in 1893 to 10.2 in 1913 and 9 in 1923.)[26] Reformers argued that this reduction in size would force the board to leave most of the work to the superintendent by making it too small to handle details directly. Chicago's board, which in the 1890s reviewed nearly every detail of school operation itself, at one time had seventy-nine subcommittees.[27] Reformers also believed, although they did not always say so, that a smaller, at-large board would be less likely to include "special-interest" members tied to neighborhood constituencies and that they themselves could control it more readily.

The report also sought to upgrade teacher preparation and increase university influence in preparing and certifying teachers. It suggested that graduates from approved colleges, other than the usual normal schools run by he school system itself, be certified to teach at the elementary and secondary level, provided they had nine months of study in education and passed an examination; and that an examination board, made up of the superintendent, one assistant superintendent, and three special examiners who were college graduates with no connection with the schools, conduct all examinations for those seeking positions or promotions. It urged further that teachers receive salary increases on the basis of prescribed criteria of merit and that advance in scholarly achievement be one of the criteria. The commission, which included no women, also believed that the public schools needed more men teachers and urged that special efforts be made to attract them, including higher pay for men. Finally, the report stressed the importance of giving principals and teachers "wider latitude" in selecting textbooks and in changing curriculum, recommended the general introduction of kindergartens and an extension of evening schools and vacation schools, and proposed that teachers' councils be organized, with direct access to the board.[28]

Not surprisingly, the Harper Commission report met stiff opposition from the teachers, ward politicians, and others who distrusted university elitism. Shortly after the report was published, Mayor Harrison wrote to Harper indicating the extent of opposition to it among the teachers.[29] They objected to giving university graduates preference in jobs and promotions and university personnel authority over promotional examinations. They charged this was a deliberate attempt by the University of Chicago, aligned with the business interests, to dominate the public schools. Women teachers, a majority in the system, objected to higher pay for men. Furthermore, they feared the concentration of power in the hands of the superintendent, since they especially disliked the current incumbent. Margaret Haley, organizer of the Chicago Federation of Teachers, testified in Springfield that the Harper plan "provided for a superintendent who would be omnipotent as well as omnipresent in all parts of the system as well as at all times, and capable of perfect justice, and that the only time in history where there had been such a visitor to the earth was nineteen hundred years ago and that he was crucified." The teachers of Chicago, she continued, were not convinced "that if he returned to earth he would come to Chicago by way of the Midway Plaisance." The teachers' union, the Chicago Federation of Teachers, backed by the Illinois Federation of Labor, favored an elected board of education, which they thought would be less responsive to businessmen. On the other hand, Nicholas Murray Butler praised the Harper report as "the most complete and most illuminating document on the organization and administration of a school system of a large American city that has ever been published," calling it "representative of the wisest experience that America has to contribute to the discussion and understanding of this important subject."[30]

In 1901 and 1903, the Civic Federation sponsored bills embodying the commission's recommendations, but the bills failed. Harper also tried in 1904 and 1905 to work the commission's recommendations into a new city charter, but the charter was defeated.[31] Most of the Harper Commission's recommendations were not enacted until the Illinois school law was completely revised in 1917.[32]

While the Harper Commission was still deliberating, Mayor Harrison told Harper that he might not be reappointed to the school board:

> You know, of course, the old charges: That the public schools are being made a feeder of the Chicago University, that graduates of the university are being given positions as teachers in preference to ordinary applicants and that the schools are drifting away from the class of instructors [*sic*] for which they are intended.
>
> While the investigations I have made of these charges show them to be absolutely unfounded, the impression is abroad in the public mind and will not down.[33]

Harper failed to win reappointment, and Andrews, his choice for superintendent, resigned shortly thereafter, insisting that the board had denied him adequate powers and had been generally hostile because of his association with Harper.[34]

Harper's short-run failures did not dampen the reformers' determination to gain control of and modernize the Chicago public schools. In the next two decades, professors from Harper's university took the lead in the battle for control of the public schools.

The two decades following the report of the Harper Commission witnessed even greater politicization and conflict within the Chicago public schools. In general, the schools suffered from internal battles among three groups: the board of education appointed by the mayor, the superintendent of schools appointed by the board, and the teachers. The board of education and the superintendent clashed frequently over who had the right to select textbooks, appoint teachers, and make educational decisions. The teachers clashed with the board over salary and tenure. Their union successfully sued the board when it tried to cut teacher salaries. The teachers often clashed also with the superintendent over promotion and rating practices. Charles Judd, dean of Chicago's School of Education, explained in 1917, "We have a body of teachers organized and critical of the board of education. We have the board of education critical of the teachers. Standing between them we have the superintendent, absolutely shorn of power." [35]

After Harper's death in 1906, leadership of public education reform became more diffuse. When reformers failed to win enactment on the city level of the recommendations of the Harper Commission, they took their fight to the state legislature. In 1907, the Illinois General Assembly passed a bill providing for a state educational commission "to make a thorough investigation of the common school system of Illinois." Northwestern dean Thomas F. Holgate chaired a committee of

the Illinois State Teachers Association, which had lobbied for the creation of the commission.[36] Edmund J. James, by then president of the
University of Illinois, served on the commission, which consisted almost
entirely of educational administrators. James's involvement in educational reform dated back to 1880, when he played a major role in the
formation of Philadelphia's Public Education Association, which fought
for abolition of the sectional school boards. The seven-man Illinois
commission appointed University of Chicago sociologist and educator
Ira Howerth to conduct its research.[37]

Howerth, using the reformers' favorite method, investigated the
administrative practices and laws affecting public schools in every state
in the country and wrote a series of bulletins on such matters as a plan
for a state board of education and county boards, a plan for certification
of teachers, recommendations concerning teachers' institutes, and proposed revision of the school law. Howerth also authored the commission's final report and recommendations.

Like the Harper Commission, this state body sought to establish
simplified, uniform, and efficient administrative agencies for public education throughout the state and to increase the authority of professional
educators. The commission recommended uniform statewide standards
for certification of teachers and urged that all schools be brought directly under the supervision of the state. The commission's only recommendation regarding the content of education was that vocational
training be introduced into all state high schools.[38] Two years after the
commission reported, the legislature authorized the superintendent of
public instruction and the state examining board to examine and certify
all Illinois public school teachers.[39] Real authority over the schools remained with local jurisdictions, however, and reformers recognized that
they must control the Chicago Board of Education in order to implement the reforms they sought.

One of the major organizations agitating for Chicago school reform was the education committee of the City Club, dominated by
Chicago professors. Mead chaired it from 1908 to 1916, succeeded by
University of Chicago industrial education professor Frank Leavitt. Di-
vinity School dean Shailer Mathews, biologist John M. Coulter, and
John C. Kennedy, a graduate student in political economy, all at the
University of Chicago, were also committee members. The Public Edu-
cation Association of Chicago, an organization of businessmen, social
workers, and professors, also played a major role in school agitation.
Mead served as vice-president of this group.

Harper and his allies had come into direct conflict with the teachers in the battles of the 1890s, but after Harper's death in 1906, reformers forged an alliance with the teachers, their union, and organized labor in general. Ella Flagg Young, who became superintendent of Chicago schools in 1909, made this possible. Young, a former student of Dewey at the University of Chicago and later a faculty member there, sought to professionalize the Chicago schools by supporting higher salaries and improved conditions for teachers and by stimulating teachers to experiment with new methods and to take greater responsibility for curriculum development. She instituted teachers' councils as a way of keeping in touch with the staff of the schools, and she conveyed teachers' grievances to the board. Young vigorously fought against board efforts to limit her prerogatives over hiring and promotion of teachers and selection of textbooks, and, therefore, antagonized many board members.

Young's superintendency received strong support from the teachers' union, because she sympathized deeply with their poor pay and insecure tenure, and from reformers like Mead and Jane Addams, who valued her rapport with the teachers and her commitment to Dewey's educational theories. In 1914, after a series of altercations with the board, Young resigned the superintendency, only to return after Jane Addams chaired a rally in Young's support and persuaded Mayor Harrison to remove several of Young's opponents on the board and appoint supporters in their places. A year later, Young retired, however.[40]

Upon Young's retirement, the City Club joined several groups in petitioning the board to appoint a committee "of the best qualified educators in the country" to suggest candidates for superintendent. Mead represented the club at a meeting of the board's school management committee, which considered the proposal; Sophonisba P. Breckinridge represented the Woman's City Club at the same meeting. The board rejected the petitions, however, and appointed Assistant Superintendent John D. Shoop as Young's successor. In general, Shoop proved willing to submit to the board.[41]

With Young gone, the disputes between the board of education and the teachers flared up again. Just after Young's retirement, the board abolished a long-standing rule that gave teachers tenure after a probationary period. In dropping what amounted to civil service guarantees for teachers, the board hoped to undermine the Federation of Teachers, and the following year it fired many of the federation's members. The abolition of tenure angered reformers. Mead wrote an official protest to the board on behalf of the club. He attended a subsequent school management committee meeting, hoping to present the City Club's objections to the new rule, but he was denied permission to speak.[42]

In that same year, "Big Bill" Thompson became mayor of Chicago. It did not take reformers long to recognize that Thompson posed a much more serious threat to their aspirations for control of public education than had the boards of education appointed by mayors like Harrison. The old boards had been pluralistic, with a variety of social groups and special interests represented. Thompson, however, moved swiftly to centralize political power in his own hands. All of his appointees to city offices were expected to be personally loyal to him. As the pattern of Thompson's administration became clear, reformers switched from advocating a smaller, appointed board of education to advocating an elected board instead. Clearly, they could not expect much influence on a board appointed by Mayor Thompson. Reformers concluded that an elected board and a superintendent with strong statutory authority held out the best hope for the kind of professionally run school system they wanted. Charles Judd, speaking to the City Club in 1917, spelled out the case for a clear role for the superintendent and a limited role for the board:

> We have in the board of education an authority so superior to the powers of any executive officer that an executive officer is utterly in the dark as to what he can do or what he cannot do. Is that right, from the point of view of expediency? I think all of you business men realize that what is necessary to conduct the schools is technical experience. A board of education can no more conduct the schools without expert operatives than you can run a railroad unless you have somebody who is trained to do so.[43]

Judd and several other professors and social workers, aligned with the Chicago Federation of Teachers, led the fight for a board elected not from the individual wards, but at-large. The board "should not represent every kind of race of people," argued Judd. "It should consist of people who know how to secure proper agents to make a careful study of the situation. The small board ought to elaborate and expand the overhead management and equipment so that experts can bring to the community a clearly defined scientific report of the needs of the city." "Under the appointive system the school board is not responsible to the people," argued Mead. At present, "school policies will be determined by those interests and individuals that have access to the school board," he insisted.[44] Democracy, he believed, meant open debate and decision making for the common good and not a balance of particularistic interests. "If we have an election for members of the board of education at large on a non-partisan basis, the men who come forward will have to have some sort of platform," he argued. "The public will demand that they define their stand upon certain issues." [45]

Professors and other reformers insisted also that those responsible for running the schools be made "acountable" for their performance. "If we are to make use of experts in a democracy," Mead insisted, "one thing is absolutely essential. We must have some method of checking up on what the experts are doing. We cannot turn our government over to experts and say: 'You understand this, therefore, you are to run it.'" Interestingly, this "accountability" of experts depended upon the work of still other experts. Mead proposed that "impersonal bureaus" be established to find out whether the schools are succeeding and expending public resources efficiently. "It is possible then for a democracy to pick out experts and give them full responsibility," argued Mead. "For we will be able to see if they produce the results, which we demand." [46]

The system of education that professors sought, then, was one over which they expected people like themselves to exert considerable influence. It would be governed by a small board that ideally would be oriented toward a single educational conception of the common good, rather than toward a variety of particularistic interests. It would rely heavily on experts, and it would test the success of its experts on the basis of impersonal data collection and analysis.

In 1917, the Illinois legislature undertook a comprehensive revision of the school law. Mead and Judd helped frame one bill that called for an elective board and fixed upon the superintendent responsibility for daily educational policy and administration. They lobbied actively for this plan as representatives of the City Club and the Public Education Association. [47] Judd and Charles Merriam were also instrumental in getting the city council to draft a proposed education law, which it submitted to the state legislature, calling for a seven-member elected board. [48]

The bill that finally passed reduced the size of the Chicago Board of Education to eleven members, but its members were still appointed by the mayor. Superintendents were officially recognized, their duties broadly defined, and their terms of appointment extended from one to four years. Ironically, this was precisely the proposal that the Harper Commission had presented in 1898. In the pre-Thompson years, reformers would have been delighted with the new education law. Tenure was restored in the new law, largely as a result of the lobbying efforts of the Chicago Federation of Teachers, Mead, and Judd. [49]

Superintendent Shoop died in 1918, and the board appointed a commission of nine "representative citizens" empowered to canvass the nation and consult with leading educators in the search for a new superintendent—which is more or less what reformers had unsuccessfully petitioned the board to do in 1915. The commission selected Detroit Superintendent of Schools Charles Chadsey, a prominent administrator and reformer, a move that enraged Thompson. He wanted instead a superintendent personally loyal to him, who would use the schools to advance the political interests of Thompson's Republican organization. When Thompson ran for reelection in 1919, he promised to "kick Chadsey out." Shortly after his victory, he had Chadsey locked out of the superintendent's office, and a prolonged court battle followed. Chadsey, realizing that it was impossible for him to function under such conditions, resigned late in 1919.[50]

Reformers now despaired of ever regaining even the partial influence over the school system they had had previously. Nor is there any reason to think that they would have been more successful in controlling an elected board. Thompson had certainly demonstrated greater ability at winning citywide elections than had the reformers. He had dramatically showed reformers the limits of structural changes in the governance of public education. The same thing happened simultaneously in other areas of public policy.

Even without gaining political control of the schools, however, professors successfully instituted programmatic changes in the public schools. In 1910, the School Extension Committee, headed by Charles Zueblin, began establishing privately financed cultural and recreational centers in public school buildings to demonstrate their importance.[51] In 1910, the board of education assumed responsibility for this work.[52]

Mead's City Club committee succeeded in establishing a permanent Bureau of Educational Standards and School Survey in the Chicago public schools. In 1916, the committee undertook a statistical study of the schools to "gather information which will make possible an estimate of the efficiency of some of the public school activities," but also to "exhibit this information as typical of the kind which should be currently and periodically gathered by the school authorities themselves." Mead and Leavitt supervised the survey work closely, and Mead raised the money for the project. The proposed bureau would "gather the 'vital statistics' of school administration such as those relating to retardation, promotional rate, truancy, over-age, failures in each subject of study, standardized tests in each subject, salaries of teachers, etc." The committee proposed that "the Chicago schools should be compared with each other and with schools in other cities as means of promoting their greater efficiency." Mead's committee presented the completed survey to the board of education, and in 1917 Superintendent Shoop established the bureau along the lines suggested.[53]

In the long run, the collection and analysis of data on educational achievement and failure through nationally standardized tests, and the correlation of these statistics with various kinds of social data, became a major activity of school systems and educational policy planners. The demand for this kind of research provided social scientists and education professors with money and influence. Along with the training of teachers, these activities bound public education irrevocably to the universities. In short, the failure of professors to win control of the public schools in Chicago and some other cities did not eclipse the growth of the education profession and of the widespread reliance of legislators, the courts, and policymakers on technical systems of measurement as a means of educational assessment.

Reformers applied their prescriptions for the public schools to other public education institutions, most notably the Chicago Public Library. Although far less important than the schools, the library constituted the major public agency for extension education beyond the classroom. With relatively little resistance, reformers successfully applied "professional" selection of the head librarian, expert assessment of the program, and "scientific" methods of efficient management of the public library.

The City Club's education committee undertook in 1908 a survey of Chicago's public library, which typically compared it to those of other United States cities. The survey, conducted by a subcommittee headed by Mead, found Chicago's system—a central library with delivery stations around the city—inefficient and costly and instead recommended that branch libraries be established. Mead's survey also concluded that the library board and the school board did not cooperate and that the poor children and immigrants who needed the library most almost never used it. The committee recommended the appointment of a commission, one of whose members would be an experienced librarian from outside the city, to study the problem more thoroughly and devise a more effective system of bringing the library to those who needed it most. The library board appointed the commission in 1909.[54]

The commission, "to secure expert advice in promoting the efficiency and extension of the public library," consisted of three persons appointed jointly by the presidents of Chicago and Northwestern universities and two by the librarian of Congress. Sociologist George E. Vincent of the University of Chicago and Thomas F. Holgate of Northwestern both served on the commission. The group recommended that the librarian be given full responsibility for administering the library as its executive head and that he be selected "on the same basis as that of other officers of similar professional standing" and that he work out with the civil service commission a plan "for the reorganization and classification of the Library service, that will secure for the Library such examinations for appointment and promotion, such tests of efficiency, and such methods of discipline as will be best adapted to its particular needs." The commission members also repeated Mead's call for branch libraries and special efforts to reach poor children.[55] The library board acted favorably on all of the commission's recommendations.[56]

VOCATIONAL EDUCATION AND GUIDANCE

In the fights to professionalize the public schools or the public library, professors usually worked closely with businessmen, lawyers, club women, social workers, and others in the reform leadership of Chicago and forged alliances with other groups like the Chicago Federation of Teachers where political interests coincided. The issue of vocational education badly split reformers themselves, however. Unable to present a united front, two groups of reformers worked at cross-purposes for several years, and neither side got what it wanted. Professors stood on one side of the issue, businessmen on the other.

The movement in the United States to replace the outdated apprentice system of industrial training with vocational schools began in the 1880s with strong backing from businessmen. The National Association of Manufacturers (NAM), organized in 1896, espoused vocational education as a major part of its legislative program. Organized labor, on the other hand, feared that businessmen wanted to create vocational schools that they would control so as to lower wages and produce scab laborers. In 1906, the National Association for the Promotion of Industrial Education began, founded by a professor at Teachers College and the director of manual training for the New York City public schools "to unite the many forces making toward industrial education" in the country. One of the founders tried to overcome the American Federation of Labor's objections to vocational schools, and at its 1907 convention, the federation appointed a special committee to study the question. The committee's 1910 report endorsed the idea that vocational schools of some sort would have to replace the old apprentice system, but vehemently opposed the NAM's plan to place such schools under the control of industry. From 1910 on, the vocational education movement gained momentum, as numerous states passed laws of some sort providing for vocational training. States like Wisconsin set up elaborate provisions for industrial training, but Illinois simply authorized local school boards to establish manual training departments in the high schools.[57]

The issue after 1910 became not whether there should be vocational education, but how it should be done and who should control it. Nowhere was the issue more polarized than in Chicago.

Mead, the leading proponent of one philosophy of vocational education, supported vocational training not only because it educated children for useful trades but also because it helped students develop intellectually. In 1908, he wrote:

> [History in the common schools] is beginning to face about toward the industrial development of the community, and in doing so comes for the first time into contact with the real problems of daily life of the majority of its citizens. The great difficulty which such a use of historical method meets is the lack of immediate contact with life which would lift the child out of story-telling into actual interpretation. How much of this difficulty would be lightened if the child were actually at work in a trade, or were preparing consciously for such work within the school system is at once evident.[58]

Like his friend Dewey, Mead sought to base teaching on the experience of the child and at the same time prepare the child for a meaningful occupation in a highly specialized industrial society.

Early in 1910, a subcommittee of Mead's public education committee at the City Club undertook a major study of vocational education, and Mead was again the prime mover. He employed several graduate students at the university to do the research, guided by faculty at the School of Education, and Anita Blaine funded the project.[59] The bulk of the completed study surveyed vocational education programs in the private and public schools at the elementary and secondary levels in Chicago as compared with New York, Boston, Cleveland, St. Louis, and Cincinnati. The investigators discovered that nearly half the children in Chicago did not complete the eighth grade in the elementary schools, and that these children did not even retain what they had learned in the lower grades. They attributed the situation to the weakness of the elementary curriculum, which lost student interest because it did not appeal to the vocational motives of the students. The major conclusion was that vocational education be introduced into the school system as an essential part of the curriculum.

The committee recommended (1) the establishment of a two-year vocational school admitting boys and girls who were thirteen years old and had completed sixth grade; (2) an elementary industrial school for children at least twelve who had fallen behind their grade level; (3) optional vocational courses in grades seven and eight; (4) specialized trade schools for those who had either graduated from the vocational schools or had at least a sixth-grade education and were at least sixteen if they were boys or fourteen if they were girls; (5) a law requiring working children between fourteen and eighteen to attend a continuation school at least six hours a week; (6) legislation raising the minimum age for leaving school to sixteen; and (7) establishment of a central high school of commerce. The report firmly insisted that these programs "appear in the American public school as an essential part of that unique institution. Nothing of the meaning of our own public school system must be lost," wrote Mead.[60]

Under existing school laws, local authorities did not have the power to raise sufficient funds for vocational training, and so some form of legislation was crucial. Shortly after the study was completed, another subcommittee consisting of Mead, Leavitt, and Ernest Wreidt (who had led the research group for the report) drafted a bill for vocational education to be submitted to the legislature. The bill provided for state support for vocational education in local communities, under the general direction of a state board of vocational training. Existing boards of education, however, would have final authority over vocational programs.[61]

In 1909, just before Mead's committee began work on this matter, the Chicago Association of Commerce committee on industrial and commercial education issued a "report of a preliminary survey" on vocational education. Nathaniel Butler, a professor of education at Chicago primarily involved in extension work, played a key role on the committee and shortly thereafter became its chairman.

In the "preliminary survey," Butler argued that, although manual training as developed by the progressive schools proved useful, it did not prepare youngsters for a trade. This task, he insisted, had to be done by special vocational schools or programs. "Industrial Education, in the view here taken . . . has direct reference to the vocations, and the welfare of the great mass of boys and girls who, from pressure of circumstances, will enter the wage earning class."[62] Unlike Mead, Butler separated vocational training from traditional academic objectives, and this difference in the rationales became a major point of contention.

In the same year that Mead began his study of vocational education in the United States, another group—the Commercial Club of Chicago—hired former school superintendent Edwin Cooley to investigate the vocational schools of Europe, especially those of Germany. In 1912, Cooley published his report and prepared a bill for vocational education in Illinois, modeled after the European system. Following elementary school, students could choose to enter vocational high schools run by a special board with strong ties to industry and labor or they could remain in the academic schools run by the board of education. The Association of Commerce committee met several times with Cooley and decided to back his bill.[63]

Thus, the lines were drawn for a debate between the proponents of the Cooley bill and those of the City Club bill. The debate raised issues of national significance and attracted attention far beyond Illinois. Mead and his supporters did not emphasize the academic value of vocational training in the debate, although that may well have been a key factor in their thinking. Instead, Mead argued that a separate vocational system would create competition between the two school systems and ultimately harm both. Furthermore, he thought separate schools were undemocratic. Parents, he said, would refuse to send their children to schools designed for one class.

> If these vocational schools are separated from the existing public school system, it will be difficult, if not impossible, to remove from them the stigma of being schools solely for the laboring classes. . . . The public school system is good in proportion as it holds the respect and interest of all classes of people. Without the regenerating influence of the struggle to keep the school close to the needs of the people, it must inevitably become even more than its critics deem it to be today, a dispenser of a leisure class, formal and "academic" education. Instead of shunting this popular interest into the narrow channels of a separate vocational system, it should be utilized to keep vigorous the whole institution of public instruction.[64]

Judd, Breckinridge, and Ella Flagg Young joined members of Mead's committee in insisting that separate schools would be undemocratic. John Dewey, who had not lived in Chicago since 1904, also wrote a pamphlet attacking the Cooley bill. That bill, argued Dewey, would "accentuate all undemocratic tendencies in our present situation, by fostering and strengthening class divisions in school and out."[65] The Illinois Federation of Labor bitterly opposed the Cooley bill in the legislature, arguing that it would supply employers with a surplus of skilled laborers and that it would create a caste system in the schools.[66]

The supporters of the Cooley bill included the Civic Federation and the Hamilton Club, a wealthy social organization, as well as the Commercial Club and the Association of Commerce. In his report on the bill,

Butler argued that the school administrators lacked expertise in the problems of vocational training. "The 'singleness of purpose, directness of method, and definiteness of results' to be desired," Butler wrote, "will be greatly endangered by placing these schools at present in the hands of boards of men and women, who, though familiar with and expert in the problems of general education, are neither by training nor by occupation specially fitted to solve the special problems of Vocational Education." Furthermore, to prevent competition between two school systems, the law provided that none of the existing school funds be used for vocational schools. The plan was not undemocratic, since it forbade admitting students to vocational schools before age fourteen and since it increased children's earning power.[67]

Both Mead and Butler were willing to work toward a compromise bill. Mead's committee did not even submit its bill to the 1912 legislature, instead using it as the basis of discussion with other groups. Butler formally proposed a compromise measure. Mead's bill had allowed for an "advisory board" on vocational education. Butler proposed that this board be appointed by the board of education, but that once appointed it have full control over expenditure of the money allocated to it.[68] These efforts were to no avail, despite dozens of meetings and conferences among the various interested parties.

One of these conferences, sponsored in 1912 by the Illinois Bankers Association, appointed a committee consisting of Leavitt, Cooley, and a number of state education officials to draft a model vocational education bill. The committee, chaired by Edmund James, drafted a bill that proved unacceptable to most supporters of the Cooley bill. Still another conference was held in October 1912 by the Illinois chapter of the American Institute of Criminal Law and Criminology, whose members felt that "crime might be materially decreased in our state" through vocational education. This conference also appointed a committee, chaired by Leavitt, to draft a compromise bill.[69] No agreement was ever reached. As a result, the legislature was divided and no vocational education bill at all passed between 1912 and 1917.[70]

Ultimately, the federal government enabled Illinois to begin a state program of vocational education. In 1917, as a result of an intensive lobbying effort by the Society for the Promotion of Industrial Education, Congress passed the Smith-Hughes Act, providing matching federal funds for states that established vocational education programs. However, a state could not qualify for the funds under the new law until it signified its willingness to participate either by act of the legislature or by proclamation of the governor if the legislature had not acted adversely on the proposition at its last session. As usual, the Illinois legislature was badly divided over the issue, and none of the various bills reached a vote in the 1917 session. Therefore, in November of 1917, Governor Frank O. Lowden appointed the Illinois Board of Vocational Education under the direction of Francis W. Shepardson, director of registration and education and a former history professor at the University of Chicago. The board, which included Ernest Wreidt of the City Club committee, drew up plans for vocational education that largely supplemented existing programs of the local school systems, and Illinois thereby qualified for federal money. A separate board for vocational education in Chicago was never established.[71] The issue arose again, however, in 1937, when the superintendent of schools once more proposed a dual school system. A citizens' committee, headed by professors William C. Reavis and Paul Douglas of the University of Chicago again defeated that plan.[72]

The conflict over vocational education was a unique episode in the history of reform in Chicago. Rarely did reformers differ so thoroughly that they failed to unite. In the vocational education debate, reform professors and educators confronted reform businessmen, with organized labor strongly behind the professors and educators. True, Nathaniel Butler was a leader on the side of the Cooley bill, but when Butler was willing to compromise, he could not get the businessmen to go along with his revised plan. Besides, Butler was something of an anomaly within the University of Chicago. He had no doctorate, published only a few popular articles, and more closely resembled the ministerial professor of the old-time college than the academic professional of the modern university. On the other hand, even Harry Pratt Judson, who was a member of the Association of Commerce education committee, a very close ally of the city's business interests and a staunch opponent of organized labor, opposed the Cooley plan!

Neither side won a total victory, but the professors and educators got more of what they wanted than did the businessmen. The proponents of a single system had the advantage of the status quo. It required an act of the legislature to establish a dual system, but it required only money to establish vocational training within the existing educational framework, and the Smith-Hughes bill provided the money after 1917. The alliance with organized labor also helped.

Closely tied to the vocational education movement was the movement to establish formal vocational guidance within the public schools.

Frank Parsons, a radical activist professor at Boston University, began counseling children in Boston as early as 1901, and by 1908 he had established a privately funded vocational bureau. Parsons died the following year, but the leadership of the bureau was taken up first by Paul Hanus and later by John Brewer, both professors of education at Harvard.[73] In Chicago, Breckinridge and Abbott pioneered in the development of vocational guidance services. In the course of their research at the School of Civics and Philanthropy on juvenile delinquency and truancy in Chicago, they were struck by the fact that, although Illinois law required children between fourteen and sixteen years to be either in school or employed, there were very few jobs available for those under sixteen who had left school.[74] There were even fewer jobs for girls than for boys, and therefore dishonest employment agencies or individuals sometimes lured girls into prostitution. In 1910, they concluded, nearly one-half of the children aged fourteen to sixteen who had left school had no job.

As a result of this situation, they put one of their students, Anne Davis, to work on a special study of the occupations available to girls fourteen to sixteen. As part of her investigation, she ran her own informal employment agency. This work was financed jointly by the Chicago Woman's Club, the Woman's City Club, and the Chicago Association of Collegiate Alumnae, the latter headed by Marion Talbot. They deemed this experiment a success, and in the fall of 1911, the three groups agreed to make the work permanent and established the Joint Committee on Vocational Training of Girls, headed by Davis and located at the School of Civics under the general direction of Breckinridge and Abbott.

Davis interviewed girls and some boys seeking employment and either found appropriate jobs or counseled the girls to return to school for further training. Gradually, other organizations in the city agreed to provide workers to assist Davis. A committee of the Association of Commerce, chaired by Nathaniel Butler, took over responsibility for the boys work. Hull House provided a worker to interview girls and ran a school that gave children special vocational training. In some cases, where a girl had to help support her family, the committee provided a small scholarship so that she could stay in school.[75] Breckinridge and Abbott conferred weekly with all the interviewers from the participating organizations.

Almost from the start, Breckinridge and Abbott urged public school officials to take over the work; they viewed their program as simply a demonstration of the need for publicly supported vocational guidance. In 1916, the board of education agreed and established a new Bureau of Vocational Guidance, and the private work was discontinued.[76] Projects like this one and the one Parsons started in Boston quickly spread and grew in size. Professors at university schools of education began writing books, conducting research, and teaching courses on vocational guidance. Before long, they had established a new profession—vocational counseling.

THE PROFESSORS who entered the battles for educational reform were troubled by the poor quality of public education in Chicago and anxious to improve it. Still, the reforms that professors proposed clearly strengthened the influence of universities and scholars over the public schools and educational policy. Professors and university presidents understood their own stake in the battles over public education, but they never doubted that their proposals would serve the common good. They certainly did not see their efforts as self-serving.

In educational reform, as on other urban policy issues, professors generally joined with other elite groups like businessmen and lawyers, who shared their faith in expertise and scientific management. The collapse of this alliance on the vocational education issue is instructive. Both groups genuinely felt they knew what kind of vocational education was best for children, and each group opted for a scheme that would maximize its own influence over the vocational programs. The professors believed that they knew better than anyone else how to educate children, and they did not want control over education shifted to the businessmen. Businessmen, on the other hand, knew industry intimately, and, from their vantage point, it was perfectly logical that vocational training be viewed as an extension of industry.

In the long run, most of the reformers' goals in public education were achieved, in form if not in substance. Educational reformers of the late 1960s and 1970s complained not of the meddling of politicians in the educational process, but of the insulation of teachers from political and community influence. The new enemy became the centralized, tenured, educational bureaucracy, immune from outside pressure and unable to meet difficult challenges. Instead of demanding that educational questions be left to educators, the new generation talked about community control and decentralization, about making schools more responsive to the public, that is, to the demands of lay people.

Of course, Mead or Dewey would have been appalled by rigid school bureaucracies incapable of responding to new situations. However, those bureaucracies grew in large measure as a result of the efforts of turn-of-the-century reformers, like themselves, to insulate the schools from outside meddling and vest responsibility in professional "experts." Yesterday's solutions became today's problems.

5

The Transformation of Criminal Justice

IN 1933 THE LEADING American journal of criminology celebrated its twenty-fifth anniversary with a series of retrospective reflections by leading criminologists on changes in the criminal justice system over the preceding two and a half decades. "In no other branch of government have such remarkable changes been made as those made in the field of police organization and administration during the last quarter of a century," wrote August Vollmer, a professor of police administration at the University of California.[1] The director of the National Probation Association shared these sentiments. "At no time in the world's history has there been such widespread interest and, I think, so great progress toward the solution of the age-old problem of the just and preventive treatment of crime as has occurred in this country since the beginning of the century." He cited in particular the rise of new agencies for dealing with crime, such as "the crime commissions, the reorganized bureaus of criminal statistics, the psychiatric clinics, scientific prison reform, and, almost all within this century, the rapid development of systems of probation and parole."[2]

Herman Adler, a professor of psychiatry at the University of California, reviewed the changes in psychiatric treatment of criminals:

> Twenty five years ago, that is in 1908, the psychiatrist was still concerned primarily with the concepts of mental disease and he restricted himself almost entirely to caring for insane patients in mental hospitals. His interests in criminology were confined largely to the determination of sanity or insanity. . . . The great mass of problems that have since come to the fore in criminologic psychiatry, that is, the psychoneuroses, psychopathic states, mental deficiency in its more

subtle manifestations, and personality problems which now bulk so large in this field, were confined to professional discussions among workers who rarely came to public notice in court actions or in any other way.[3]

William Healy, who as director of the Juvenile Psychopathic Institute of Chicago had pioneered in the individualized study of juvenile delinquents, stated that "about twenty five years ago, the case study method of individuals and causations began—studies in which the structure and qualities of the individual, his conditioning experiences, and his environmental life were put together in one picture for interpretation. . . . Knowledge of how to check and prevent anti-social tendencies must be based, it was discerned, on understanding causations."[4] Just a year earlier, the founder of the journal, Dean John Henry Wigmore of the Northwestern University School of Law, reflected that when the journal had been founded, "the editorship seemed to require an incumbent outside of the field of law; for at that period few if any lawyers (or professors of law) had enough knowledge of the workers in the other fields to be able to evoke contributions which should represent the composite field of the Journal."[5]

This dramatic transformation of the criminal justice system could not occur without both the development of new ideas about crime and criminals upon which institutional innovations could be based and a group of people ready to demand the changes and staff the new institutions. The emergence of new academic professionals in fields like psychology, law, sociology, political science, psychiatry, statistics, and social work proved indispensable in the development of a new theory of crime. These men and women did not just write about crime. They struggled to change the institutions of criminal justice in such a way as to increase the influence of experts and professionals upon them. The juvenile court, probation, parole, psychiatric treatment of criminals, police science, sophisticated methods of crime reporting and collection of crime statistics, and the emergence of criminology as a field of study all bear witness to their success.

Of course, reform in the criminal justice system was hardly unique to this period. Humanitarian impulses had fueled a variety of movements from the beginning of the United States designed to turn prisons into correctional institutions instead of places for vindictive punishment. Throughout the nineteenth century, reformers experimented with more effective ways to treat juvenile offenders and to keep them from becoming adult criminals. Police forces in the major

American cities had been periodically investigated by reformers and reorganized along "professional" lines. Nor was the study of criminology new. Throughout the nineteenth century criminology emphasized genetically inherited tendencies toward crime, but by the end of the nineteenth century, social scientists began talking about the influence of social environment on criminality.[6] This environmental analysis held up prospects of changing criminal behavior and thereby opened up numerous possibilities for expert influence over the criminal justice system.

The early-twentieth-century reformers differed from their nineteenth-century predecessors in their faith in science and their reliance upon expertise. Nineteenth-century reformers and theorists, they insisted, had based their ideas upon speculation, whereas the present generation could develop theory through application of the scientific method to all phases of crime and justice. "Very recently there has been a remarkable awakening of interest in the scientific study of crime and penal methods," wrote University of Illinois political science professor John Garner in 1910, "an interest which is beginning to manifest itself in a productive research and investigation as well as in destructive criticism of antiquated methods and in constructive proposals for reform."[7] In 1914 William Healy put it this way:

> How has progress been made in dealing with other human conditions? How has conquest been made of diseases? Simply by the growth of human knowledge, gained through reasoning and experiment, leading to appreciative understanding of the essentials which underlie the problems involved. There is no other road to success. We might take the thesis of Herbert Spencer's old essay, "What Knowledge is of the Most Worth," and apply it here—it is scientific knowledge; scientific understanding of the basis of conduct.[8]

Like so many scientists of the day, the new criminologists believed that science could devise more effective methods of crime control and treatment. "It is because criminalistics is a science dealing primarily with dynamics, with the forces that make for criminalism, that it is, and will be still more, in a position to suggest many advantageous alterations in the field of criminal procedure, penal administration, and progress in preventive phases of criminalistics," wrote William Healy in 1914:

> As it develops, it is going to be, and already partially is, in a position to apply the test of efficiency to the law. The law has not seen fit to develop any accurate criteria for judging whether or not its methods are effective, but it should heartily welcome any genuine science

which can tell the tale of success and failure. . . . The relation of this science to the reform that is ever called for now-a-days in many aspects of the practical treatment of delinquency ought to be obvious. It furnished the only criteria by which one can sanely judge of the values of many reforms.[9]

Of course, the new criminal science meant that the criminal justice system would rely more heavily on the work of experts. The new criminologists made no apologies for this. In an article in 1915 calling for adult probation in Cook County jails, Northwestern psychologist Robert Harvey Gault urged that the decision on whether or not to grant probation to a particular inmate ought to be made upon the basis of a thorough expert investigation of "the sociological, psychological and medical aspects of the case."

If it be objected that this plan would place too much power in the hands of experts, we have but to reply, in the first place, that the power is not necessarily placed in the hands of one alone, and in the second place, that at present the disposition of the applicant for probation is in the hands of one expert—the judge who has heard his case. Then the question is: which expert is the more able by training and experience to estimate the possibilities of an individual, and to make a forecast of his future reactions; the expert in legal precedent or the expert in human nature?[10]

The goals of criminal justice reformers, then, mirrored the goals of urban school reformers—greater control for scientific experts like themselves over criminal justice apparatus.

CRUSADES FOR WOMEN AND CHILDREN

The new criminal justice reformers first tackled the problem of juvenile crime. Chicago and Illinois pioneered in the special treatment of juvenile offenders with the creation of the Juvenile Court of Cook County in 1899.[11] Before 1899, juveniles arrested for any offense were tried, convicted, and sentenced just as adults were and went to jails with adult criminals. The juvenile court allowed youngsters to be placed on probation and returned to their homes and provided flexible courtroom procedures and a more sympathetic judge. These early changes in the treatment of juvenile offenders stemmed largely from the efforts of Hull House residents, but as the movement for individualized treatment advanced, professors played an important role.

Chicago's Juvenile Protective Association (JPA) provided an important agency through which professors could develop supposedly scientific methods of treating juvenile offenders and preventing juvenile delinquency. When the juvenile court first opened in 1899, no money had been allocated for probation officers. Therefore, a group of citizens organized the Juvenile Court Committee, which provided probation officers and other services for the juvenile court. Later, when the court finally received an appropriation for these purposes, the committee changed its name to the Juvenile Protective Association, investigated individual cases of child mistreatment or illness, and sought to remedy social conditions that were harmful to children.[12]

A professional staff performed the daily work of the association, supervised by trustees who raised money and formed policy. Allan Hoben of the University of Chicago Divinity School held the staff position of field secretary from 1910 to 1913. Like Henderson, Hoben was a minister whose interests had moved from otherworldly to this-worldly concerns and eventually led him to a career as a sociologist. The association had about a dozen neighborhood affiliates throughout the city. It was Hoben's job to organize new neighborhood leagues, assist those already in operation, and publicize the work of the Juvenile Protective Association by public appearances and addresses. "In the last analysis," wrote Hoben in one of his annual reports, "there is little hope of rectifying the city's sinister treatment of its children except by informing and enlisting the rank and file, and the value of the work of the Juvenile Protective Association is measured largely by the number of people it awakens and sets to work." Hoben believed his work prevented delinquency. "In the long run," he wrote, "the officer who can discover and organize the protective forces of a district will do more for the children than one who is engrossed, however heroically, in the pathetic cases which continually occur."[13]

Hoben attended numerous meetings and conferences for the association and helped to organize three new local leagues, inducing churches, clubs, and other city organizations to establish juvenile protective departments in affiliation with the association. He also helped to organize classes on juvenile delinquency and moral education for public school teachers and principals. Hoben's affiliation with the JPA advanced his academic position at the university, and he taught a course in the Divinity School on juvenile delinquency and moral education. He collected data from the JPA for his course and his writings, and he placed a number of his students in youth agencies affiliated with the association.[14]

Hoben resigned as field secretary in 1913 and became a member of the board of directors. There he joined other University of Chicago faculty, including psychologist James Rowland Angell, Edith Abott, and Sophonisba Breckinridge. In 1913, Angell induced several state officials to endorse the association's proposal to send delinquent boys between the ages of twenty-one and twenty-five to the state reformatory at Pontiac instead of to an adult prison.[15] Hoben helped secure a workshop for boys in the county jail and prepared a bibliography of books on children for use by the staff of the association; with Angell, he served on a committee in 1917 to consider the advisability of pressing for a new child labor bill.[16] Both men headed also the Hyde Park Center, a JPA affiliate founded in 1909 in the university district, which was supported primarily by University of Chicago professors.[17]

Reformers fought continually with machine politicians over control of the juvenile court and its probation system. Reformers insisted that probation officers be selected through civil service examinations administered by experts like themselves. Naturally, machine politicians also sought control over appointments. In 1911, the conflict came to a head in Cook County, when the chairman of the Cook County Board of Commissioners fired a member of the Civil Service Commission and appointed another in order to remove the court's chief probation officer and get his own person appointed. At the same time, the *Chicago Examiner* printed a series of attacks on the court, centering on alleged abuses of children who had been taken from their homes by the court and sent to institutions. Reformers called the *Examiner*'s charges grossly exaggerated or entirely untrue and demanded that a special committee be appointed to investigate the juvenile court and the probation system. In response, the Cook County Board of Commissioners named an investigatory committee, headed by the dean of Northwestern's business school, Willard Hotchkiss. The board made no blanket appropriation for the costs of the investigation, however, apparently hoping to control the committee by retaining control over its funds. Hotchkiss, determined to keep the committee independent, secured private financing.[18]

The committee sought to avoid entanglement in charges and countercharges made against specific persons. Rather, the committee stated in its report that it "conceived its primary function to be the discovery of merits and defects in the system. . . . It has not thought necessary to fix blame for every failure to obtain good results, but has applied itself rather to consideration of legal or administrative changes which might lessen failure in the future." The final report, however, clearly vindicated the former chief probation officer and criticized the tactics of the chairman of the Cook County board. Hotchkiss thus employed a common reform strategy—to posture scientific detachment and deny any political stake in the issue.

Juvenile reformers throughout the country hailed the committee's extensive recommendations. Its report, written by Hotchkiss, called for much closer cooperation between the juvenile court system and the public schools and recommended that the court system increase its supervision over the children it sent to reformatories. Unless the court could control the conditions of a child in a reformatory or school, Hotchkiss argued, the court could not be sure that the child actually received the type of care mandated by the court. In many instances, Hotchkiss noted, the institutions returned a child to his or her original home without authorization from the court. The Hotchkiss committee also called for stricter enforcement of civil service laws as applied to probation officers, and made extensive recommendations about the appropriate kinds of examinations for this post. It proposed raising the standards of reformatories and industrial schools and expansion of the staff that supervised children placed in foster homes. Finally, the committee proposed that a better system of bookkeeping be used to account for state money given to private institutions for care of delinquent children.[19] Thus, Hotchkiss used an attack on the probation system to advocate expansion of the reformers' control over it.

Reformers also insisted that society make special efforts to assist adult women through the juvenile court system, just as it did children. Innocent women, they maintained, could easily become the victims of prostitution (the contemporary term was "vice"). Therefore, they undertook a broad attack on prostitution per se and lax sexual morality generally. Here, perhaps more than on any other crime issue, the cultural gap between the upper-class world of the reformers and the lower-class world of crime and vice became apparent.

Vice reformers placed heavy emphasis on education. The Chicago Society for Social Hygiene was organized for "education of men concerning transmissible diseases, and the consequent protection of wives and children from venereal contamination." Charles R. Henderson helped found the group and headed it for many years. By 1907, the society boasted that it had distributed 225,000 circulars "among young men, with the cooperation of officers of over 450 educational institutions, heads of business houses, officers of railways, physicians and others."[20]

In the fight against prostitution, as in other reform crusades, research and investigation were major tools. Under the leadership of Columbia economist E. R. A. Seligman, New York's Committee of Fifteen prepared a study of vice conditions in their city in 1902 and revised it ten years later.[21] The American Social Hygiene Association, founded in 1914, did similar work. Charles W. Eliot was its first president, and David Starr Jordan served as an officer.

In January 1910, after several years of local agitation against prostitution, a group of Chicago clergymen asked the mayor to appoint a "commission made up of men and women who command the respect and confidence of the public at large," to investigate the "social evil." In March, he reluctantly appointed thirty people to the commission, including University of Chicago Semitic language professor Herbert L. Willett and W. I. Thomas of the sociology department, and Northwestern president Abram W. Harris. Henderson later replaced a member who died. The commission received an appropriation from the city council and undertook a major investigation of prostitution.

Willett, an ordained minister, and Henderson were active commission members. Thomas, who had done research on the sex impulse and held "advanced" views on sex, had little impact on the group and in fact antagonizd some of its members. Henderson, of course, had written extensively on the subject through the Society for Social Hygiene and apparently he had considerable influence; the commission's final report echoed Henderson's views expressed in his writings.[22] The commission insisted that suppression was insufficient: "The Social Evil in its worst phases may be repressed," it announced, but "so long as there is lust in the hearts of men it will seek out some method of expression. Religion and Education alone can correct the greatest curse which today rests upon mankind." The commission therefore backed sex education, both in the home and in the school, arguing that "many of the immoral influences and dangers which are constantly surrounding young children on the street, in their amusements, and in business life, may be counteracted and minimized by proper moral teaching and scientific instruction." The commission concluded that "the teaching of sex hygiene in schools is an important movement which, while not yet past the experimental stage, promises great advances in the promotion of child protection for the future."[23] The report also exposed widespread collusion between the police and the vice world and announced, to no one's surprise, that prostitution was blatant and extensive in some parts of the city. Many commission members had previously favored segregation of vice in certain areas, but the commission strongly recommended elimination of the vice districts. The report sparked a major anti-vice crusade in Chicago and numerous publicly financed commissions elsewhere.

In one sense, the commission proved extremely successful. The extensive publicity which the commission gave to vice practices in Chicago forced the mayor and police commissioner to crack down on the red-light district, and the district was suppressed and its establishments closed. The commission's recommendation that a permanent morals commission be established was implemented quickly. However, prostitution neither disappeared nor sharply declined; it simply became less evident. With the suppression of the central vice district, prostitution houses moved into poorer neighborhoods throughout the city. Furthermore, police crackdowns were inevitably sporadic, and the election of Thompson in 1915 severely limited the influence that the vice reformers exerted on the city police force. Their major success, then, was in making prostitution less blatant, less public, and more dispersed.[24]

PRISON REFORM, PROBATION, AND PAROLE

Early reforms in juvenile justice led to the same prescriptions for correctional institutions for adult males. Charles R. Henderson's interest in prisons developed in the 1870s and 1880s, when, as a minister in Terre Haute, Indiana, he worked at the local house of correction. At the University of Chicago, Henderson wrote several books on prison methods, headed the National Prison Association in 1902, and in 1910 represented the United States at the International Prison Conference where he was elected president.

Henderson typified the Christian and humanitarian impulses of pre-twentieth-century prison reformers. After his conversion to professional sociology, he urged reform on "scientific" instead of "sentimental" grounds. For example, like many of the new criminologists, he opposed capital punishment because he concluded that it was ineffective. In 1911, he joined with Jane Addams, Graham Taylor, Breckinridge, and others in urging Governor Charles S. Deneen to change a death sentence to life imprisonment for a group of young men convicted of murder. Life imprisonment, Henderson wrote Deneen, would "have more deterrent influence than hanging."[25]

Henderson played a crucial role in applying the principle of probation developed in the juvenile court to adult offenders. In the 1890s, several states passed parole laws, which gave the governor or a state board authority to release prisoners for good behavior before they had completed their entire sentence. Illinois passed a parole law in 1895, but, like many other states, made almost no provision for supervision of prisoners once they were released, and large numbers of parolees returned to prison for new offenses. To remedy this problem reformers proposed that prisoners released before completing their sentences be placed under the careful supervision of probation officers attached to the courts.[26]

Henderson, one of the leading advocates of adult probation in Illinois, explained the need for the system:

> The paroled men are either wicked or weak, or both. . . . These men, after a long period in prison, require a gradual adjustment to the atmosphere of liberty. Men who are working in compressed air at high pressure suffer greatly, and sometimes are even killed by too sudden transition to the ordinary atmospheric pressure, and therefore they are put through what is called a "hospital lock," in which they gradually become adjusted to the regular pressure. So also men who come from the strain of prison into an entirely different world should be put through the hospital lock of state watch care.[27]

Since the Illinois parole law of 1895 made almost no provision for supervision of convicts, the Civic Federation established a committee on parole and probation in 1909 under Henderson's chairmanship, to "ascertain . . . the defects in the parole system of Illinois." Characteristically, a committee publication claimed complete detachment and objectivity, arguing that the problem needed study by "those who, besides being impelled by feelings of philanthropy, are equipped by knowledge gained from scientific research." The group drafted a proposed law providing for a "system of adult probation under proper regulations" and the appointment of parole officers. The bill passed the Illinois legislature in 1911. Henderson's committee then demanded that an expert in criminology be appointed chief probation officer.[28]

The new law allowed those on probation to work and pay back money they had stolen. After three years of experience with the new system, Henderson's committee suggested some modifications. Most important of these was that before any judge would grant probation, a probation officer should "make a preliminary examination and file a written report." The public "should not expect the judge to exercise, in addition to the all-important judicial function, the activities of a detective and the powers of a mind reader." Obviously, such an arrangement would further individualize the correctional system and vest greater responsibility in the new probation officers.[29] The committee also raised money so that the chief probation officer could tour prisons and courts in New York and Massachusetts "in order that he might gain helpful information and ideas inaugurating the new system in Cook County." It also sponsored the Illinois Probation Conference in 1913 to create greater public interest in adult and juvenile probation.[30]

COPS AND SCHOLARS

The new criminologists confronted the most vigorous opposition when they sought to wrest control of municipal police forces from the politicians and police officers. In the eyes of reformers, police were not only poorly trained and brutal, but in cities like Chicago, they worked closely with gangsters and corrupt politicians. Historian Mark H. Haller has shown, however, that the police, politicians, and criminals shared common social experiences and values that were different from those of reformers.

> In Chicago, criminal activity and the criminal justice system were rooted in the city's ethnic neighborhoods and were means of social mobility for persons of marginal social and economic position in society. The strength of the criminal underworld lay in the fact that its members . . . could frequently maintain mutually satisfactory, if somewhat ambiguous, relations with enforcement officials. They were tied to politics by a shared belief that the system should operate on the basis of friendship and favors. They played a part in organized labor and in many aspects of business activity. Within the red-light district and in other parts of the city, they participated in a social life of saloons, hangouts, and gambling parlors.[31]

Of course, this system was anathema to professors and other elites, whose thoroughly different experiences caused them to judge the police by their efficiency and professional expertise. In the early twentieth century, these reformers began to devise new ways to penetrate the urban police systems from which they had been effectively excluded.

Reformers characteristically called for the "professionalization" of the police force through the development of scientific training programs for police officers. The first formal training school for police in the United States began in Berkeley, California, in 1908, an outgrowth of its School of Pistol Practice, which had been started in 1895. New York started a training school in 1909, Detroit in 1911, and Philadelphia in 1913. None of these were tied to universities, however.[32]

In 1912, the Chicago Civil Service Commission released a report on the Chicago police force, undertaken after reformers accused the police of widespread corruption. The report found, to no one's surprise, that "a bipartisan combination or ring exists by which the connection between the Police Department and the criminal classes . . . is fostered and maintained." In addition to advocating extensive administrative and organizational reforms, the commission urged that "an effort be made to secure the establishment of courses in police work in one or

more of the city's universities or training schools.[33] In 1915, another
investigation of the police by a special city council committee on crime,
headed by Charles Merriam, discovered widespread collusion between
the police and criminals and generated extensive publicity.[34] In 1919,
the Chicago Association of Commerce's committee on prevalence and
prevention of crime, on which Northwestern's law school dean John
Henry Wigmore and Robert H. Gault served, established a permanent
body to monitor crime and the police. This permanent investigative
body, the Chicago Crime Commission, employed a staff of a hundred
investigators to look into individual crimes as well as the general operation of the criminal justice system in order to expose inefficiency and
corruption and propose corrective legislation. The commission operated
in this way throughout the 1920s, financed and directed almost entirely
by businessmen.[35]

It was small wonder, then, that professors quickly seized the opportunity to enhance their influence by proposing scientific training at universities for police officers. Wigmore headed a committee of Northwestern faculty that studied the curricula of European police schools and in
1915 drew up a proposed one-year curriculum for police officers consisting of courses in criminal law, physiology and anatomy, hygiene,
legal evidence, psychology, practical sociology, criminal procedure, and
comparative police administration. Gault, who served on the committee, readily conceded that the program provided an opening wedge for
extensive university involvement with the police. In the *Journal of Criminal Law and Criminology* he wrote:

> Far reaching results for the next and subsequent generations will be
> attained if the universities will take hold of the problem of education
> for police service and management as intelligently and with as much
> zeal as they have already taken up the problems of the management
> of industrial corporations. To do so will be quite compatible with
> university dignity and with proper regard for public virtue as well, if
> not with academic prejudices. And the universities are arising to their
> obligations in this matter. They have in their curricula much of the
> wherewithal to contribute to the professionalizing of our future
> police forces, and it is in their power also to mold the conventional
> attitude of the next generation toward the police function in our daily
> life.

Wigmore failed to induce the Chicago police chief or Mayor
Thompson to implement the training program as a requirement for
entry or promotion in the force even though Northwestern offered to
carry the entire cost of the program itself. Thus, the plan fell by the

wayside. In 1916, the first university police course in the United States began at Berkeley, and the next year Harvard offered a course for Cambridge police officers. It would be more than decade, however, before a university-related police course would be offered in Chicago. In 1929, August Vollmer, the Berkeley police chief who had instituted the nation's first university police course, came to the University of Chicago as professor of police administration, largely through the efforts of Charles Merriam. His courses became part of the regular undergraduate curriculum.[36] In the same year, Northwestern established its Scientific Crime Detection Laboratory and shortly thereafter began offering special courses for police officers. Neither program, however, became a part of the official apparatus of the Chicago police department, and therefore both programs served a national rather than a local police clientele.[37]

It is not surprising that Chicago's professors were among the first to propose programs for law enforcement or that its government was so slow to adopt them. Governing a city notorious for police corruption and organized crime, Chicago politicians were hardly inclined to give the elite universities leverage over the police force. Living in such a city, Chicago professors naturally felt an urgent need for scientific training of law enforcement officers.

THE SCIENTIFIC STUDY OF CRIME

Juvenile courts, adult probation and parole, and scientific training for police, like most demands of the new criminologists, required that crime be subjected to systematic scientific study. Judges needed accurate psychological, sociological, and medical profiles of adult criminals and juvenile offenders before they could determine whether to grant probation, for instance. Scientific police training demanded an ever-expanding body of knowledge on the causes of crime and the constant application of this knowledge to practical methods of prevention. To measure the efficiency of the criminal justice system required the collection and interpretation of elaborate statistics of crime and prosecution. Thus, underlying all of the reforms of the criminal justice system in the early twentieth century lay the movement for the scientific study of crime and criminals. Professors quickly saw the possibilities that the demand for knowledge about crime held out for their professional and institutional advancement.

Individual researchers and theorists had examined crime and criminals for many years, of course; yet at the beginning of the twentieth century, no institution, association, or journal in the United States was devoted exclusively to the systematic analysis of crime. In 1909, Wigmore, seeing the opportunity, celebrated the fiftieth anniversary of Northwestern University Law School with a national conference "representing the various classes interested in the problems connected with the administration of punitive justice, including the treatment of criminals." The conference established the American Institute of Criminal Law and Criminology, a national organization of professionals interested in all phases of work with crime and criminals. Wigmore became the first president of the institute, which was headquartered at Northwestern University Law School.

The institute organized committees to report on various topics. For example, Edwin Keedy of Northwestern Law School chaired a committee that reported on "Reform of Expert Testimony." Others served on investigatory and recommending committees on probation and parole, recording criminal data, the indeterminate sentence, the organization and training of pardon and parole boards, and the like. The institute also commissioned translations into English of several treatises on criminology by Europeans. Finally, the institute established a journal, the first in the United States to treat the problems of crime from the point of view of all the relevant disciplines. James W. Garner, the University of Illinois political scientist, edited the journal for its first years, succeeded by Gault, who held the editorship for most of his professional life. "The institute . . . is engaged in developing and crystallizing into practice a rational public opinion with respect to all phases of the administration of justice and the prevention of crime in America," wrote Gault to Anita Blaine in a letter seeking financial assistance. "Our method is investigation by special committees, dissemination of information, and contact with legislative committees." [38]

Five years after the establishment of the institute, the Chicago City Council financed a major study of crime, under the general direction of alderman Merriam, "for the purpose of investigating and reporting . . . upon the frequency of murder, assault, burglary, robbery, theft and like crimes in Chicago," and upon their causes and methods of prevention. The committee's report went beyond the usual exposés of widespread collusion between the police and the criminal underworld, presenting in addition analyses of criminal statistics and of the underlying causes of crime. [39]

Merriam hired Edith Abbott for the statistical study. Using virtually every available source, Abbott put together the most complete statistics to date on "complaints and arrests, trial and disposition, together with the statistics relating to social status—age, sex, nationality and occupation—of persons arrested." Abbott found the criminal justice system grossly inefficient. Only a very small percentage of those arrested were charged with serious offenses. The majority of those tried in court were discharged without conviction—only about 3 percent of the total number charged were sentenced to imprisonment, and nearly 89 percent of those sentenced to the House of Correction were there for nonpayment of fines.

In a second study on the social status of offenders, Abbott found that most of those arrested were young men, with the arrests of women confined largely to vice offenses. Arrests of native-born Americans accounted for a larger proportion of total arrests than those of immigrants, and, although "statistics relating to conjugal condition and occupation" were not satisfactory, Abbott found that the majority of men and women arrested were unmarried and poor. "It is not that the poor are more criminal than the rich," she concluded, "but that their offenses bring them so easily within the reach of the law." Abbott's report also contained a plea for more careful collection of statistics relating to crime. "Criminal statistics show us where we are going in the treatment of persons convicted and accused of crime," she asserted.[40] In addition to publishing her findings in the final report of the crime committee, Abbott used the data gathered in her study in popular pamphlets designed to publicize the need for prison reform.[41]

Robert H. Gault prepared the report on the underlying causes of crime with the assistance of Herman C. Stevens, a psychologist and physician in charge of the University of Chicago Psychopathic Laboratory. The investigation focused both on psychophysical characteristics of delinquents and environmental causes of crime. "If one's nervous system is badly out of gear so that nerve impulses, in one part of the system or another, become sidetracked or retarded or accelerated, the parts of the system must fail to work together harmoniously," explained Gault. If the nervous system were weak or defective, Gault believed, a person was more likely to commit illegal acts. Knowledge of the nervous system and its relation to crime was essential for intelligent decisions by courts or officials deciding whether or not to grant probation or parole to a prisoner. "Studies in the psycho-physical nature of the individual delinquent, therefore, are the cornerstone of investigations of criminology." On the other hand, Gault acknowledged that a person's biological disposition toward crime was substantially modified by the environment in which he or she functioned and that scientists must also look to the economic and family conditions of criminals, for instance, to understand the causes of crime.[42]

Gault and Stevens therefore investigated (1) the physical and mental conditions of prisoners in the House of Correction; (2) the adult probation system; (3) physical, mental, and some environmental factors affecting juvenile delinquents, and (4) the defense of poor people accused of crime in Chicago.[43]

Stevens examined sixty-one female prisoners in the House of Correction and found that the average mentality of these prisoners was of "the moron class"—86 percent had a mental age of between nine and thirteen. At least 50 percent showed evidence of serious disturbances of the nervous system. Venereal disease was common among the women. "Prisoners with these physical and mental illnesses," he concluded, "should be segregated on farm colonies or in hospitals until cured."

Similarly, Stevens examined sixty-three male juvenile delinquents aged twelve to seventeen. Approximately one-half of the boys demonstrated "a deplorable condition." One-quarter of them suffered from venereal disease. "Their physical condition," he found, "besides offering no guarantee even of the probability of establishment of steady habits, leaves no doubt in our minds that these boys, if they were at liberty now, would be as great a menace to the health of the community as adults in the House of Correction."[44]

Gault reported that 76 of 132 men found insane by the medical staff of the House of Correction during eight months of 1914 were not sent to institutions for the insane because "it was deemed by the medical staff impossible to get a lay jury to commit them to an insane asylum" since "to the inexpert . . . each . . . would . . . appear sane." He also found that "the letter of the adult probation law utterly fails to establish a satisfactory criterion of fitness for probation."[45]

The findings of the Merriam Crime Committee were widely publicized. Merriam believed the report embodied "the first attempt at a scientific study of the crime problem in an American city."[46] Scientific study of this sort provided the foundation on which reformers ultimately built a new criminal justice system.

THE EXPANSION OF LEGAL AID

Although the criminal justice reformers of the early twentieth century were primarily interested in the control of criminal activity, they did not entirely ignore the need to guarantee that justice was fairly administered to the poor. Gault's report, for instance, noted that poor people were often the victims of unscrupulous attorneys.[47] The first agency founded to give legal assistance to the poor in Chicago was the Bureau of Justice, begun in 1888. In 1904, Wigmore became a member of its board of directors. The next year, the bureau consolidated with the Protective Agency for Women and Children, which had been doing similar work, to form the Legal Aid Society, and in 1919 the society became a department of the United Charities of Chicago.

Wigmore was a prime mover in legal aid work from 1905 on. In addition to serving on the board of directors and the executive committee of the various agencies, he was chairman of the Legal Aid Society's law committee in 1910 and became its vice-president in 1911. Under Wigmore's guidance, many law students at Northwestern volunteered their services to the society. In 1919, at Wigmore's instigation, Northwestern Law School and the Legal Aid Society agreed that senior law students would be required to work at the society's Legal Aid Clinic for credit under the direction of a member of the Law School faculty, the first program of its kind in the United States.[48] Again, professional activism enhanced the work of the university proper.

THE RECORD OF CONCRETE achievement by the professors and other advocates of the new criminology in Chicago in the early twentieth century was hardly impressive. True, reformers in Illinois successfully introduced the juvenile court and the adult probation system into their state, and the study of crime became an established enterprise. However, in the real struggle over control of the mechanisms of the criminal justice system, reformers remained primarily outsiders.

Nearly every reform proposed by professors and their allies had the practical effect of increasing their control over the system and decreasing that of political representatives of poor and working-class people. The juvenile and adult probation system, if properly administered, gave power over the fate of offenders to psychiatrists, psychologists, and professionally trained probation officers and limited the power of politicians and judges who held office by virtue of the popular elections that reformers usually lost. The scientific training of police would have significantly changed the social origins of policemen, excluding large numbers of poorly educated working-class people for whom the police force provided a means of mobility. The demand for higher educational standards and strict civil service procedure in selecting probation officers likewise excluded lower-class persons in favor of professionally trained social workers and college graduates. The anti-vice crusade sought to eliminate an institution that reformers found morally repugnant and socially dysfunctional, but it had the practical effect also of limiting the number of brothel keepers and gambling-house entrepreneurs who paid off politicians like Hinky Dink Kenna or Bathhouse John Coughlin in exchange for protection from the police. Even the legal aid movement, like charity work generally, minimized the dependence of poor people on precinct captains who used their influence to see that a loyal voter in trouble with the police got off easily.

In the struggle for control over the criminal justice system, professors and their allies believed that they could make things better for everyone. If professors knew more about the nature of crime than any other group, reasoned the new academic professionals, should they not rightly determine who became a policeman or a probation officer? If psychologists or sociologists understood better than anyone else the causes of crime, should they not design and administer the new institutions to control lawlessness? Others, with a stake in the old order, distrusted experts who aggressively sought control over them and who spoke a language they could not understand. Our own generation, living amidst the failures of probation and the juvenile courts, recognizing the dangers of professional police insulated from political and community control, can empathize with the opponents of the new criminology.

6

A Foundation for the Welfare State

ALTHOUGH AMERICANS ACCEPTED the principle of local government responsibility for the poor inherited from the Elizabethan Poor Laws, until the twentieth century, they relegated primary responsibility for the protection of people from devastating illness, unemployment, or old age to the family, private systems of insurance, and voluntary charity. In the years after the founding of the University of Chicago, reformers struggled not only to gain control over the meager state and local poor relief systems, but also to establish entirely new concepts of social welfare and to dominate new specialized institutions and agencies to do for urban dwellers what they and their families could not do for themselves.

The American welfare state more or less assumed its modern form during and after the New Deal. For several decades before the depression of the 1930s, however, professors, social workers, and philanthropists steadily constructed a foundation for large-scale government intervention in peoples' lives to guarantee minimum standards of social and economic well-being. They built this foundation from two elements —an elaborate network of privately funded agencies that pioneered in new forms and methods of helping people, and a protracted struggle to convince state and local governments to undertake new social welfare responsibilities. Chicago's activist professors played a critical role in both and thereby helped to forge a welfare state that relied heavily upon people like themselves.

CHARITIES AND SETTLEMENTS

Private charitable institutions were affected very early by the late
nineteenth century's faith in science and the concomitant emergence of
professional social scientists and social workers. As early as the 1870s,
those involved in charity work in American cities began to criticize the
traditionally haphazard and "unscientific" manner in which the rich
gave alms to the poor. Under the pressure of increasing urban poverty
and the resulting pressure on resources, charity workers established central agencies to coordinate the relief work of the entire community. All
requests for aid were typically referred to the central agency, which sent
out volunteer "friendly visitors" to investigate the requests and determine whether assistance was warranted, and, if so, which of the various
agencies in the city would be the most appropriate to give the kind of
help needed. Charity organization, they believed, would eliminate poverty by forcing those who were able-bodied to work and by making life
difficult for those who lived as professional beggars.[1]

At meetings of the American Social Science Association and its
offshoot, the National Conference of Charities and Correction, the experiences of cities with the new "scientific charity" methods dissemi-
nated rapidly. "Scientific" poor relief proved enormously attractive to
new urban universities seeking to prove their usefulness to society.
President Gilman, a member of the American Social Science Association, helped organize the Charity Organization Society of Baltimore,
after hearing an account of the work of the London Charity Organization Society at the 1881 meeting of the Social Science Association. The
Baltimore group remained closely tied to Johns Hopkins. Gilman served
as president of the society from 1891 to 1901. Amos G. Warner, a Hopkins graduate student in social science, served as general secretary and
Jeffrey R. Brackett, another Hopkins Ph.D., as chairman of the executive committee. Brackett and Herbert Baxter Adams taught courses for
charity workers at Hopkins beginning in the 1880s. Columbia social
scientists Richmand Mayo-Smith, Franklin H. Giddings, and E. R. A.
Seligman all served on the board of the New York Charity Organization
Society, and Giddings initiated the appointment of Edward T. Devine, a
University of Pennsylvania Ph.D., as general secretary of the society.
Devine later taught social economy at Columbia as well. The founder of
Harvard's social ethics department, Francis Peabody, was a leading organizer of the Associated Charities of Cambridge, Massachusetts, and
another Harvard professor, John Graham Brooks, also played a major
role in that association.[2]

When the University of Chicago opened in 1892, Chicago still did not have a central coordinating agency, however, although the Chicago Relief and Aid Society, founded to furnish relief after the Chicago fire, still dispensed aid directly. The nationwide depression of 1893 was especially severe in Chicago because the conclusion of the Columbian Exposition put many people out of work. In response, over a hundred prominent civic leaders met and formed the Civic Federation, whose first task was to put thousands of idle men to work cleaning city streets, for which they received food, clothing, or shelter.

After meeting the immediate crisis, one of the federation's major projects was the formation of the Bureau of Charities. In this project, Albion Small and especially Charles R. Henderson were prime movers. Henderson had already done charity work while a pastor at Terre Haute and Detroit, and charity organization was one of his major research and teaching interests. Henderson took charge of educational work, organized conferences, designed the forms to be used by visitors in interviewing applicants for aid, and helped raise money. Small helped prepare proposed legislation regarding the care of the insane, reorganized several competing child-care agencies in the city, and chaired the committee on registration.[3]

Small ceased his active involvement with the Bureau of Charities around 1900, but Henderson's influence continued to increase. He frequently discussed the latest developments in charity practices in the United States and Europe with the businessmen on the board and led campaigns to educate the public to the nature of charity and the work of the bureau. After the Bureau of Charities merged in 1909 with the Relief and Aid Society to form the United Charities of Chicago, Henderson helped organize more effective infant welfare and tuberculosis treatment programs.[4]

In 1912, Henderson became president of the United Charities. The organization had changed considerably from what it had been in 1894. Professionally trained caseworkers had replaced the volunteer friendly visitors. Many of these caseworkers were former students of Henderson at the University of Chicago proper or in the extension program for social workers. Henderson was now Chicago's leading expert in charity and also an authority on the problems of workingmen in general. He headed a municipal commission on unemployment. When a new and severe unemployment crisis developed in 1914, Henderson used his affiliation with both the United Charities and the commission on unemployment to establish a city program in which the United Charities processed applications of men for public works jobs paid for by the city.[5]

Faculty at the School of Civics and Philanthropy also maintained intimate ties with the United Charities and other charitable agencies, and the majority of the school's graduates entered the employ of Chicago's voluntary charitable agencies. The earliest concerns of the scientific charity movement involved centralized record keeping and coordination of agency work, but soon its concerns extended to centralized fund raising and dispersal as well. Breckinridge took the first step toward centralized control over fund raising in Chicago in 1911, when she proposed to establish a voluntary system of investigating and certifying private charitable agencies soliciting public support. Originally, she hoped to publish the results of these investigations at the School of Civics and Philanthropy, thereby giving social workers primary control over the process, but Chicago's businessmen/philanthropists sought to control the process themselves, and Breckinridge acquiesced.

The Association of Commerce appointed a subscriptions investigating committee in 1911 "to investigate the solicitors and beneficiaries by or for whom donations are solicited" and make its findings available. This committee, composed of businessmen, worked in cooperation with an advisory council of social service and church people, on which Henderson served. Beginning in 1912, the association published an annual *Classified List of Local Philanthropic and Charitable Organizations*.[6] In Chicago and other cities, the charities endorsement movement soon led to cooperative fund raising and fund dispersal systems through the Community Chest or United Fund in each city. It is not surprising that nonprofessional charitable agencies, particularly the Catholic charity agencies, opposed this movement. Many Catholics feared that Catholic charities run by nuns rather than social workers would fail to win endorsement and saw the movement as an effort by Protestant elites to gain control of all voluntary social welfare work. The charities endorsement issue was hotly debated by the National Conference of Catholic Charities. Father Siedenburg of the Loyola School of Sociology, one of the few Chicago Catholics who shared the outlook of the new professionals and who traveled freely among them, favored the endorsement system. Many Catholic leaders disagreed. One speaker at the National Conference of Catholic Charities in 1914 insisted that "we have too many professionals . . . may the Lord protect us against the professional sociologist."[7]

After Henderson's death in 1915, Chicago's sociology department failed to sustain Henderson's work in methods of charity organization, and the major academic influence within the United Charities and charitable work in Chicago generally shifted to social work scholars, especially Breckinridge and Abbott. In the 1920s, after the School of Civics and Philanthropy became the University of Chicago's School of Social Service Administration (SSA), Breckinridge and Abbott placed a continuing stream of students in fieldwork within the United Charities and obtained substantial support from United Charities for several major research projects. Numerous SSA graduates obtained jobs with United Charities or its affiliated agencies. As private social agencies developed ever more elaborate techniques of psychiatrically based work beginning in the 1920s, they depended increasingly upon the expert knowledge produced by university scholars and the services of trained graduates of social work programs. The growth of the university-based schools and departments of social work since the 1920s stemmed largely from a continuing close relationship between professors of social work and charitable social agencies.

The social settlement movement, nearly two decades younger than the scientific charity movement, maintaind strong university connections almost from the start. The earliest American settlements were inspired by London's Toynbee Hall, founded in 1883 by a minister and students at Oxford to bring the culture of the university to the slums. In the United States, both the program of the settlements and their relationship to the universities departed from the limited social uplift goals of the English settlements. American settlements became not only centers of classes, clubs, and a variety of community services, but catalysts for political agitation within their communities and outposts for launching local and national reform movements. American professors and students, like their English counterparts, devoted considerable time to the cultural activities of the settlement houses. The most important university connection with the settlements, however, and one of the things that distinguished it from the English pattern, was the use, by professors, of the settlements for social research.

The importance of the Hull House kindergarten for John Dewey's work in education is well known. The settlements provided an even greater stimulus to the development of empirical urban social science, however. Almost from the beginning, settlements undertook detailed neighborhood surveys such as *Hull House Maps and Papers: A Presentation of Nationalities and Wages in a Congested District of Chicago*. The new professional social scientists in economics and sociology quickly saw how settlements could facilitate empirical neighborhood investigations and help provide financial support for such research.

Zueblin, Breckinridge, and Abbott all began their careers in urban research as Hull House residents.[8] Presidents and professors at private urban universities recognized the public service potential of establishing their own settlement houses. Northwestern's settlement, located near Division Street and Milwaukee Avenue in the Sixteenth Ward, provided the customary classes, clubs, and services, and sponsored a conference on tenement house conditions. Its major support came from President Rogers and Northwestern faculty and students.[9] Harper similarly gave strong backing to the establishment of a University of Chicago settlement and also sought, unsuccessfully, to affiliate Hull House with the university. Unlike Northwestern, however, Chicago's own settlement played a major role in reform-oriented social research in Chicago.

During the spring of 1893, graduate students under the direction of J. Laurence Laughlin canvassed an area just north of the stockyards and a few miles west of the campus with a view to establishing a university settlement. The students prepared a map of the region, showing the location of churches, schools, and saloons. On January 1, 1894, a group of students moved into rented quarters in the neighborhood, and the University of Chicago Settlement got its start. The settlement soon incorporated with its own board of directors and hired Mary E. McDowell as head resident. (It was not an organic part of the university and therefore had to raise its own funds.) Harper helped organize the settlement and raise money for it and appointed a Chicago Divinity School graduate as director of university settlement work on campus, with responsibility for coordinating campus involvement with the settlement.[10]

For several years, the settlement performed the usual services, but in 1909 its trustees decided to conduct a "scientific survey" of the entire situation in the district. The study was to consider the "chief factors determining standard of living," namely, the types of men and women who came into the district for employment, working conditions in the packinghouses, purchasing power of workers' income, housing conditions, health conditions, educational facilities, and social institutions.[11]

By that year, the national social survey movement reached its height with the first published results of the massive Pittsburgh Survey, an examination of living and working conditions throughout Pittsburgh financed by the Russell Sage Foundation. This survey and others like it sought to collect data for the purpose of demonstrating the need for social reform. Chicago's stockyards study was one of numerous undertakings inspired by the effort in Pittsburgh; it was initiated and directed by Henderson and Mead.

A staff of ten worked on the project, which lasted two years. John C. Kennedy, an advanced graduate student in political economy at the university, was in charge of the research. He personally collected and correlated data on wages and family budgets, as well as on working conditions, health and sanitary conditions, and housing. He arranged for families in the area to keep detailed records of their daily expenses for several months, in order to determine scientifically the real cost of living in the stockyards district. Ernest L. Talbert, who held a doctorate in philosophy from the university and taught psychology in the extension division, made a study of boys and girls who left school between the ages of fourteen and sixteen. Other staff members studied retarded children and the problems faced by the daughters of immigrants in adjusting to American conditions.[12]

Mead insisted that the survey be designed in such a way as to fit easily into a larger survey of Chicago as a whole and hoped that the stockyards survey would inspire a full-scale city survey as a foundation for intelligent social policy.[13] In 1910, after collection of the housing data was completed, the board wrote to the Chicago Planning Commission, insisting that the housing problem was "of central importance in any scheme of city planning," and urging that housing be subjected to "competent, impartial, public control." The City Plan, the settlement board insisted, did not deal with housing, even though experience had proved that satisfactory results could not be obtained if housing were simply left to private contractors and landlords. "The working population, through no fault of their own, are, for the most part, obliged to accept the kind of living conditions which they find already in existence." The board also urged the Chicago Association of Commerce to back a proposed investigation "of all the crowded districts of the city," which would afford a "basis upon which intelligent relief and constructive measures might be had through our municipal authorities," citing the famous Pittsburgh survey as an example of what was needed in Chicago. The association agreed and established a committee on the housing problem shortly thereafter.[14]

Board members expected their survey to improve neighborhood conditions and, therefore, sought the support of the packers throughout. Data on conditions of work, hours, and wages paid could be obtained only with their cooperation, and Armour and Company agreed to allow investigators to study conditions in their packinghouses provided that the information gained therefrom would not be used in an "unfair way" to the packers. Undoubtedly, the packers still had vivid memories of Upton Sinclair's *The Jungle*, which only four years before had depicted horrifying scenes of miserable workers and filthy food. Board members assured Armour that "none of the information given to, or obtained by, our Mr. Kennedy or any of his assistants will be used by the Settlement, or any of its employees as the basis of sensational articles." They insisted that the "reports . . . will have the form of scientific brochures," and that "no sensational or misleading use shall be made of their contents." The board also agreed, at Armour's request, "to submit [to Armour] any of the statements and data prepared for publication" relating to the company "for inspection, and correction if necessary, before publication." "If you can point out to us any misstatements of facts, or any statements of facts which while they are true would carry a false impression, we shall be glad to correct them," they wrote in a letter of reassurance.[15]

Two years later, as Kennedy was completing his section of the report on wages and family budgets in the stockyards, Mead wrote to Henderson expressing concern over some of the wording Kennedy had used. Mead indicated that the final report ought "first of all . . . be directed to the attitude of the Packers and afterwards—perhaps with modifications—published." It was most important to invite the packers "to confer with us upon the conditions and to discuss general plans for alleviating and where possible remedying conditions." Through such a conference, Mead hoped to get the packers to understand

> the facts in regard to actual wages and their actual decline since the unions were destroyed . . . to emphasize the evils that must result from lowered wages, to emphasize further that in other industries within this period, such as the steel industry, wages have actually risen . . . and finally to emphasize the necessity of finding some other method of controlling the downward trend or stationary position of wages under our conditions of increasing cost of living.[16]

When Kennedy's report was completed four months later, the board at Mead's suggestion voted to change some of the wording and then submitted it to the packers as previously agreed. Armour and Swift representatives posed a few objections to the revised report. Mead met with the packers' representatives and reported that "the report could easily be modified so as to meet these criticisms." In addition, the board appointed a committee, which included Mead and Tufts, to draw up recommendations for the packers and to meet with them. Most of the packinghouses sent representatives.[17] No immediate improvement in wages resulted, however.

Why did the settlement trustees settle for such scant immediate results after three years of effort on the stockyards survey? In part it was
because men like Mead and Henderson felt that influencing the packers
provided the only chance for immediate improvement of conditions. An
unqualified indictment of the packers, they believed, would do no more
to raise wages than had Sinclair's novel. Furthermore, they objected to
sensationalism on principle—it was unscientific.

More important, however, the settlement trustees had reached the
limits of acceptable faculty activism. The survey clearly indicated that
inadequate wages were at the heart of the social problems of the
neighborhood, but the packers were among the leading contributors to
the settlement and the university. Harold Swift became chairman of the
university trustees only a few years thereafter. There is no formal evidence that Judson urged the settlement trustees to change the report's
wording, but such intervention was unnecessary. Mead and Henderson
understood that the men who endowed the university were willing to
support scientific charity, kindergartens and clubs in settlement houses,
laws protecting women and children, even social survey research. However, most of them refused to condone outside interference with wages
or working conditions, matters over which they considered themselves
more "expert" than social scientists or professors. The board's offer to
"correct" true statements in the report that "would carry a false impression" was a concession to the well-established limits of faculty activism.

The failure of the survey to bring about significant reform in the
stockyards might have discouraged Mead and Henderson from attempt-
ing further survey projects, but they were so committed to the concept
of research as a foundation of social policy that it simply stimulated
them to devise more elaborate and (hopefully) more effective vehicles
for social survey research. In June 1912, as the stockyards project
neared completion, Mead approached Anita Blaine to interest her in a
study of the different social surveys that had been conducted in Chicago,
in the hope of providing a rationale for the creation of a social research
bureau. Such a bureau, as Mead envisioned it, would "avoid dupli-
cations, . . . help toward profitable criticism of the methods of the different organizations, . . . bring the facts together that are needed to
interpret each other," and "make it possible to plan intelligent common
campaigns."

Mead expected the bureau to be a voluntary agency. As a prerequisite to its work, Mead thought it "necessary to make evident
the importance of the work, the scope which the bureau would have,
and the amount and character of the material that should be brought to

the bureau." Ernest Wreidt was again employed to conduct such a study, at Blaine's expense. Wreidt's research, completed the next year, reviewed the several dozen surveys already undertaken by different groups in Chicago, described potential sources of data like the census, outlined the activities that could be undertaken by the proposed bureau, and prepared suggestions as to organization and budget. Wreidt proposed that the bureau's work be divided into five categories: records and reviews, information and assistance, research, exhibits, and special surveys.[18]

Before Wreidt began his study, Mead and Blaine had called a meeting of over a dozen prominent reformers to win backing for the plan. Wreidt's final report was submitted to this group in January 1913. Present at that meeting were Blaine, Mead, Breckinridge, Henderson, Merriam, Graham Taylor, and a number of other reform leaders. The group strongly favored the proposed bureau, but Merriam announced that he planned to introduce an ordinance in the city council creating a public welfare department, which would perform all of the proposed functions of the social research bureau. The committee therefore decided to hold the matter in abeyance until Merriam's proposal reached a vote.[19]

By 1913, Merriam had become a major advocate of systematic social surveys. "I believe that nothing would contribute more to the health and happenings of our communities than . . . [social surveys] impartially and intelligently conducted and energetically followed up with wise, constructive measures," he proclaimed to the Illinois Conference of Charities and Correction that year. "It is not possible to remedy all the wrong that has been done in our communities, but it is entirely feasible to adopt measures for the future which will prevent the wholesale exploitation of the weak and helpless by the strong and unscrupulous."[20] New academic professionals who, like Merriam, had devoted their careers to scientific study and research understood that the demand for social survey data as the basis for social planning would inevitably increase their leverage over social policy.

The Chicago City Council accepted Merriam's ordinance, and what began as a movement for a private agency culminated in the creation of the Department of Public Welfare. At first, the department relied heavily on the expertise of professors. In 1914, for example, it decided to study housing problems in Chicago. Students at the School of Civics and Philanthropy had recently completed a series of housing surveys, and the department turned to Breckinridge and Abbott for assistance.

They let the department's investigators use the housing data cards and instruction sheets they had worked up for their own investigators and held a few special classes at the School of Civics for the department's survey workers to familiarize them with proper survey techniques.[21]

Reformers had tremendous expectations of the new department, but they were bitterly disappointed. Mayor Harrison appointed people to head the department whose qualifications reformers questioned, but Thompson, assuming office the next year, fired the department's civil service workers and replaced them with his own people, who had little interest in conducting social surveys. Finally, the director of the department revealed that she had been forced to split her salary with certain politicians. The city council withdrew appropriations for the department and suspended its operations.[22]

The stockyards survey, the ill-fated Department of Public Welfare, and similar activities in Chicago and throughout the nation helped to demonstrate the possibilities of systematic data collection and analysis as a basis of social policy. Social workers and social scientists continued to conduct policy-oriented empirical studies, funded at first by private individuals and foundations and later on increasingly by government. Large, general surveys of a single city gave way to studies of particular problems designed for a specific purpose, and the methodological sophistication of data collection and analysis increased enormously over the crude empiricism of the 1910s. Social scientists had already infiltrated the United States Bureau of the Census and other federal government agencies engaged in data collection and research on social welfare.[23] As the number and extent of these agencies and the scope of their work expanded in the 1930s and thereafter, the role of empirical social scientists in social welfare policy was insured. That development grew naturally from the early survey work of Henderson, Mead, Merriam, Breckinridge, Abbott, and others like them elsewhere.

THE PROBLEMS OF IMMIGRANTS AND BLACKS

Professors and their reform allies also applied their characteristic methods and solutions to the special problems of groups like immigrants and blacks. Education, specialized casework, data collection and analysis, and demands for new government programs characterized their efforts on behalf of immigrants and blacks, and in these endeavors also voluntary associations frequently preceded government agencies.

The Immigrant's Protective League, founded in 1908, employed

caseworkers to prevent the victimization and exploitation of newly arrived immigrants at Chicago's Union Station and to aid immigrants in
adjusting to America by helping them find employment and housing,
learn English, and understand American ways. The league's founders
included Freund, who served as president; William Rainey Harper's son,
Samuel, who was a Russian-language scholar at the University of
Chicago; Breckinridge, who was secretary; and Mead, vice-president;
Adolph Carl Von Noe, a professor of Germanic literature, later served
on its board. Edith Abbott's sister, Grace, became its executive director.[24]

As they did in other voluntary associations, the league's leaders
used the organization not only to provide services directly but also to
agitate for new laws and the assumption of their work by the government itself. Their efforts to create a federal immigrant protective bureau
in Chicago and a state immigration commission illustrate the process.

Freund was the chief architect of a bill creating a federal bureau in
Chicago. For years, the Immigrants' Protective League had tried to shelter immigrants arriving at Chicago's Union Station from exploitation,
and the new bureau was designed to take over this work. Members of
the league lobbied in Congress for the bill, which passed in 1912.[25]
Congress authorized expenditures of $75,000, for 1913–14, but only
$20,000 was budgeted by the administration and all of that was spent
on equipping the office. Thus no immigrants were aided by the bureau
during the first year. The league then pressed the Labor Department.
Breckinridge was especially active, working through Louis F. Post, a
one-time Chicago reformer who was then assistant secretary of labor,
and United States Senator Johnson M. Camden of Kentucky, an old
friend of the Breckinridge family. She had succeeded in making head-
way among key members of Congress when the outbreak of war in
Europe shut off the flow of European immigrants and pushed the problem to the background.[26]

The 1913 federal immigration bureau theoretically extended to
Chicago the federal government's traditional responsibility for regulating the arrival and admission of immigrants, but, once they were settled,
the newcomers received no assistance from any government agency. By
1917, Massachusetts, New York, New Jersey, and California had state
immigrant bureaus for this purpose. In 1916 Breckinridge tried unsuccessfully to interest Anita Blaine and Julius Rosenwald in a privately
funded study of immigrants in Illinois, which could "be the basis of
proposed legislation."[27] In 1918, however, Freund presented a detailed

plan for an immigration commission to Edgar Addison Bancroft, a reform lawyer and close friend of Illinois governor Frank O. Lowden,
urging him to present the plan to the governor. According to Freund's
plan, the commission would

> keep in constant touch with the needs and interests of the alien popu-
> lation, and with the needs and interests of the people of the state as
> they are specifically affected by the presence of a large alien element.
> It would see to it that these needs and interests are brought to the
> attention of the state and local administrative organs, and devise the
> best methods of remedying evils and meeting dangers. It would advise
> the governor if it finds defect or conflict of action. It would formulate
> and recommend legislation for executive consideration and eventual
> presentation to the General Assembly.
>
> Among other things the commission should undertake a survey
> of the foreign born population and its distribution.

"The taking over of the entire work [of the Immigrants' Protective
League] by the state," he wrote to Anita Blaine the next year, "will be
the consummation of the League's effort for over ten years. To fail to
bring this about would be a great disappointment and loss."[28] In 1918
the state legislature passed Freund's law, creating the Illinois Immigration Commission, and with Grace Abbott as its director, the new state
agency began to take over the functions of the league, only to be abolished in June 1921, when, as an economy move, Governor Lennington
Small vetoed its appropriation.[29] Once again, political factors frustrated
the apparent successes of reformers.

Professors applied similar remedies to the economic and social adjustment of newly arrived black migrants from the South and to the
special problems of anti-black prejudice. Breckinridge helped found and
raise funds for a black settlement, the Wendell Phillips Settlement, and
induced Julius Rosenwald to provide scholarships for two black women
to attend the School of Civics so that they could then run the settlement.
For several years, she served as the settlement's president.[30] Breckinridge
and Marion Talbot also served on the board of the Chicago chapter of
the National Association for the Advancement of Colored People. Talbot, as head of its education committee, protested racially segregated
dance classes at a Chicago public high school.[31] Breckinridge and Edith
Abbott played a major role in founding and sustaining the Chicago Urban League, begun in 1916. Robert E. Park, the Chicago sociologist of
urban life and ethnicity, served as the league's first president. In addition
to providing child welfare, employment, and housing services for newly

arrived black migrants, the league maintained a department of investigation to collect data on black social conditions, headed by Park's student, Charles S. Johnson.[32]

Those Chicago reformers concerned with the problems of blacks remained in the minority, however. Until the mass migration of World War I, blacks constituted too small and inconspicuous a part of Chicago life to warrant very much attention. That situation changed when race riots disrupted numerous American cities during and after the war. In Chicago, the bloody race riot of 1919 caused professors, social workers, and other reformers to urge that an expert commission study the status of black people and the causes of racial strife. The Chicago Commission on Race Relations, appointed by Governor Frank O. Lowden, but privately funded, resulted. It is not surprising that the reformers' major response to the racial strife of 1919 was a study commission. Unlike problems of public health, poverty, labor unrest, or juvenile delinquency, the problem of racial equality and race relations was a relatively new one for Chicagoans, and one for which most reformers had few solutions. In the absence of solutions to the problems of prejudice, reformers characteristically placed their faith in a prestigious study commission, in the sincere hope that detached and objective analysis would chart a course for future action. This was an attractive option also for Governor Lowden, who could thereby show concern with a problem without doing anything that might alienate voters. This sort of study commission became an increasingly common tool of government as it expanded its social concerns in the twentieth century.

The commission chose Graham Romeyn Taylor, son of Graham Taylor, and Charles S. Johnson to direct a comprehensive study of race relations. Johnson took the lead in developing the research design, supervised closely, although unofficially, by Park. Three of the commission's other researchers were also students of Park, and one other had studied with Henderson.[33] Johnson and Taylor drew heavily upon Park's knowledge of race relations and survey techniques and consulted with him frequently. At various stages in their work, the executive secretaries also consulted Breckinridge, Merriam, and University of Chicago sociologist Ernest Burgess. Breckinridge also had students at the School of Civics and Philanthropy collect housing data for use by the commission.[34] The final report of the commission stands as one of the earliest and most comprehensive considerations of northern race relations in the United States.

In their struggle for immigrants and blacks, Chicago's social workers, social scientists, and other reformers sought to establish acceptance of the idea that cultural differences of newcomers and racial or ethnic prejudices fundmentally affected the social welfare of foreigners and American blacks and that, therefore, these cultural differences and prejudices required special attention. Their solutions were the familiar ones—specialized casework and services to meet special needs, broad social scientific analysis of their problems to devise more effective solutions, and an enlarged role for government in protecting these groups from exploitation and providing them with the means to help themselves. These solutions broadened still further the demand for the expertise of university social scientists and their students.

PUBLIC HEALTH AND HOUSING

In the movement for improved public health and housing standards in Chicago and other large cities, the expertise of social scientists was united with that of chemists, bacteriologists, and physicians. The earliest towns in the American colonies had passed laws to protect the public from disease and fire, and these measures expanded as cities grew larger and more dense. With the enormous breakthroughs in scientific learning of the late nineteenth century, cities turned to highly specialized scientists for solutions to problems of public health, and their expertise soon became indispensable.

A considerable number of university natural scientists undertook the study of municipal health and sanitation problems. Professor Charles Frederick Chandler at Columbia did sanitary studies for the New York City Board of Health as early as 1866, and he became president of the board in 1873. Dr. William H. Welch, professor of pathology at Johns Hopkins Medical School, worked actively for improved water supply and sewage in Baltimore and in 1898 became a member of the Maryland State Board of Health. The university's second president, Ira Remsen, a chemist, served on a commission on installation of a modern sewer system in Baltimore in 1906.[35] Similarly, Chicago's Edwin O. Jordan and Northwestern's John Harper Long assisted a number of government and private agencies in purifying their water supplies.

As early as the 1870s, civic groups demanded that the city do something about the impurity of Chicago's drinking water. Chicago drew its water from Lake Michigan, but also used the lake for disposal of sewage, and it did not take extremely advanced knowledge of public health to link the city's high rate of disease to its drinking water. In 1871 the city made the first of several attempts to reverse the flow of the Chicago river, the repository of the city's sewage, so that it would flow into the

Illinois River and eventually down the Mississippi, instead of into the lake. In 1890, after several efforts had failed, the Sanitary District of Chicago began construction of a drainage canal that would join Lake Michigan with the Mississippi. Construction began in 1892. By this time the situation was critical. A typhoid epidemic in 1890 and 1891 caused largely by impure water took 1,997 lives in twelve months. The Chicago death rate from typhoid in 1891 was seven times greater than that of New York and eleven times greater than that of London.[36]

Both the Sanitary District of Chicago and the Illinois State Board of Health needed expert assistance to ascertain the effect of the drainage canal on the city and town water supplies drawn from the Illinois or Mississippi rivers. Jordan's credentials for this work were unique. As chief assistant biologist for the Massachusetts Board of Health and a graduate student at Clark University, Jordan had worked closely on questions of water and sanitation, and at Chicago he offered a course in sanitary biology. In the spring of 1895, Jordan had gone abroad to study the water supplies of several European cities.[37]

The following year, Jordan wrote to Harper, volunteering his services to the city if Harper deemed it advisable. When the chief engineer of the Sanitary District asked Harper to recommend "competent chemists, bacteriologists and microscopists" to make "a series of analyses . . . of the water of Chicago, the Desplaines, the Illinois and the Mississippi Rivers to show the extent of pollution under existing conditions, and after the water is let into our Channel," Harper nominated Jordan.[38] His extensive tests indicated that the enormous numbers of colon bacilli in Chicago sewage disappeared completely in less than 150 miles of flow and that the water of the Illinois River at Grafton, where it emptied into the Mississippi, showed no effects of the drainage canal.[39]

The Illinois State Board of Health was also interested in the impact of the drainage canal, not only on Chicago, but on the other towns and cities in Illinois that drew their water supplies from the Illinois River. The board, established by the legislature in 1877 to "make such rules and regulations and such sanitary investigations as they deem necessary for the preservation and improvement of the public health" consisted almost entirely of practicing physicians, who had no training and little expertise in public health and sanitation.[40]

John Harper Long, a chemist educated in Germany, had taught at the Northwestern Medical School since 1881. His work for the Illinois board confirmed Jordan's findings. In a series of tests made between 1899 and 1904, Long concluded that "in the stretch of the canal and river between Chicago and Peoria a remarkable destruction of organic matter is constantly taking place, not by sedimentation . . . but by organic oxidation."[41] Subsequently, the State of Missouri brought suit against the Sanitary District claiming that the drainage canal polluted the water supply of St. Louis, drawn from the Mississippi. The case went to the United States Supreme Court, and Jordan's testimony for the defense was a key factor in its ruling in favor of Chicago.[42]

While the drainage canal was under construction, Jordan, Long, and F. Robert Zeit, also of Northwestern Medical School, studied the purity of the drinking water in the Chicago public schools, at the request of the board of education. Jordan conducted experiments "to determine the number of colonies and types of sewage bacteria present in the water." Zeit "carried out animal experiments in which cultures from the waters were tested as to their pathogenic or disease producing properties," and Long carried out chemical analyses. The committee found the water highly contaminated, but noted that there was little the schools could do, since the "real source of the difficulty is the quality of the general public water supply."[43]

In the movement for pure water supplies, professors of chemistry or bacteriology were in considerable demand, but in other areas of public health, professors had to fight vigorously to influence policy. In 1910, for example, Breckinridge wrote to the city health commissioner urging him to use a study by one of her students on the disposal of waste matter on South Water Street and in the stockyards district. The commissioner responded quickly, describing the methods to be employed and stating that the study would "be of value in the further elaboration of this question."[44]

The City Club's public health committee fought for a number of reforms. Jordan, Edward Scribner Ames of Chicago's philosophy department, and Anton J. Carlson, chairman of Chicago's physiology department, served on this committee. In 1911, the committee investigated conditions at Cook County Hospital and then discussed their findings with the chairman of the Cook County Civil Service Commission. He, in turn, included several of the committee's proposals in his report to the county board.[45]

More important, the committee participated in a campaign in 1914 for a Chicago milk protection ordinance. When a milk inspection bill was defeated in the city council, the committee joined with the ad hoc Citizens' Milk Committee (on which Henderson served) formed under the auspices of the Civic Federation to work for enactment of the bill. As a result of the campaign, the bill was subsequently reconsidered and passed by the council.[46] Jordan and Paul G. Heinemann, another Chicago bacteriologist, were especially active in the pure milk campaign. Jordan wrote several popular articles advocating milk inspection, and together with Heinemann drew up regulations for pasteurization, which were endorsed by the American Medical Association.[47]

The City Club's housing committee, chaired by James Hayden Tufts, helped revise the municipal and state housing codes. In 1908, the committee learned that a commission had been appointed by the city council to rewrite the building laws, and the committee successfully obtained appointment of three of its members to that commission. The new 1910 building code that emerged spelled out building requirements in such a way as to leave less room for arbitrary interpretation by city officials.[48] Tufts, who had recently completed a study of housing in Illinois cities, helped secure appointment also of a state commission to revise the state housing laws. The City Club committee met with this body too, and Tufts presented his study to it.[49]

No major group in Chicago really opposed these health and housing measures. But the willingness of city officials to use Breckinridge's findings on garbage disposal or include the City Club's recommendations on Cook County Hospital in a report was a gesture that had no real impact on the quality of public health in Chicago. Milk inspection was an important step, and reformers needed only to educate the press and the city council to win approval of the inspection ordinance. The real opposition to milk inspection came from the downstate dairy interests in the legislature. In 1911, the legislature passed a law *forbidding* any city in the state to require a tuberculin test of cows whose milk was sold within city limits. Thus, in spite of the council's ordinance, there was no effective milk inspection in Chicago until 1925, when the city health commissioner announced that he was going to inspect milk sold in the city and would go to jail to do so. The dairy interests, not willing to allow him to become a martyr, backed down.[50] Virtually all interests in Chicago united in favor of milk inspection, but they lacked the political power to defeat the dairy interests in the state legislature.

The reformers' success in improving the housing code also proved illusory. The new law was not adequately administered, and in any case the problem of poor housing proved difficult to combat, even years later when large amounts of federal money were allocated to the task. In 1935, reflecting on the history of housing reform in Chicago, Edith Abbott sadly concluded that "very few improvements have come as a result of these efforts."[51]

SOCIAL INSURANCE AND THE PROTECTION OF EMPLOYMENT

At the center of the welfare state forged during the New Deal stood the idea that industrialization had made the economic security of workers and their dependents unpredictable and that therefore government had to find ways to stabilize family income. Systematic efforts of reformers and local or state governments to improve the social security of urban populations began more than three decades before the landmark reforms of the 1930s. Professors played a critical role in this early social security movement. Genuinely concerned over the effects of industrialism, they believed that the same scientific expertise that they applied to public education, crime control, or public health and housing could be applied also to the problem of economic stability in American life. Their efforts to rationalize the economic system helped establish new, centralized social welfare agencies over which they, as experts, expected to exert considerable influence.

Especially appointed study commissions, which in the case of the 1919 race riot provided an excuse for avoiding action, sometimes proved very useful to professors in their efforts to develop social insurance programs. When a coalition could be formed in support of a particular kind of insurance program, then professors, with their special knowledge of the problem, could often dominate a commission and produce concrete results.

One of the earliest problems that social welfare reformers sought to tackle was industrial accidents. At the start of the twentieth century, the laws of every state allowed injured workers or their dependents to sue employers if the accidents were attributable to the employer's negligence, but no laws guaranteed compensation for routine industrial accidents. Furthermore, it was difficult and expensive to win a settlement in court. In practice, therefore, workers and their families went unprotected.

In the first decade of the twentieth century, several states attempted to establish some form of industrial accident insurance. In 1902, Maryland became the first state to enact a compensation law that provided benefits regardless of fault, but the courts declared it unconstitutional in 1904. In the following years, Massachusetts, Connecticut, and Montana considered compensation laws.[52] So did Illinois.

Henderson played a leading role in the national movement for workmen's compensation. He chaired a committee of the National Conference of Charities and Correction that studied the question and in 1906 recommended that workingmen's insurance be fostered by state legislation.[53] Henderson helped secure passage of a joint resolution in the Illinois legislature in 1905 creating the Industrial Insurance Commission, appointed by the governor to "formulate a plan for industrial insurance and workingmen's old-age pensions." The governor subsequently appointed Henderson as secretary and a voting member of the commission.

The legislature made no appropriation for the commission, however, so the members decided to restrict their study to accident insurance and based their recommendations on accident reports, statistics, and information concerning European practices supplied by Henderson. Because of his extensive knowledge, the other commission members looked to Henderson for leadership. He drew up the lines of inquiry and formulated the major decisions the commission would have to make, and he furnished the other members with bibliographies on workingmen's insurance and copies of laws passed in Europe and other states.[54]

Two bills embodied the commission's final recommendations. The first provided for compulsory insurance like that of Germany. The commission members recognized that the courts would certainly overturn this; they submitted it only to stimulate discussion and to set an ultimate goal. The other bill, drafted by Ernst Freund, represented the most comprehensive plan the commission thought the legislature would accept and the courts uphold at present. The bill required that employers provide some form of insurance for their workers and that at least half the cost be paid by the employer. If an injury resulted in death, a sum equal to the wages of the deceased for the previous three years and not less than one thousand dollars would be paid to any dependents; in the case of total disability, weekly benefits of not less than 50 percent of the worker's wages for the preceding year were to be paid during the period of disability, and in case of partial disability, weekly benefits were to be paid in amounts fixed by contract between employer and employee. This bill created state supervisory machinery, but it required employers to submit copies of insurance policies used to the superintendent of insurance and to make quarterly reports of all payments and settlements.[55]

A slightly altered version of the latter bill was submitted to the legislature, where it died in committee. Trade union representatives opposed it because they considered the compensation inadequate and because they did not want workers to pay 50 percent of the cost. Nevertheless, the issue had been raised and a good deal of discussion followed, culminating in the appointment of another commission in 1910, consisting of six labor and six industry representatives. By this time, work-men's compensation was experiencing rapid success in several states. Minnesota, Wisconsin, and New York passed laws in 1909, and in 1910 eight other states followed suit. In 1911, the first workmen's compensation act passed the Illinois legislature, and it was extended by amendment in the following years.[56]

Henderson's commission had recommended that another body be appointed by the legislature to investigate occupational diseases and suggest appropriate legislation. The next year the legislature appointed this commission, and again Henderson was a member and secretary. The study took two years and spent fifteen thousand dollars in one of the country's earliest efforts to explore the different kinds of health hazards in industry, especially the use of poisons and their effects. The commission employed several doctors and bacteriologists and drafted a bill designed as a first step in protecting workers against industrial disease. The bill required that employers of workers in lead-refining plants and other poisonous industries take proper precautions to insure the health of their workers, provide laborers with adequate protective clothing, and give workers a monthly medical examination. The bill became law in 1911.[57]

By 1912 reformers in Chicago and Illinois had so many different legislative proposals in the area of social welfare that they formed a coordinated lobbying organization, the Committee on Social Legislation. Tufts, its chairman, represented the Illinois Association for Labor Legislation. As chairman, Tufts conducted much of the organization's correspondence, supervised the paid executive secretary, raised funds, and brought together people interested in a particular piece of reform legislation. Breckinridge headed the group's committee on labor. Freund chaired the legal committee, which passed upon "the constitutionality and form of bills which the Committee desires to approve." Walter Wheeler Cook, University of Chicago law professor, also served on the committee, but Freund did most of the work. Every bill submitted to the committee for endorsement received Freund's critical attention before coming to a vote, and many of the organizations and individuals sponsoring bills asked explicitly for Freund's opinion. The committee did not have much time to prepare for the 1913 session of the legislature and, therefore, had little impact on it. In the 1915 session, however, five measures that the committee actively supported became law.[58]

Tufts personally developed several bills, particularly one establishing a state commission on health insurance. In April 1916, Tufts proposed that the committee make a special effort in the coming legislative session to advance health insurance. The American Association for Labor Legislation organized by University of Wisconsin economist John R. Commons, had just drafted a model health insurance bill and urged its state branches to push the bill in their respective legislatures. Tufts formed a committee of representatives from Illinois groups interested in health insurance. The committee spent several months discussing the problem and then decided to seek a commission to study health insurance. Tufts went to Springfield several times to testify in favor of this proposal and to speak privately with lawmakers. The bill passed in the 1917 session, and the commission was appointed shortly thereafter, with University of Chicago economics professor Harry A. Millis, a specialist in labor, as its secretary in charge of research.[59]

Under the direction of Millis, the commission gathered a massive amount of data on health care in the state, and Millis and others believed that this information clearly demonstrated the need for health insurance. A majority of the commission disagreed, however, and recommended only extension of current state health activities. Specifically, it called for increasing the power of the state department of public health, payments to wage earners under treatment at county tuberculosis sanatariums, a legislative appropriation for control of venereal disease, establishment of hospitals and public health nursing services in every county, and creation of study commissions on mortality in childbirth and occupational diseases. Two commission members wrote a sharp dissent. The unfavorable report and the organized opposition of the insurance companies and the medical profession effectively killed public health insurance as an issue in Illinois, as in the rest of the country.[60]

Academic professionals also played an important part in making employment and unemployment a matter of government policy, although in these pre-Keynesian years, reformers focused primarily on city and state government. British and American reformers called for the establishment of public employment agencies very early as one solution to unemployment. In 1899, Illinois became the fifth state to establish a public employment agency, when it set up one free employment office in each city of more than 50,000 population and three in Chicago. By 1907, thirteen states had public employment offices. In Illinois, as in other states, these agencies received inadequate appropriations and were poorly coordinated, and therefore, reformers thought, they failed in their purpose.[61]

By 1911, the City Club committee on labor conditions, chaired by Northwestern economics professor Frederick S. Deibler with strong support from Chicago economist Robert F. Hoxie, investigated state free employment agencies and concluded that Chicago's three state agencies needed greater intercommunication and a better system of registration. Members of the committee met with the state commissioner of labor, who agreed "to secure a greater degree of cooperation between the heads of these three offices." In 1918, Governor Lowden appointed Deibler to the state advisory board of the Illinois Free Employment Office, and he subsequently became the board's chairman. The next year Deibler represented Illinois at a conference in Washington, D.C., "to consider plans for the continuation and expansion of the work of the employment service." Some of the administrative difficulties of the employment agencies were ironed out in the course of these efforts, but public employment agencies never had the impact on unemployment that reformers expected.[62]

Reformers similarly sought to regulate the practices of private employment agencies. Such agencies frequently charged exorbitant fees and sent workers to jobs that did not exist. A 1903 law established maximum fees and explicit rules for private agencies, but its ambiguous language made it easy for the agencies to evade many of its provisions. Freund achieved a major revision of the law in 1909. As president of the Illinois Association for Labor Legislation and chairman of the legislative committee of the Immigrants' Protective League, Freund met with the secretary of the Illinois Bureau of Labor Statistics, the inspector of private employment agencies in Chicago, and representatives of the Employment Agents' Association of Chicago, and worked out a mutually acceptable revision of the law. The bill, introduced into the 1909 legislature, received the endorsement also of the City Club labor committee. Freund's bill set up apparatus for inspecting and supervising agencies and required both that the terms of work be stated explicitly and understood by the client and that all travel costs be refunded if a person was sent to a job that did not materialize. With all parties agreed, the bill faced little opposition and passed easily.[63]

On the city level, Henderson initiated extensive government activities to relieve unemployment. In December 1912 Henderson wrote to Mayor Harrison asking him to appoint a commission to study the unemployment problem, emphasizing "the utter hopelessness of relieving sufferings and evils caused by unemployment in all its forms by private or public charity, working alone." Henderson's concern over unemployment had been stimulated by his attendance at the meetings of the International Commission on Unemployment in 1909 and 1911. He sent Harrison a series of questions about unemployment and a bibliography on unemployment and suggested a budget of one thousand dollars. Harrison asked the city council to establish the commission, which it did in 1912. He then appointed twenty-two people to the commission and made Henderson its secretary. From beginning to end, Henderson was its moving force and acknowledged leader. The commission's committees prepared reports on the nature of unemployment and its extent, immigration, vocational guidance, adjustments of employment, relief, and laws repressing vagabonds, and consulted Freund on the reorganization of state employment bureaus.

In November 1913 Henderson again wrote to Mayor Harrison, this time pointing out the urgency of the present unemployment problem for the coming winter and the current pressure on voluntary relief agencies. Harrison therefore induced the city council to reconvene the unemployment commission. The commission this time decided to work on immediate solutions to the crisis. The group proposed a series of stopgap measures, the most important of which was a program of municipal works for unemployed men, paid for jointly by public money and private charity.[64]

In 1914, with unemployment still critical, Mayor Harrison appointed still another body, the industrial commission, headed by Henderson, to "stimulate employment in private trade and industry; encourage part or short-time work among private employers; strive to dovetail seasonal occupations so as to provide for as great an amount of continuity of work as possible and obtain the cooperation of private employers to increase the number of their employees as far and as soon as this may be practicable." Once again, Henderson's commission first found temporary work or permanent jobs for some of the unemployed and then set out to frame long-run recommendations. It again called for passage of a bill improving the state employment agencies; it asked the city and state to enlarge their public works, urged development of a state or national program for unemployment insurance, and called upon city, state, and national authorities to arrange plans and contracts for public works so that they would demand labor at depressed periods. Late in 1915, the commission's bill on the state employment agencies passed the legislature and became law. Before the bill was passed, however, Henderson died of a stroke, apparently brought on by overwork on the employment problem.[65]

Freund helped develop a bill guaranteeing "one day rest in seven" for laborers. An 1845 Illinois law prohibited Sunday labor only if it "disturbed the peace and good order of society." In practice, large numbers of factories and commercial concerns required seven days' work of

Class at the University of Chicago Settlement House. Courtesy of the Chicago Historical Society.

(top) *Excavation for the Chicago Drainage Canal, 1895. Courtesy of the Chicago Historical Society.*

(bottom) *Illinois National Guard in front of homes damaged during the 1919 Chicago race riot. Courtesy of the Chicago Historical Society (DN 71,302).*

United Charities of Chicago work relief client. Courtesy of the Chicago Historical Society.

Police loading striking garment worker into a patrol wagon during the 1910 garment workers' strike. Courtesy of the Chicago Historical Society (DN 56,132).

their employees.[66] Late in 1911, John A. Fitch, a staff member of the social work periodical *Survey* in New York, drew up a model bill for "one day rest in seven," and sent it to Freund for his comments. Freund thought Fitch's bill weak because its definition of jobs that could be excepted from the requirement was "so wide that it practically throws the determination of what is permissible work entirely upon the courts." Freund suggested instead "more elaborate and detailed provisions, either within the act itself, or by administrative regulation" of work that might be allowed on Sunday. After a good deal of correspondence, Freund convinced Fitch and suggested how the wording of the bill could be strengthened.[67]

At the same time, the American Association for Labor Legislation appointed its own committee on "one day rest in seven" and made Freund a member. The association's secretary, John D. Andrews, sent Freund a copy of its bill applying only to those industries that operated continuously. Again, Freund had considerable correspondence over the questions of defining what constituted a "continuous industry" and of the differences between Fitch's bill and that of the association.[68] Freund modified the "model bill" that the association finally produced so that it would conform with Illinois state law and worked to win passage of it. In 1915, the bill passed the senate, but it was badly amended in the house and died after the house refused to accept further amendments reinserted by the senate.[69]

The Illinois Association for Labor Legislation lobbied for numerous other bills as well. Tufts succeeded Freund as its president, and Henderson served on the executive committee. In 1909 the group urged Governor Deneen to propose legislation for industrial safety, factory sanitation, expansion of the Bureau of Labor Statistics so that it might issue bimonthly publications and further study of methods of relieving hardships resulting from industrial accidents. On these, the first two passed the legislature during that session. The association also successfully petitioned the legislature to defeat a bill relaxing child labor restrictions.[70] In 1913, Tufts and Deibler urged Governor Edward F. Dunne to establish a commission "to revise the labor laws of the state, with the special end of securing greater economy and efficiency of administration," and the next year, Freund set forth the association's views on the organization and administration of Illinois labor laws to a legislative committee studying the state's entire administrative system.[71] In 1917, the legislature reformed the Illinois administrative structure, including those agencies involved with labor law.

Chicago professors were not unique in this extensive commitment to social insurance and labor legislation. The name of John R. Commons was associated with labor legislation in this period perhaps more thoroughly than that of any American. Henry R. Seager, an economist who established the field of labor problems at Columbia University, served as vice-chairman of a New York State Commission on Employers' Liability and Workmen's Compensation. Edwin F. Gay, the first dean of Harvard Business School and an economist, played a critical role on a Massachusetts commission appointed in 1910 to investigate factory inspection and authored a bill to reform the state's inspection laws. The following year he became first president of the Massachusetts branch of the American Association for Labor Legislation. Edward Devine, head of the New York School of Philanthropy and professor of social economy at Columbia played a leading role in the establishment of a public employment agency in New York.[72]

Chicago professors concerned with labor and social insurance generally won support for these efforts from reform-oriented businessmen and lawyers, who recognized the importance of a more rational and predictable system of economic security for prosperity and also for social control of the working-class population. On the issue of labor unions, however, reformers parted company. In general, social workers and many professors accepted trade unions as at least a necessary evil in guaranteeing adequate wages, whereas businessmen and lawyers saw nothing redeeming in them. Chicago's 1910 garment workers' strike highlighted the efforts of Chicago professors to gain acceptance for unions and to develop mechanisms for minimizing labor-management strife.

The strike had twenty-five thousand workers out for several weeks. Related industries and businesses began laying off workers, and the charity agencies were flooded with requests beyond their means. Worst of all, as the strike wore on each side seemed to harden into its position, and the potential for violent confrontation increased. For these reasons, some twenty-five prominent reformers met one night to attempt to break the deadlock. The group formed itself into a citizens' committee, which then appointed a subcommittee of five, including Mead as chairman, Henderson, and Breckinridge, to "investigate the grievances which the workers allege as the occasion of their striking."[73]

The subcommittee spent the next few days interviewing both workers and owners. The major grievances of the workers centered around conditions of work rather than pay as such. The shops used a system of fines to insure shop discipline. If a spool of thread or a bobbin was lost, it came out of the worker's pay; cutters were given just enough cloth to cut a garment and if the garment did not quite fit the cloth, the cost of a small additional piece was taken out of their pay; the company deducted twenty-five cents a week from the pay for use of company soap in the washrooms. Problems of this sort were exacerbated among newly arrived immigrants, who did not immediately catch on to the rules and who found it difficult to communicate with the foreman. On top of this, the work was very seasonal. During the busy months, the bosses resorted to speeding up techniques and made the workers sew at home during the evenings. In the lean season, large numbers of workers were either unemployed or were forced to remain in the shop all day, even though there might be no work or only a few hours' work; of course, they were paid only for the time they actually worked.

The subcommittee also interviewed Harry Hart of Hart Schaffner and Marx; Harry Pfalum, president of the Wholesale Clothiers' Association, and E. J. Rose of the National Wholesale Tailors' Association—thereby reaching representatives of nearly the entire Chicago garment industry. All three men insisted that the fines helped to enforce factory discipline, and Hart maintained that there were no grievances.[74]

The subcommittee came down strongly on the side of the strikers. The strike was not fomented by outside organizers, they concluded, but by "the continued irritation arising out of the conditions in the shops." The procedures followed in the shops resulted in "the unwholesome methods of speeding up," and foremen and inspectors gave "their first, and frequently only, attention to the efficiency of the operatives, and will have every interest in increasing this even to the possible injury of the laborers themselves." Finally, they concluded that the "natural method of removing the causes of irritation in the shops and making a more healthful social life there possible, is some form of organization among the workers in the shop." Mead and Breckinridge wrote the report, which was accepted by the larger committee on November 4, 1911.[75] The next morning, Hart Schaffner and Marx signed an agreement with their striking employees. The agreement was reached through negotiations under the auspices of the city council.

The Hart Schaffner and Marx agreement submitted all grievances to a committee of arbitration, composed of one representative of the workers, one of the company, and a third person agreed on by the first two. This committee worked out a long-range agreement whereby a board of arbitration settled all disputes between workers and the company. The board, like the committee that created it, included representatives of both sides and an impartial chairman selected by the other two. The system kept peace in the shops for over a decade. From the inception of the system until the early 1920s, Northwestern University professor of economics and business Earl Dean Howard served as Hart Schaffner and Marx's labor manager, representing the company on the board. In 1919, James Hayden Tufts became the impartial chairman of the board. No further strike occurred in the Hart Schaffner and Marx shops in the 1910s. (During World War I, Columbia's Henry R. Seager served similarly as secretary of the Shipbuilders' Labor Adjustment Board.)[76]

The other clothing manufacturers refused to settle in 1910, and eventually the strike was broken. Mead, Breckinridge, and another member of the subcommittee framed an angry resolution calling for arbitration:

> The impropriety of their [the employers'] attitude is emphasized by the fact that they know their employees are ready to accept the fair agreement adopted by Hart Schaffner and Marx and their striking operatives. This agreement refers all grievances to an impartial committee and leaves their settlement to this committee, as well as the means of avoiding strikes in the future. This is the principle of arbitration and it is not too much to say that at the present time the community demands that industrial struggles should be ended by arbitration, and that either party that refuses to submit its case to arbitration must meet the just condemnation of the community.[77]

This citizens' attempt to mediate labor conflict on the surface seemed one of the reformers' least successful efforts. The Hart Schaffner and Marx settlement emerged from negotiations sponsored by the city council, and both parties signed it just a few hours after the citizens' committee released its report—not enough time for the report to have influenced the employers. The rest of the garment industry refused to settle, in spite of the committee's efforts and its stinging denunciation. Nonetheless, the social workers and professors who supported arbitration articulated important assumptions about the nature of industry and industrial conflict that eventually became widely accepted in the United States. Just as they believed that existing practices in education, criminal justice, and social service had to be made more rational so as to avoid inefficiency and human suffering, they believed that America's late-nineteenth-century methods of factory labor management, characterized by gross exploitation of workers and occasional violent conflict between workers and management, could be replaced by a more stable and humane system in which everyone would benefit.

Earl Dean Howard articulated most systematically the outlook of professors and social workers on this question. Howard, the representative of Hart Schaffner and Marx on the board of arbitration, was nonetheless a vocal advocate of systematic procedures for resolving worker discontent in American industry. In a "statement of principle" drafted in 1920, "Rectification of Industrial Relations," Howard argued that modern industry required coordination and that "industrial coordination is achieved by obtaining the cooperation of the persons necessary to the functioning of industry (managers, workers, proprietors, capitalists)." Fundamental human morality or "righteousness" must guide all those involved in bringing about industrial harmony, but the task was still a complex one requiring complex solutions framed by experts:

> The industrial problem is too fundamental to yield to superficial treatment, panaceas merely obscure the case. When conflicts of interest generate hatred, particularly when incorporated in class consciousness, the disintegrating poison can be expelled only by a general application of the principle of righteousness. . . .
>
> The labor of translating the principle of righteousness into specific plans and policies of action must be the joint work of the experts in ethics and religion and in industrial management. The industrial world is already a vast laboratory of experiments in economic justice and practicable schemes of cooperation. Research will bring them to light while scientific study will interpret and adopt them to wider use.[78]

This view was thoroughly consistent with the efforts of reformers to create more rational and scientific methods in other areas of public policy and to rely upon experts to frame complex solutions. A majority of the businessmen who usually supported such solutions opposed unionization so categorically that they failed to recognize that collective bargaining would ultimately be good for industry because it would make production more stable and predictable. The professors and social workers, who had no personal financial or managerial stake in the issue, were more consistent, with more foresight. They also recognized that "rationalized" labor arbitration would give social scientists and business management specialists greater leverage over industry.

IN THEIR MULTIFACETED efforts to expand the social welfare functions of American urban society, professors and their reform allies applied the same kinds of remedies that they proposed for public education and criminal justice. Through their voluntary associations, they first attempted to apply "scientific expertise" to the poor, immigrants, blacks, workers, and other deprived groups. They quickly realized, however, that private initiative was insufficient. Their voluntary associations trained those who later staffed the government agencies, identified the complexity of the problems, and developed concrete solutions.[79] This was no small achievement, and one in which professors had a substantial part.

As the period moved on, reformers increasingly turned to government for more lasting solutions. "The 'voluntary benevolent efforts' of an earlier day have become state services with large numbers of salaried positions in the field of social welfare," wrote Edith Abbott in 1931.[80] She might have added that her own generation recognized at the time the relationship between voluntary effort and government. Voluntary associations provided no permanent solutions; they were experiments designed to discover and demonstrate what government could and should do more completely. "The voluntary association is often best for a narrow local enterprise, for pioneer experiments . . . ," wrote Charles R. Henderson in 1913, "but when the need for co-operation affects a great people the organs must be clothed with the dignity and force of regal or national power."[81] Herein lies the significance of the voluntary welfare efforts. Through them reformers showed what could be done and how it should be done, and then they set about trying to convince the government to do it. The voluntary efforts of the progressive period have, of course, bequeathed an ongoing tradition of voluntary social service, embodied in the numerous agencies supported by Community Chest fund drives, and these agencies remain an important part of our contemporary welfare system. However, the cornerstone of that system has become government.

Government in 1900 had the potential power and resources to protect the health and welfare of city dwellers, but reformers recognized the drawbacks of reliance on the state. It was controlled by politicians answerable to particular constituencies, and reformers could not always convince politicians to accept their claim to expertise. As in public educational reform, immigrant, Catholic voters and politicians legitimately distrusted programs that elevated "experts" of Protestant middle- and upper-class origin. Small-town and rural politicians, who usually dominated state legislatures, did not understand why government suddenly had to undertake so many new activities. Therefore, when reformers finally won adoption of a new program, there was no guarantee that appropriately trained experts like themselves would be appointed to administer it; nor could reformers be sure that a new law would be adequately enforced.

Nonetheless, retreat to the voluntary associations was unrealistic. Their resources were too meager, and improvement of industrial conditions, wages, housing, public health, or poor relief demanded not only money but the power of government modifying the free play of economic forces.

Professors had no master blueprint for social reconstruction, only a series of proposals forged from what they thought constituted the best available data on a particular problem. Professors and their reform colleagues envisioned in the future a continuing series of responses to new problems based upon popular determination to do what was just and efficient and upon the expertise to analyze problems and find workable solutions. Thus they envisioned a future society that would call upon them continuously for assistance and would demand the knowledge and skills that they imparted to their students. In laying a foundation for the welfare state in these early years, professors helped to create a crucial place for themselves in the elaborate government social service apparatus that would characterize American society at midcentury.

7

The Fight for City Government

JULIUS ROSENWALD WAS NOT ordinarily given to excesses in
rhetoric. Nor was he inclined to spend his time or money on candidates
for political office. Yet in 1911, during Chicago's mayoral election, he
declared that "Mr. Merriam's defeat would be the greatest calamity that
could overtake Chicago."[1] Rosenwald's unequivocal support for Merriam's candidacy was hardly idiosyncratic. Throughout Chicago, reformers echoed these sentiments.

There was more than a touch of irony in the enthusiasm generated
by Merriam's candidacy. Since the mid-nineteenth century, businessmen
had commonly sought to reform municipal government by replacing
"evil men" with "good men." When professional social scientists first
arrived in the new urban universities, they usually joined economy-
minded businessmen in the struggle for control of municipal government. By the beginning of the twentieth century, urban social scientists,
and their business allies, recognized that they could exert most lasting
and profound influence over city government by developing a "science"
of municipal administration, which would require greater expertise
than practical experience in government or business provided. The
modern public administration and urban planning professions grew directly out of this phase of municipal reform.

Reformers' demand for honesty, efficiency, and economy in city
government, whether of the older variety or the new scientific species,
derived from an honest analysis of city problems. Here again, however,
the solutions they proposed had the practical effect of increasing their
political power at the expense of the poorer classes. As Samuel Hays

has written in an extremely perceptive analysis of the battles for municipal reform:

> The movement for reform in municipal government . . . constituted
> an attempt by upper-class, advanced professional, and large business
> groups to take formal political power from the previously dominant
> lower- and middle-class elements so that they might advance their
> own conceptions of desirable public policy. . . . Reformers . . .
> wished not simply to replace bad men with good; they proposed to
> change the occupational and class origins of decision-makers. To-
> ward this end they sought innovations in the formal machinery of
> government which would concentrate political power by sharply cen-
> tralizing the processes of decision-making rather than distribute it
> through more popular participation in public affairs.[2]

Reformers genuinely believed that centralization of authority and agencies for "scientific" decision making and administration offered the
most rational ways to conduct city business and, therefore, served the
interests of all of the people. In practice such changes had potential
benefits for the reformers. They thought they could more easily
influence a centralized government than one in which power was dispersed among numerous political bosses and particular constituencies,
and they believed they had the knowledge and training to staff and
influence the new administrative agencies.

Charles Merriam, more than any individual in Chicago, led the
fight for the new *system* of public administration in the city government. Yet reformers like Merriam were caught in a bind. No matter how
well they developed the science of municipal administration, they would
never have the opportunity to use their scientific methods to reshape the
machinery of city government unless they won control of that government through conventional electoral politics. At the same time, reformers struggling to impose scientific and expert methods in education,
social welfare, and criminal justice also found their paths blocked by
unsupportive elected officials. The history of government reform in
Chicago, culminating in the political career of Professor Charles E.
Merriam, dramatizes this ultimate irony of urban progressivism.

RESTRUCTURING CITY GOVERNMENT

Upper-strata reformers, when faced with corruption and misman-
agement, first sought to replace dishonest and incompetent men with
honest and competent ones. In Chicago, reform-oriented businessmen

and attorneys started the Municipal Voters' League in 1896. Headed by George E. Cole, a stationery manufacturer, the league investigated the records of all candidates for city council, endorsed those candidates who appeared honest, and saturated the wards with information about the corrupt activities of dishonest incumbents. In its first years, the league was spectacularly successful, and in 1901, reformers also began the Legislative Voters' League, which monitored candidates for the state legislature.

Two professors worked actively with the Municipal Voters' League in the 1890s—John Henry Gray of Northwestern and William Hill of Chicago, both political economists. Hill gave numerous speeches against candidates the league had targeted for defeat. Gray vigorously opposed William Lorimer, a west-side Republican boss who controlled heavily immigrant wards through patronage and personal services to constituents. At the 1898 Republican State Convention, Gray fought aggressively to nominate an anti-Lorimer slate.[3]

To complement these honest government campaigns, urban elites for many years advocated civil service reform to undercut the power of lower-class politicians over government service. Throughout the progressive period, reformers in Chicago and elsewhere continued to press for extension of the civil service laws and for their strict administration. Several professors, especially Gray and Freund, worked actively with businessmen and lawyers in the Chicago and Illinois civil service reform associations.

The reformers of the progressive era were not content with the older techniques of the good government reformers alone. It was not sufficient to replace one group of politicians with another group, they reasoned. Instead, one had to build new government structures to guarantee efficiency. Antiquated city charters constituted a major obstacle to adequate government structure in most American cities. "Our greatest troubles in city government have been (1) the lack of adequate power, and (2) the lack of unity and responsibility in government," wrote Charles Merriam. Cities must be freed from the domination of the state legislatures, reformers insisted, and granted enough "home rule" to solve their own problems. Benjamin Park DeWitt, the author of a widely read book on progressivism in 1915 that became the unofficial manifesto of the movement, posed the issue as follows:

> The first problem of the city, as of the nation or the state, . . . is to become free. But because of the peculiar position which cities occupy in our scheme of government, freedom in the case of the city means more than it does in the nation or the state. . . . To realize itself fully,

a city must, in so far as the exercise of purely local functions is concerned, be free from the domination of the state legislature—must, in
other words, have municipal home rule.

Once freed from the domination of special influence and from
the interference of the state legislature . . . the city is ready to modify
its machinery of government so as to make it more readily controllable by its citizens.[4]

Reformers also sought home rule so avidly because legislatures
were notoriously partisan bodies, and political bosses wielded considerable power within them. "By both tradition and law, the state legislature
is the most thoroughly political body in the country," wrote Gray. "For
that reason it is the least well adapted for determing the policy of a great
municipality, which, of all our governmental agencies, is the most dis-
tinctly administrative, and therefore non-political."

Gray also echoed a familiar refrain of reformers when he insisted
that "the work of a great municipality requires as great ability and as
much expert knowledge as the management of any large private industry."[5] Here we have the remedy: power to the city, exercised by expert
administrators.

The movement for strong municipal government drew heavily
upon univesity professors from its inception in the 1890s. The annual
good-government conferences of the National Municipal League,
founded in 1893, attracted numerous academic types. In alliance with
the traditional groups that had sponsored clean-government crusades in
the past—businessmen, lawyers, and other city elites—the professors
developed a national movement for municipal government reform
whose central objective was strong city government. Among those active in these good-government conferences in the 1890s were presidents
Eliot and Gilman, and social scientists like Richard T. Ely, Edward Bemis, Herbert Baxter Adams, Edmund J. James, Frank Goodnow,
economist Francis A. Walker, political scientist E. P. Ellinson, and
economist Jeremiah W. Jenks.[6]

The 1870 Illinois constitution prohibited the legislature from passing "special" legislation for any city or village, so in theory the same
laws applied to both a village of a few hundred people and the city of
Chicago. The movement for charter reform began in 1894, when a
committee of the Civic Federation proposed a constitutional amendment granting Chicago a new city charter. Gray headed a federation
subcommittee on charter revision. "The law does not embrace the latest
accepted theories of municipal government in many respects," one Civic
Federation report announced. In its place, Gray's committee proposed a

number of measures to concentrate power and undercut the influence of small constituencies. The mayor's term was to be extended from two to four years, and the mayor was to appoint the heads of all departments, who would form his cabinet. Chicago was to be divided into six districts for city council elections instead of the current sixty-eight, with six aldermen elected for two-year terms from each district, three chosen each year. Furthermore, twelve other aldermen were to be elected at large, six each year, with voters allowed to vote for only four candidates, to insure minority representation. Clearly, Gray's plan sought to undercut the power of political bosses in relatively small and homogeneous wards. The proposal never progressed very far in the legislature.[7]

In 1902, a group of twenty-three city organizations met to inaugurate a movement for a new city charter for Chicago. Harry Pratt Judson served on the executive committee for this meeting and University of Chicago English professor Oscar Triggs was a delegate, although neither played an active role. The charter movement won its first major victory when, in 1903, the state legislature approved a constitutional amendment allowing Chicago to elect delegates to a charter convention.[8] In June of the next year, the charter convention convened to draft a document that would go to the legislature for approval.

Merriam was an active member of the charter convention. He was instrumental in getting the body to commission his colleague, Augustus R. Hatton of Chicago's political science department, to prepare "a convenient book of reference for use during the drafting of a new charter for the city." The 351-page *Digest of City Charters* brought together the main provisions of the charters and constitutions governing Chicago, eleven other North American cities, and six European cities, as well as unique features of other charters.[9] Hatton's work for the charter convention was his first major activity in a lifelong career devoted to municipal charter reform. The commission also employed Ernst Freund as its draftsman. In that capacity, he worked closely with the convention's committees and wrote most of the charter.[10]

Merriam formulated many of the charter's provisions on finance. As chairman of the convention's committee on municipal taxation and revenue, he undertook a major study of city finance in preparation for the convention. In January 1906, one month after the convention began its work, Merriam published a *Report on an Investigation of the Municipal Revenues of Chicago* under the auspices of the City Club. This document traced the development of the city's revenue system from 1871 to the present, compared it with those of other cities, analyzed the sources of revenue of Chicago, and proposed possible new sources.[11]

Merriam identified three difficulties "of paramount importance" in Chicago's financial situation: "the constitutional limitation of the borrowing power, the lack of unity in the scheme of local finances, and the scantiness of revenue in relation to the extensive territory to be governed." Merriam thought the lack of unity was the most serious. Eight different governments, Merriam showed, had substantial taxing authority over the city—the city government, the board of education, the public library, three different park boards, the Sanitary District of Chicago, and the Cook County government. Consolidation in some form, he urged, was essential to efficiency and orderly growth. It would allow a central body to view the needs of the entire city and allocate money accordingly; it would allow taxpayers to keep track of how their money was spent; and it would pin responsibility for city finances on one body.[12]

The charter that emerged from the convention included Merriam's recommendations for increased sources of revenue and fiscal consolidation by making the parks, the library, the schools, and the sanitary districts all council-funded city departments.[13]

The completed charter of 1907 went to the legislature, which removed many of its most important features. It curtailed home rule provisions allowing the city to make its own regulations regarding sale of liquor and Sunday observance, establishment of a direct primary and a corrupt practices act, and the extension of civil service to employees of the municipal courts. The legislature left the unification of the schools, parks, and public library under one government intact, however. Reformers split over the document that emerged from the legislature. Merriam favored ratifying the charter in the municipal referendum, arguing that the new charter was better than the old, but many reformers opposed it because of the legislature's amendments.[14]

When the voters defeated the charter, Merriam was active in discussions among reformers regarding the next step for charter revision. Reformers agreed to divide the main provisions of the proposed charter into separate constitutional amendments and submit them to the legislature, but in succeeding years they discovered that it was just too difficult to amend the state consitution. In March 1913, Walter F. Dodd, a law professor at the University of Illinois, wrote an article in the *Illinois Law Review* suggesting the need for a constitutional convention and proposing that the legislature appoint a special commission to gather material for a convention. Wigmore read the article and suggested that, since the legislature was not likely to provide for such a commission, the work should be done by a private group.

Discussions began among the representatives of the state's three major universities—Illinois, Northwestern, and Chicago—and finally the presidents of the universities asked members of their faculties who had special knowledge of constitutional problems to form the Universities Committee on the State Constitution.[15] About twenty persons joined this informal group, which gathered material for a state constitutional convention. Merriam took charge of the work on elections and their machinery, Freund on legislative procedure, Breckinridge on social legislation, University of Chicago law professor Walter Wheeler Cook on the initiative and referendum, Mead on education, charities, and correction, and Wigmore on constitutional changes. Chicago Law School dean James Parker Hall was secretary of the group.[16] The three universities split the committee's expenses.

When the committee completed its work in 1915, the movement for a constitutional convention picked up momentum. Several civic groups backed the proposal. Merriam, a member of the advisory council of the Constitutional Convention League of Illinois (an organization formed to bring about a convention) and of the constitutional convention advisory committee of the Citizens' Association of Chicago, helped to galvanize supporters. In 1916 he submitted a resolution to the city council calling upon the legislature to place the question of calling a convention on the ballot, and it passed the council unanimously. In 1917 the legislature agreed to ask the voters whether or not to call a convention.[17]

Merriam continued to use his influence in the subsequent campaign to win voter approval. His colleague and former student Frederick D. Bramhall conducted a series of five conferences to inform voters on the most important subjects likely to be considered in the proposed convention.[18] In November 1918 the voters approved the calling of a constitutional convention.

The convention assembled on January 6, 1920. A major battle developed between Chicago and downstate delegates. The latter wanted the new constitution to limit permanently the number of Cook County representatives in the legislature regardless of population, in return for Chicago home rule. The document that finally emerged from the convention in 1922 limited Cook County to one-third of the state senate, but apportioned the assembly strictly by population. Furthermore, it provided that should a future constitutional convention be called, Cook County would be limited to 45 of the 121 members. These provisions made the proposed constitution unpopular in the city, despite its home rule features. In the referendum, it was defeated overwhelmingly, and in

Cook County only one voter in seventeen supported it.[19] Illinois did not get a new constitution until 1971.

Professors, in alliance with other reformers, had a double interest in the nearly three-decade battle for charter and constitutional reform. They wished to centralize authority in the city government and also to develop the mechanisms needed for "scientific" administration, and they sought to write as much of this as possible into the governing documents. Machine politicians, who felt similarly constrained by the power of rural interests in the legislature, shared the interest in home rule, but for different reasons. They had no concern for "scientific" administration, but favored anything that would increase their political influence. Had Chicago won home rule, it is doubtful that reformers would have beaten machine politicians in the scramble to control a more powerful city government—a point these optimistic reformers failed to grasp.

The intense commitment of Chicago professors, particularly political scientists, to charter and constitutional reform mirrored the activities of their urban colleagues elsewhere. In 1899, New York governor Theodore Roosevelt appointed Columbia's Frank Goodnow to a commission to draft a new charter for greater New York. William B. Munroe, who taught municipal government at Harvard, served on the Cambridge Charter Commission (1913–14), the Boston Budget Commission (1915), and chaired a commission to collect data for a Massachusetts constitutional convention (1917–19). His Harvard colleague, Albert Bushnell Hart, served in that constitutional convention. Dr. William H. Welch of the Johns Hopkins Medical School served on a nine-member charter revision commission appointed by the city's reform mayor in 1909.[20]

Political scientists and economists especially shared Merriam's interest in municipal taxation and revenue. Richard T. Ely served on a Baltimore tax commission as early as 1885, and on a Maryland tax commission the following year, although unlike Merriam two decades later, he failed to win those bodies over to his viewpoint. In 1916, two years after assuming the Hopkins presidency, Goodnow chaired the Maryland state budgetary commission. E. R. A. Seligman induced New York's reform Mayor John P. Mitchell to appoint a committee to study the city's tax system in 1914 and served actively on it. One of Seligman's colleagues in the Columbia economics department, Robert Murray Haig, prepared its report. Seligman also advised the Joint Legislative Tax Committee of New York State in 1919 and 1920.[21]

Charter and constitutional revision were necessary prerequisites to the "scientific" municipal administration that social scientists sought, but reformers simultaneously tried to change the way in which city government performed its functions under admittedly adverse statutory circumstances. Home rule, they argued, was itself simply a means to an end. Benjamin Park DeWitt put it this way: "Good city government . . . does not necessarily result when cities are given the right to frame their own charters and regulate their own affairs under a constitutional home rule provision; for cities may never take advantage of the opportunity, and even if they do, they may provide for themselves a worse government than that given to them by the legislature." To guarantee sound administration, DeWitt argued, cities must make efficient administration a matter of ongoing concern:

> The fundamental ideas underlying the efficiency movement are that there is no panacea for municipal ills; . . . that municipal problems depend for their solution upon the same scientific study and analysis that banking problems or railroad problems require; that any attempt to remove inefficiency and waste must be continuous and not intermittent; that honesty and good intentions cannot take the place of intelligence and ability; and finally that city business is like any other business and needs precisely the same kind of organization, management, and control.[22]

A system for providing city officials and legislators with adequate information on any given problem constituted one essential prerequisite to intelligent administration, reformers believed. In an early effort to provide basic information about cities, a dozen prominent Chicagoans, including Charles Zueblin, founded the Municipal Museum of Chicago in 1904. Early in that year, the group raised fifteen thousand dollars to purchase a number of city exhibits displayed at the St. Louis World's Fair. Mayor Carter Henry Harrison endorsed the plan, and the Chicago Public Library agreed to give space in its building for the exhibits. The Municipal Museum of Chicago opened in 1905, with George E. Vincent as its president and Charles Zueblin as a member of the board of directors. They conceived the museum as a place where the experiences of the world's cities could be compared. This, the founders believed, would be of immeasurable value to Chicago and all cities in formulating policy. "Its purpose is the promotion of intelligence concerning the administration of cities and the problems of urban life," they announced.[23]

More important, however, was the establishment of a reference bureau to assist legislators in drafting laws. Wisconsin pioneered in the Legislative Reference Service, headed by Charles McCarthy, who tapped the expertise of University of Wisconsin social scientists in developing progressive legislation. Other states and cities soon followed Wisconsin's lead. Legislative reference bureaus typically had close ties with university scholars in the social sciences and law. The first such bureau established in a city began in Baltimore in 1905, headed by a young Ph.D. in political science from Johns Hopkins.[24] Charles E. Merriam agitated actively for such a bureau in Illinois. Working closely with James W. Garner at the University of Illinois, Merriam rounded up support from prominent individuals and from organizations like the bar association. He arranged to have McCarthy address the City Club and obtained from him data on the costs of the bureau and the size of the staff. Merriam and Garner hoped for passage in the 1908 legislative session, but the bureau was not created until 1913.[25] Similarly, Frederick D. Bramhall, who had been legislative reference librarian in New York before coming to Chicago, campaigned actively to establish a municipal bureau of information and publicity for the city. As chairman of the City Club's committee on publicity and statistics, he and members of his committee testified in favor of the ordinance establishing the Chicago bureau, which was passed in January 1912.[26]

In their efforts to rationalize urban government, reformers also demanded systematic city planning. "The era of haphazard, happy-go-lucky, hit and miss city growth is rapidly passing away," announced Charles Merriam at a city planning conference in 1917. The outstanding example of systematic urban planning in Chicago, and indeed in the nation, during the early twentieth century began when the Commercial Club of Chicago employed architect Daniel H. Burnham to draw up a plan for improvement and beautification of the city. His *Plan of Chicago* was published in 1909, and in subsequent years the businessmen of the Commercial Club fought vigorously to implement Burnham's design.[27] Professors quickly became a part of the new planning movement.

The creation of parks and adequate recreational facilities required advance planning, so that land in a given area could be reserved for this purpose before it was put entirely to private residential or commercial use. As early as 1899, park advocates persuaded the city council to establish the Special Park Commission to examine proposed new sites for parks and playgrounds. Zueblin served on this commission and coauthored a major report on the park problem.[28] In 1910, largely at the behest of the Chicago Geographical Society and some of the woman's clubs, Illinois governor Deneen appointed a special five-person commission to select sites within the state to be preserved as parks because of their historic or geographic features. Northwestern history professor James A. James chaired the body, and University of Chicago geologist Wallace A. Atwood was also a member.[29]

Park commissions planned for one kind of urban need, but the planning movement soon recognized that more comprehensive planning was required. In January 1908, Mayor Fred A. Busse appointed a harbor commission "to consider the question as to whether any part of the lake front should be reserved for possible future harbor uses" specifically, and generally to "report on Chicago's harbors and their relation to railway terminals and park plans." The commission was created because the city's South Park commissioners were in the process of completing plans to develop the entire downtown lakefront for park purposes, and many civic and business leaders felt that the needs of Chicago's water commerce ought to be considered before final lakefront plans were completed.[30]

Merriam got himself appointed secretary of the commission in charge of conducting its research. The commission wanted someone with "special knowledge and training" to make a "concise report on the commerical advantages obtained by improvements on harbor facilities in leading cities of the United States and abroad."[31] Merriam hired John Paul Goode, a colleague at the university. Goode, a specialist in commercial geography, spent several months studying eighteen harbor cities in the United States and Europe. His final report described the growth and operations of these ports, and, based on an analysis of their experience, Goode argued that it was Chicago's "manifest destiny" that it become "the commercial focus between the rich central plain and all the rest of the world." To do this, Goode urged, "one absolutely essential step is plain—Chicago must become her own seaport."[32]

"The whole drainage canal should be looked upon as a harbor for development as a manufacturing region," he urged, "and suitable provisions made for adequate docks and turning basins. But for the commerce of the Great Lakes and the ocean boats which may come from the East and Northeast, extensive areas on the lake front should be reserved." The experience of European ports indicated that it was unwise to develop the river in the downtown area into a harbor because that would necessitate drawbridges which would hinder both street and water traffic. Furthermore, Goode argued, a lakefront harbor would make connection with the railroads easy. Many of Goode's suggestions were adopted by the commission, including his idea of harbor construction on the lakefront. The commission called for reserving the lakefront from the Chicago River to Randolph Street for harbor development and

from the Chicago River to Chicago Avenue for future harbor development.[33]

Merriam wanted the commission to produce a plan that would
balance the requirements of shipping, commerce, railroads, and parks;
the final report, which recommended that a portion of the lakefront be
reserved for harbor development, attempted to do this. The proposals of
the commission were not readily accepted, however. It took nearly a
decade of court fights and negotiations before a municipal pier was constructed, the railroads' needs met, and the lakefront park developed.[34]

Reformers faced constant frustration in their efforts to restructure
and centralize municipal government and to improve the quality of social welfare, education, and criminal justice in the city. Therefore, they
looked for ways to alter the machinery of electoral government. It was
the will of the people that society's problems be solved, they said. If
government responded to the people, it would adopt reformers' scientific solutions for society's various ills, they self-confidently asserted.
Throughout the country, men and women rallied behind measures that
they claimed would bring government back to the people—the initiative
and referendum, nonpartisan municipal elections, the short ballot, and
many others. Many of these same men and women also urged that
women be given the vote.

Here too reformers had several motives. Many really believed that
a more perfect democracy would bring about necessary change. Reformers also thought that direct democracy provided a tool for under-
cutting the power of political bosses and legislative bodies responsive to
particularistic concerns. They thought, naively, that they could win a
citywide referendum more easily than a vote in the council or state legislature. In short, reformers saw direct democracy as a means of winning
the substantive battles in which they were engaged.

The initiative allowed the electorate to bypass the legislature and
enact a law, and the referendum allowed the electorate to review an act
already passed by the legislature. Merriam, a founding member of the
Initiative and Referendum League of Illinois, served on its executive
committee from its inception in 1911. He constantly gave the league's
officials advice and assistance, suggesting appropriate men in the legislature to endorse or manage the initiative and referendum bill. Illinois did
not pass an initiative or referendum law, however.[35]

Similarly, reformers expected to undercut the power of politicians
by limiting the number of elected offices. In 1913 Freund helped organize the Short Ballot Association of Illinois, with Judson's endorsement. Judson also served on the City Club's committee on the short

ballot. The short ballot also failed to win legislative approval, however.[36]

Through nonpartisan elections, reformers likewise hoped to limit machine influence over municipal elections, arguing that party labels gave no indication of a person's abilities to perform the largely managerial tasks of city government. By 1917, this proposal had picked up wide support in the city, with endorsements from the Association of Commerce, the Woman's City Club, and the city council. Merriam lobbied actively for nonpartisan election bills in the state legislature and used his influence with Governor Frank O. Lowden and Hyde Park's representative to the assembly to push it along.[37] A law establishing nonpartisan election of the city council passed shortly thereafter, but in practice it made little difference. The two parties still continued to put up candidates and political machines had little problem in getting voters to support their candidates, even if there was no party label next to the name.

The proponents of woman suffrage throughout the nation used much of the same rationale as the proponents of the initiative and referendum, nonpartisan elections, and the short ballot. The feminist demand for suffrage dated back to the mid-nineteenth century. Since large numbers of women entered municipal reform in the early twentieth century, leaders of the suffrage campaign argued that as mothers and housewives, women voters would demand adequate welfare, good schools, and proper public health and housing protection more readily than men. "The housekeeper cannot adequately and intelligently do her work unless she can share in deciding under what conditions it is to be done," insisted Marion Talbot at a 1913 suffrage hearing in Springfield.[38]

In Illinois as in the rest of the nation, women themselves led the suffrage movement, with strong endorsement from many men reformers. Breckinridge, Abbott, and Talbot played major roles in the Illinois campaign, writing propaganda pamphlets and testifying before legislative committees.[39]

In 1912 the national Progressive party endorsed suffrage, and the Illinois branch of the party, in which Merriam was a key figure, strongly lobbied for it. Merriam served as a liaison between the party and the Illinois Equal Suffrage Association and brought the association's bill to the party for endorsement. In 1913 Illinois granted women the vote in municipal elections and for many state offices, the first state outside the far West to do so.[40]

Now the suffragists sought to show that Illinois women were voting wisely and in large numbers. Breckinridge helped organize a Woman's

City Club campaign to educate women for voting.[41] In 1915 Edith Abbott analyzed the women's vote in Chicago's municipal elections in an article entitled "Are Women a Force for Good Government?" By law, special women's ballots were used and counted separately, so it was clear for whom the women had voted. In the Republican and Democratic primaries for mayor, women gave a larger percentage of their vote to the "better" candidate than did men, Abbott argued. Neither candidate in the regular election was desirable, said Abbott, but the "least undesirable candidate" received no more support from the men than from the women. Furthermore, Abbott showed that in two wards the women's vote changed the outcome of the aldermanic elections, and in both cases the women put over the candidate backed by the Municipal Voters' League.[42] Abbott wrote similar articles for other popular periodicals.

THE POLITICAL CAREER OF CHARLES E. MERRIAM

The advocates of charter and constitutional reform, modernization and centralization of government machinery, expert legislative drafting, and systematic city planning assumed that the older "good-government" crusades that replaced one set of politicians with another were less effective than new, scientific methods of public administration. Direct democracy and woman suffrage, they argued, increased the likelihood of implementing these systemic changes. At the same time that they struggled aggressively for new methods and acceptance of new ideas, however, reformers stayed in the rough-and-tumble of Chicago electoral politics. By the second decade of the twentieth century, they vested virtually all their hopes for implementing the changes they sought in the political candidacy of one man—Professor Charles E. Merriam. Here we have the ultimate irony of the new municipal reform. Reformers claimed to place their faith in impersonal experts and systems, not in good politicians. Yet to implement their proposals they had to win control of the city government through the conventional electoral process. Thus the very people who eschewed electoral politics as a permanent solution to municipal ills embraced it, at least once more, in the hope of electing a man who would finally establish the new order.

Merriam's background mirrored that of many of Chicago's elite reformers. Hopkinton, Iowa, his hometown, had a population of about six hundred. Merriam's father was a bastion of respectability—a staunch Republican politician, an elder in the Presbyterian church, and a successful storekeeper and banker. His mother wanted her two sons to become ministers. (Charles's brother John became a natural scientist and eventually head of the Carnegie Institution.) Charles married a Catholic, although he remained a nondenominational Protestant most of his life.

At Columbia Merriam studied with William A. Dunning, but he learned as much from the rough-and-tumble of New York City politics as he did from his classes and books. While at Columbia, for example, he watched Theodore Roosevelt's flamboyant performance as police commissioner and took part in Seth Low's campaign for mayor. In 1899 Merriam went to study in Berlin, where he organized a group of Americans interested in observing the German methods of municipal administration. The next year, he joined the faculty of the University of Chicago.[43] He soon became a member of the Republican party organization in his ward, served on the Chicago Charter Convention, made many contacts through the City Club, and directed the research of the Chicago Harbor Commission.

In 1909 Merriam sought the Republican nomination for alderman in the primary election in his ward, which included most of the university community. There was strong reform sentiment in the area, and despite opposition from the Republican organization and Mayor Busse, Merriam scored a substantial victory, which guaranteed his success in the regular election in this heavily Republican ward. He was then thirty three years old.

As alderman, Merriam quickly became the acknowledged representative of good government forces and reform in the city council. If the Woman's Club, the City Club, or the Juvenile Protective Association needed information about the city government, they turned to Merriam. He was always looking into complaints or suggestions made by reform groups and individuals. Later, as a member of the finance committee, Merriam continually used his influence to see that one reform project or another received adequate funding. Through his access to information and to government personnel, Merriam performed vital services for Chicago's network of reform organizations.

As alderman, Merriam first undertook an examination of the city's finances, a task that he had already begun through the charter convention and the City Club. A few weeks after he took his seat, Merriam moved that a commission be appointed to conduct a comprehensive inquiry into the expenditures of the city government. Merriam became the head of this body, and the Merriam Commission, as it was commonly called, quickly uncovered gross waste in city expenditures and several cases of graft. For example, the commission discovered that a particular firm had been paid to remove shale rock from a tunnel under construction, although it turned out that there never had been any rock in the tunnel at all. Records had been falsified to cover up the crime. In another instance, Merriam's investigators found that the city purchasing agent constantly violated a law requiring that all purchases over five hundred dollars be made by formal contract. To evade the law, the agent broke down his purchases into several small five-hundred-dollar units. Thus, the Department of Public Works had taken bids for purchase of castings at a particular price, but the purchasing agent ignored the bids and divided the purchase into small units, which cost the city an extra forty thousand dollars. In one city department after another, such practices prevailed. The commission, although not a prosecuting body, turned its material over to the Cook County state's attorney. Several indictments were handed down, but few convictions resulted.

According to Merriam, there were three great sources of loss to the city: outright graft, political favoritism, and lack of a proper system. The commission exposed graft and favoritism, and temporarily forced out those most guilty. However, it recommended a series of new budgetary procedures designed to avoid waste and make it harder to plunder. The council adopted the most important of these, an itemized budget.

Those threatened by Merriam's exposures tired unsuccessfully to discredit the commission's work. They sought a court injunction barring the commission from expending any further public money, on the grounds that expenditures for such investigations were illegal. In addition, those commission members unsympathetic to Merriam's purposes tried to undermine it from within. Their actions so angered Julius Rosenwald, who had previously avoided political activities, that he announced that he would personally underwrite the commission's work if necessary. The injunction was never obtained, however.

The commission's disclosures stimulated establishment of a private Bureau of Public Efficiency, formed to keep track of how the city government spent its money. Rosenwald was its first president, and Merriam served on its board of directors for many years. The bureau's staff published reports on expenditures of the different city departments.[44] A similar development had already occurred in New York, where William H. Allen, who had earned a doctorate in economics from the University of Pennsylvania under Simon Patten, convinced several businessmen to support establishment of a bureau of city betterment, to conduct independent, nonpartisan research on the financial procedures of city government. Allen and others associated with this group soon won backing for the New York Bureau of Municipal Research, begun in 1907, which was devoted to the study of New York municipal administration. Seligman, Goodnow, Charles A. Beard, and numerous other social scientists worked closely with the bureau in succeeding years.[45]

Merriam also looked into public utilities, and here too he found widespread corruption. Shortly after he entered the council in 1909, he discovered that Mayor Busse's administration was backing a plan granting a fifty-year franchise to a company for construction and operation of a pier on the downtown lakefront. Merriam had just finished his work with the harbor commission, which had recommended municipal construction of the pier. He then realized that many people had supported the creation of the harbor commission to provide publicity for this private pier development. Merriam protested loudly, and eventually the pier was constructed by the city.[46]

By 1911, Merriam had embarrassed Republican Mayor Busse, and Republican reformers felt that they had to push Busse out. Furthermore, in Illinois as elsewhere President Taft had alienated reform Republicans who were preparing to challenge him for the presidential nomination in 1912. Finally, progressive Republicans in Illinois were angered by the national scandal stemming from state Republican boss William Lorimer's bid for a seat in the United States Senate. Chicago's progressive Republicans determined to challenge the regulars in the mayoral election, and Merriam seemed the logical choice.

Busse eventually withdrew, realizing he could not win reelection. In the Republican primary, Merriam scored an upset victory over two regular candidates, one backed by Busse and one by Governor Deneen.[47] In the general election, former mayor Carter Henry Harrison, Merriam's opponent, tried to exploit the fact that Merriam as a professor lacked practicality and was elitist. One piece of campaign literature argued that Merriam had submitted an ordinance requiring building inspectors to be trained engineers so that "the Building Engineers would come from the University of Chicago."[48]

Wealthy reform elements in the city strongly backed Merriam's campaign. Julius Rosenwald summed up the feelings of the hard-core reformers of Chicago. "In my opinion," he wrote, "this is, without exception the most important epoch in Chicago's history. We have, for the first time, the opportunity of electing a Mayor who can give us an administration unhampered by party influences. . . ."[49] Merriam lost, but impressively, polling 161,000 votes to Harrison's 178,000. Merriam believed, not unreasonably, that his defeat stemmed from the Republican organization's failure to work for his election.[50]

The election of 1911 foreshadowed the national Republican split in 1912, with progressives leaving the Republican party to form the Progressive party. Merriam participated actively in the state and national negotiations that led to the founding of the Progressive party in Illinois. He served as temporary chairman of the Progressive party convention of 1912 and continued to work in the new party after Roosevelt's defeat. The party made a respectable showing in 1912, carrying Chicago for Roosevelt by 35,000 votes.[51]

In 1913, regulars in the Republican party strongly opposed Merriam's bid to return to the city council, but Merriam was extremely popular in his ward and won as an independent in spite of substantial gerrymandering. Back in the council, Merriam kept hammering away at the old issues and added several new ones. In 1914, he became a member of the council's finance committee, which prepared the budget and reviewed all requests for city money. Here again, he kept his eyes open for suspicious projects and misuse of public funds. He also exposed city officials who pocketed for themselves the interest earned on city monies and pension funds.[52]

Merriam continued promoting city planning as well. In 1914, he launched a drive for city zoning regulations by preparing a special report detailing the problems that developed when people lived in industrial districts. Merriam gained wide support for zoning, and the council endorsed a resolution asking the legislature to give the city authority to zone. It took several years for the zoning bill to emerge from the legislature, but in 1921 a zoning commission began preparing tentative plans.[53] Merriam also unsuccessfully pushed a bill, originally drawn by the National Playground Association, which would have required that one-tenth of all new land subdivisions be reserved for playgrounds and schools.[54]

Merriam had a hand in planning the city's railroad terminals too. In 1913, when the Pennsylvania Railroad applied to the city council for permission to construct a major terminal, Merriam insisted that the request be studied in relation to the larger city plan, and a railroad terminal commission was appointed. As a result, the original plans for the terminal were altered to square them with the overall needs of the city. Among other things, the railroad agreed to electrify its south-side lines, thereby counteracting heavy smoke pollution, which had been a special source of annoyance to Merriam's Hyde Park constituents.[55]

Throughout this period, reformers scrutinized the rates charged by franchised public utilities. In his first term in the council, Merriam had studied a telephone company's request for a $900,000-a-year rate increase necessitated by losses in the preceding years. He discovered the company had altered its figures to show a loss when actually it had earned a substantial profit. As a member of a subcommittee appointed to review the rate issue, he submitted a bill in 1911 lowering current rates. When Merriam returned to the council in 1913, he found the ordinance still pending. After further investigation and study by rate-making experts, he won approval of a $900,000 cut in telephone rates. In 1913 Merriam unsuccessfully sought an ordinance reducing the rates for electricity. However, shortly after its defeat, the electric company voluntarily lowered its rate to the level Merriam had proposed. He also took part in a long and intricate series of maneuvers involving gas rates, in which, among other things, the gas company's books mysteriously disappeared and it was discovered that Mayor Thompson had a major financial interest in the gas company. The case finally went to court, and the ruling was against Merriam's demand for a reduction in the gas rates.[56]

While most of Merriam's early activities as alderman concerned honesty, efficiency, and planning in city government, after 1913 he also took a strong interest in the problems of social welfare. It was his idea to make Mead's proposed private bureau of research a municipal Department of Public Welfare.[57] Merriam's central preoccupation in the years after his return to the city council in 1913, however, was crime.

In 1913, Merriam introduced a resolution into the council calling for investigation of the contract labor system in the city prisons. Under this system, prisoners worked for private companies, which paid the city only a fraction of the costs of free labor. As a result of this investigation, the council abolished contract labor in the House of Correction, and thereafter prisoners worked directly for the city.[58]

More spectacular was Merriam's investigation of crime through the council committee that he headed. This body was created on Merriam's resolution in May 1914 to investigate "the frequency of murder, assault, burglary, robbery, theft and like crime in Chicago; upon the official disposition of such crimes; and upon the best practical methods of preventing these crimes." It was this body for which Robert Gault, Edith Abbott, and Herman C. Stevens made studies. Merriam hoped the committee could combat growing crime by making the first truly scientific and comprehensive study of crime in an American city.

The committee's final report, published nearly a year later, revealed gross inefficiency and corruption in the city's criminal justice system. Not only were the prisons ineffective in deterring further crime and the courts overwhelmed with cases that did not bring convictions, but the

committee's investigators discovered that crime in Chicago was conducted largely by an organized network, whose members were well
known to the police and were frequently protected by them. Indeed, two
of Merriam's investigators, after getting themselves arrested, were
quickly taken into the underworld, which arranged pickpocketing ven-
tures for them under police escort! To prove how easily such information could be obtained, the committee's investigators also prepared a list
of five hundred known criminals operating in Chicago. The final report
contained four pages of detailed recommendations, including proposals to prevent collusion between police and criminals and suppress
criminal hangouts, and suggestions for more effective courtroom practices and a better penal system.[59]

One of the committee's recommendations was that a commission
be appointed by the chief justice of the municipal court and the pre-
siding judge of the criminal court to "study the criminal practice and
procedure in the courts of Chicago" and recommend necessary changes.
In September 1915 Merriam was asked to serve on this body, and he
continued his efforts here, heading the commission's committee on
police.[60]

Merriam wanted to run again for mayor in 1915, but realized that
he could not win without support from Governor Deneen. Deneen refused to back Merriam, but both men agreed to support Judge Harry
Olson, who nevertheless lost in the Republican primary to William Hale
Thompson. Thompson's defeat of Harrison was the beginning of the
end for reform. Thompson freely violated civil service rules to build up
his power base and made numerous deals with disreputables. Reformers
found it hard to cope with Thompson's political tactics. Merriam attacked him head-on in the city council, and Thompson determined to
defeat Merriam in the 1917 aldermanic elections. Thompson now controlled the election machinery, and Merriam was defeated by five votes
in the primary. His petition to get on the ballot as an independent was
thrown out by Thompson's people. In the election Merriam nevertheless
received over ten thousand write-in votes, which was still fifteen hundred short. Thompson was victorious.[61]

When America entered the war, Merriam enlisted, serving briefly in
Italy as American high commissioner of public information. He returned to Chicago in time for the 1919 mayoral election. Hard-core
reformers naively thought Thompson vulnerable because of his strong
public opposition to United States involvement in the war and believed
Captain Merriam even stronger because of his army service. Thompson's ruthless political tactics, his blatant disregard of civil service

laws, and his unwillingness to deal with reformers made him the antichrist of elite reform.

Again Deneen would not back Merriam and supported Olson, but Merriam's backers urged him to run anyway. They saw in Merriam the only hope for a really effective and honest municipal government. Mary McDowell appealed to "the freedom loving people of [Chicago] to support the one man who by his training, his sympathy, his experience and his loyalty to the democratic cause, is fitted to give Chicago that high quality of leadership which the city's place in the nation demands." Jane Addams urged that "the elction of Capt. Charles E. Merriam as mayor of our city would make Chicago the pioneer in scientific administration of American cities. . . ." Anita Blaine insisted that "to have Mr. Merriam win in the mayoralty contest would be not so much the success of Mr. Merriam as the success of Chicago."[62]

Thus the Republican primary saw a strong progressive and a moderate progressive challenging Thompson. The result was stunning. Thompson polled more votes than Merriam and Olson combined, and Merriam trailed far behind Olson. Thompson easily won reelection against his Democratic opponent in the general election.[63] The defeat ended Merriam's career in electoral politics. But its significance went far beyond one man.

Merriam had become the symbol of reform and the embodiment of everything elite reformers had worked for since the early 1890s. Victor Elting, a lawyer prominent in many reform groups before World War I, wrote in 1940 that the years between 1915 and 1918 were years when "Chicago started on its retrogression. Then descended upon the city two blights," he wrote. "One was the election to the mayoralty of William Hale Thompson, and the other was the World War."[64] Merriam's defeat symbolized the end of an era in which elite reformers had developed hundreds of programs with boundless optimism. Of course, elite reformers did not simply withdraw from civic affairs after 1919. They continued to hammer away at the same problems, but their faith in progress and science was shaken by the national disillusionment of war and the local frustration over Thompson. Increasingly, they despaired of solving urban problems at the local level.

Merriam's defeat was no accident. Here and there, when local conditions were right, upper-strata elites might win the mayoralty of major American cities. But industrialization guaranteed that American cities would be inhabited overwhelmingly by the poorer classes. Elite reformers honestly believed that they were operating in the interests of "the people" but, in the short run at least, they sought to replace politicians closely tied to lower-class constituencies with politicians and experts from the upper strata of income and social status.

Indeed, Merriam should have known as much. As a graduate student at Columbia, he had seen how much hope reformers there had placed in Columbia president Seth Low's successful bid for mayor of greater New York in 1898, and Merriam joined literally dozens of Columbia social science faculty and graduate students in Low's campaign. Low ran an honest and efficient administration for two years but failed to win reelection.

Facing defeat on the local level, in the 1920s and thereafter Chicago's elite reformers increasingly looked to the federal government and its bureaucracy as a means of implementing the changes they sought. Further removed from the electoral power of lower-class urban populations, the federal government proved the most suitable agent for the bureaucratic rationalization to which professors and other elite reformers were so committed. Ultimately, Merriam and his fellow social scientists would find a stable and permanent role for themselves in the executive branch of the federal government.

With the perspective of hindsight, it is apparent that professors like Merriam could lose all the battles but win the war. Even though professors failed to gain control of local government, they won the support of business elites for the new concepts of scientific administration that depended so heavily upon ongoing research and social science expertise. The rise of public administration, urban and regional planning, and administrative law, in which scholars like Merriam, Freund, Goodnow, and Seligman played such a major role, attests to their success. Win or lose, these scholars and universities generally prospered from the alliances and experiences they developed in the largely unsuccessful struggle in the progressive era to wrest control of urban government from the political leaders of lower-class constituencies. As the federal executive came to dominate and even dwarf local and state administration after the 1930s, academic experts secured their continuing influence over urban social policy.

8

From Chicago to Washington

THE WAVES THAT the new academic professionals made in Chicago eventually flooded Washington. Seeking a high position in the emerging social structure of urban industrial America, the presidents of the University of Chicago and many of its faculty worked aggressively to forge an indispensable role for themselves in practical affairs. Like their counterparts in academia elsewhere, they established a host of university programs to educate people for particular careers, extend education to those for whom it was usually unavailable, and expand or transform the activities of local government in ways that would increase their own influence. In private urban universities at the turn of the century, alliance with local elites provided the surest means of both financial support for the university itself and success in the struggle for influence.

Chicago provided unusually fertile soil in which to nurture this relationship. A boom town of the mid-nineteenth century, by the last decade of the century it had a large group of wealthy people ready to build cultural institutions to equal the city's commercial and industrial enterprises. Chicago's boosterism and civic pride spilled over into politics. The addition of academic professionals to the ranks of the already active businessmen, lawyers, settlement house workers, and club women produced a reform movement of extraordinary vigor and breadth.

What difference did professors and their universities make to this reform movement? On the simplest level, professors provided much of its leadership. It is difficult to imagine a reform movement in Chicago in these years without Charles E. Merriam, Charles R. Henderson, Edith Abbott, Sophonisba P. Breckinridge, George Herbert Mead, James

Hayden Tufts, John Dewey, William Rainey Harper, Robert H. Gault, Charles Zueblin, John Henry Wigmore, or Ernst Freund. It was not just the tangible activities of the professors that made them important, but their influence on other leaders. Merriam helped convert the traditional business concerns for honesty and efficiency in government into a movement for what we now call public administration. Sophonisba P. Breckinridge deeply influenced Julius Rosenwald's ideas regarding social welfare. In virtually every area of local reform, professors provided a seemingly scientific ideology to underpin the proposals that reformers instinctively favored on the basis of their experiences.

Unlike many of the other members of the reform community, professors belonged to nationally based professions and therefore always looked beyond Chicago. Education, criminal justice, social welfare, urban planning, health, housing, and home rule constituted the concerns of a national movement that fought its battles in various cities and states. Activist professors, in Chicago as elsewhere, wrote for national or international audiences and attended conferences that brought together scholars from the rest of the country and often from much of the western world. Henderson belonged to international associations concerned with prison reform and social legislation, and chaired the social insurance committee of the National Conference of Charities and Correction. He, Freund, and Tufts helped develop the programs of the American Association for Labor Legislation, usually in the form of "model" bills to be introduced into the various state legislatures. Merriam could compare notes with numerous reformers elsewhere simply by attending meetings of the American Political Science Association. Locally rooted reform leaders like Charles L. Hutchinson, George Cole, or Louise deKoven Bowen, for example, lacked this cosmopolitan orientation.

Professors affected Chicago's reform movement in one other way. The solutions to urban problems that reformers proposed required an ongoing staff of trained persons to perform specialized tasks. Universities facilitated the development of formal training programs for teachers, police, probation officers, legislative reference experts, budget analysts, statisticians, social workers, and numerous other persons in occupations fostered by urban reform programs. Without universities it would have been difficult to establish a legislative reference service, a probation system, a bureau of educational standards, or an office of social survey.

A tough-minded observer of the Chicago scene in 1920, reviewing the struggles for control of local affairs since the opening of the University of Chicago in 1892, would nonetheless have concluded that, although professors profoundly affected the reform community, that community itself had gained little real influence in Chicago. Although reformers could point to a long list of accomplishments—the juvenile court, a smaller school board, bureaus of educational survey and vocational guidance, a workmen's compensation law, the Chicago Plan, adult probation, reorganized employment bureaus, and numerous others—the election of Thompson in 1915 greatly reduced their influence and dramatized how easily apparent gains could be undone by a hostile mayor.

Time changes perceptions of success and failure. From the vantage point of the present, it is clear that reformers' objectives have been substantially realized. Elaborate and specialized agencies relying upon expert knowledge and employing trained functionaries, insulated from interference by politicians, today characterize government to a degree that reformers in 1920 could not have anticipated. On the other hand, the substantive objectives of urban reformers—quality mass education, elimination of poverty and economic insecurity, control of crime, efficiency in government—have not been realized. Indeed, many observers today attribute the failure to achieve these objectives to the very solutions that reformers articulated in Chicago and other cities during the progressive period.

Today's reformers attack large centralized bureaucracies for their inability to provide adequate services, and some call instead for neighborhood government, decentralization, community control, or competitive private institutions. Urban school systems, police forces, and welfare departments are accused of insulation from political control, the secure job tenure of their employees making it impossible for elected officials to bring about badly needed change. Today, critics on both the Left and the Right perceive specialized bureaucracies as part of the problem.

The success of universities and academic professionals in gaining prestige and resources through an alliance with urban reformers is beyond question, however. American higher education and scholarly research in the twentieth century have been supported lavishly in large measure because universities have assumed primary responsibility for recruiting and training people for numerous occupations and because academic professionals have convinced government and private benefactors that research has practical uses.

The involvement of social scientists in urban reform in Chicago and elsewhere is part of the success story of the American university.

University scientific and technological work for national defense in the nuclear age, the achievements of land grant colleges in American agriculture, and the activities of economists in managing the national economy are other ways by which the modern university made itself indispensable to American society. This academic prosperity through service has not been uniformly hailed. Veblen's critique of university public service is more readily appreciated today than when he wrote it in the early twentieth century. Government, foundation, and corporate support of teaching and research has influenced the kinds of problems that scholars study and the nature and relative size of the various academic programs of the modern multiversity, sometimes to the detriment of high-quality scholarship and rigorous education.

For better or for worse, however, the modern university has become one of our most important institutions, and the experience of professors in urban progressivism had a good deal to do with bringing this about. Despite their failure to win major influence over local affairs, Chicago professors and their colleagues elsewhere continued to seek influence over public education, social welfare, criminal justice, urban planning, and government administration. Their influence in these areas expanded enormously with the dramatic growth of the federal government during and after the New Deal.

Political historians usually portray the years from the 1930s to the end of the 1960s in terms of a series of ideological battles in which the proponents of a vastly expanded role for the federal government in domestic affairs triumphed over the proponents of a limited state. Several developments help explain this rapid expansion of federal responsibility. Industrialization continued to create an ever more integrated and interdependent economy, and problems like the control of poverty or unemployment could not be solved locally. Administratively, centralized federal supervision of domestic mobilization during World War I demonstrated the possibilities of federal action.[1] Politically, the Democratic party under Al Smith and then Franklin D. Roosevelt emerged as a majority party because it advocated and then enacted extensive federal social programs that wedded working-class and ethnic city dwellers, blacks, liberal reformers, and intellectuals to the party. The depression created the sense of national urgency that facilitated a quantum leap in federal domestic activities during the New Deal. The modern civil rights movement, beginning in the 1940s, demanded federal intervention in local affairs to guarantee equal treatment under the law for all Americans. The cold war made domestic strength seem more urgent and thereby fostered federal programs in such areas as education.

Against this backdrop, the experiences of progressive reformers in the major cities were transferred to the federal level. The dynamics of this process, and in particular the role of the social science disciplines in it, have not been fully explored, but some tentative observations are in order.

Professors played a major role in this expansion of federal activity. Progressive social scientists like Charles E. Merriam and Frank Goodnow helped forge the modern federal administrative apparatus. As early as 1910, leaders in the public administration movement, particularly those at the New York Bureau of Municipal Research, induced President William Howard Taft to establish a Commission on Economy and Efficiency, in which Goodnow played a critical role. The leading participants on the commission later organized the Institute of Government Research in Washington "to assist, by scientific study and research, in laying a solid foundation of information and experience upon which . . . reforms may be successfully built." [2] In 1937 Merriam, described by one scholar as "something of a social scientist in residence in Roosevelt's New Deal," served on FDR's committee on executive reorganization, where he applied the lessons of Chicago in the organization of the federal executive. [3]

Merriam played a similar role in bringing the planning movement to the federal level. Within a few years of his defeat in the 1919 mayoral election, Merriam initiated the formation of the Social Science Research Council, a multidisciplinary organization of professional social scientists devoted to advancing social science research and encouraging its use by policymakers. Shortly after Herbert Hoover's election to the presidency, Merriam, William F. Ogburn, who taught sociology at Chicago and before then at Columbia, and several other council leaders organized and directed the Commission on Recent Social Trends to examine and report upon recent social trends in the United States so as to provide a basis for intelligent national planning. Numerous social scientists took part in the commission's research. Charles Judd, Mead's ally in the Chicago public school battles of the previous decade and dean of the Chicago School of Education, authored the report on education; Sophonisba Breckinridge prepared the volume entitled "The Activities of Women Outside the Home." [4]

The depression and Hoover's failure to win reelection doomed this effort at national social planning, but in 1933, Secretary of Interior Harold Ickes, who had been Merriam's campaign manager in the 1911 Chicago mayoral race, created the National Planning Board to stimulate local and national planning activities. Its members included Merriam,

Columbia economist Wesley C. Mitchell (a Chicago Ph.D.) and Frederic
A. Delano, a prominent businessman who had been instrumental in developing Burnham's *Plan of Chicago* in 1909. In 1935, the board established the research committee on urbanism to make the first national
study of American cities. Its report, *Our Cities: Their Role in the
National Economy*, presented a detailed analysis of American cities and
proposed a variety of social programs. The committee enlisted the services of, among others, University of Chicago sociologist Louis Wirth, a
former student of Albion W. Small and a colleague and associate of
Robert E. Park, and Louis Brownlow of the Public Administration
Clearing House on the University of Chicago campus, a longtime associate of Charles E. Merriam. The report urged establishment of a
clearinghouse of urban information in the Census Bureau and a division
of urban research somewhere in the federal executive; it also called for
efforts to raise family income and to increase economic security, and for
federal programs to coordinate local planning efforts, help alleviate the
financial plight of the cities, house the urban poor, and prevent crime.[5]
    Social scientists played an especially active role in initiating and
implementing the social welfare legislation of the New Deal, especially
the Social Security Act. A committee of the Social Science Research
Council undertook administrative planning for the social security program before its passage, and social scientists served on FDR's committee
on economic security and its advisory council, which drafted the social
security bill. Grace Abbott, Edith Abbott's sister who headed the Illinois
Immigrants' Protective League, directed the United States Children's
Bureau until 1934, when she returned to the University of Chicago to
teach at its School of Social Service Administration. As a graduate student at Chicago, Grace had studied with Charles E. Merriam. An intimate partner of Edith and Sophonisba Breckinridge in almost all their
reform activities, Grace, according to someone in a position to know,
"above everyone else, was responsible for the child welfare provisions
which occur in the Social Security Act."[6]
    The appearance in Washington between the wars of professors or
their associates previously active in Chicago social welfare and social
planning reform suggests that significant transfer of local experience to
the federal executive occurred during these years. The influence of professors who held major positions on prominent commissions and committees is more easily documented and assessed, however, than other
less celebrated and more subtle kinds of transference. Federal welfare
programs would have been impossible without the corps of trained social welfare professionals who gained their experience in local voluntary

welfare associations and at schools like the Chicago School of Civics and Philanthropy. Ideas such as social security or public works were drawn from the experiments of an earlier day. The programs of urban reformers often moved to the federal level in ways that obscured their relationship to urban progressivism.[7]

To illustrate, in 1929 Martin H. Bickham, an official of the United Charities of Chicago who had studied with Henderson fifteen years earlier, proposed a program of privately funded public works to a committee of wealthy Chicagoans, who accepted his plan and financed it. "I went back to my studies with Dr. Charles R. Henderson in the unemployment difficulties of 1913 and 1914," Bickham wrote years later, "and drew some experience and inspiration from his lectures and insights. . . . From these Henderson sources and ideas there developed in my mind a plan for the unemployed of Cook County and the ghettos of central Chicago." Under Bickham's direction, unemployed men went to work cleaning the city, improving parks and forest preserves, working at settlements, and the like. The Civil Works Administration of Cook County eventually took over these projects. In 1933 Harry Hopkins called Bickham to Washington for consultation on his public works program, and Bickham thereby contributed to the development of the Works Progress Administration, of which he was appointed Illinois director.[8] Detailed research can reveal the extent to which this sort of transfer of experience occurred and its impact on the welfare state forged by the New Deal.

Professors also played a major role in the dramatic increase of federal anti-crime activities in the 1920s. "The federal government now exercises law-enforcement functions which are in no way auxiliary to other federal services," noted a 1937 Brookings Institution study of crime control by the national government. Unlike earlier federal activities in this area, the report suggested, "the new functions are aimed directly at crime control as such; and are designed to supplement, if not supplant, state and local activities."[9]

The National Commission on Law Observance and Enforcement, popularly called the Wickersham Commission, provided a major springboard for expanding federal involvement in crime control. Appointed in 1929 by President Hoover to study prohibition enforcement and other aspects of criminal justice, the commission employed numerous professors and other experts to prepare an exhaustive study of the criminal justice system. Edith Abbott prepared the report on crime and the foreign-born, and August Vollmer, the Berkeley police chief who had pioneered in the development of a university-based police training course, wrote the report on police. Vollmer, a close associate of Merriam, came to the university of Chicago in 1929 to teach police administration.[10]

The commission's report on criminal statistics noted that the earliest attempt to create national interest in the development of adequate crime statistics occurred in 1909 at the National Conference of Criminal Law and Criminology, which had been organized in Chicago by John Henry Wigmore and Robert H. Gault. In 1929, the International Association of Police Chiefs published a plan for uniform crime reporting. The plan was developed by a committee of police, of which August Vollmer was a member, and by an advisory committee on which Robert H. Gault served. The following year, based upon the work of the police chiefs association, the Federal Bureau of Investigation began collecting and publishing uniform crime statistics.[11] When the FBI established its "Technical Laboratory" shortly thereafter, J. Edgar Hoover sent a special agent to enroll in a course at the Scientific Crime Detection Laboratory established by Gault and Wigmore at Northwestern University.[12]

Public education first became a subject of major federal discussion in these years, although substantial federal intervention in education did not occur until the 1960s. Hoover appointed a commission to investigate and make recommendations on the federal role in education. Charles Judd served as a member, as did Yale University president James Rowland Angell, a psychologist who taught at the University of Chicago for nearly three decades. President Roosevelt also appointed a committee on federal involvement in education, and in 1936 it urged an active federal role. Charles Judd once again served on this committee, and its chairman and director of its extensive research activities was University of Chicago professor of education Floyd W. Reeves.[13]

Detailed studies could reveal how traditional local issues like these became federal concerns and the precise relationship between local prewar experiences and the national initiatives of the 1920s and 1930s. Professors in this period worked actively to affect policy and to gain influence just as they did on the local level in the preceding decades. Progressive reformers in most cities had failed to win lasting influence over local affairs because they could not be sure of winning elections in heavily working-class and immigrant cities. They won establishment of new bureaus or agencies, but they had no control over the actual functioning of the bureaus. By the end of World War I, the prospect of gaining and holding control of local government machinery must have appeared bleak, especially in Chicago, where reformers confronted Thompson. Under these circumstances, professors turned to the federal government, especially to the executive branch, to overcome the barriers posed by hostile politicians who held the loyalty of a majority of the big-city voters.

In this sense, Charles E. Merriam's disastrous defeat in the 1919 mayoral election frames not only the end of an era of intense and optimistic local reform, but the beginning of a new era for professors who now looked to the federal executive as the place where their influence could firmly take root and flourish.

After World War II, American universities and professors greatly expanded the already intricate web linking higher education, service, the vocations, and public policy. In the early 1960s, the American university had a measure of national support and influence far beyond anything William Rainey Harper could have imagined. Clark Kerr, one of the most optimistic and prolific promoters of American higher education in the 1960s, heralded the university's seemingly boundless capacity for public service and practical endeavors. In *The Uses of the University*, published in 1963, Kerr wrote that "The basic reality, for the university, is the widespread recognition that new knowledge is the most important factor in economic and social growth. . . . Because of this fundamental reality," Kerr continued, "the university is being called upon to produce knowledge as never before—for civic and regional purposes, for national purposes, and even for no purpose at all beyond the realization that most knowledge eventually comes to serve mankind. And it is also being called upon to transmit knowledge," he added, "to an unprecedented proportion of the population."[14] Kerr truly inherited the tradition of William Rainey Harper.

A decade later Kerr's optimism had disappeared. A period of student protest, declining enrollments, decreasing support, and fundamental criticism had shaken the American university. A special volume of *Daedalus* caught the new mood in its title—*American Higher Education: Toward an Uncertain Future*. Kerr, in the opening article, declared, "Seldom has so great an American institution passed so quickly from its Golden Age to its Age of Survival."[15]

In historical perspective, the changes occurring in the American university do not appear as cataclysmic as Kerr and others have suggested. The strains felt by universities, however real, reflect a temporary imbalance in academic supply and demand, not a radical change in the functions of the university. Unemployment among scholars in the humanities and some of the sciences is growing as students increasingly opt for study in subjects that will lead to employment after graduation. But this is hardly a new development. The modern university, as distinct from the old-time college, consciously linked itself to the emerging oc-cupational structure of modern American society. As changes occur in demographic trends and in the economy, it is only natural that univer-sities reflect these changes. Veblen's seminary of learning for its own sake might be immune to the exigencies of the economy, but few Ameri-can university professors, past or present, have been willing to forego middle-class comforts and social prestige for the life of the seminarian.

Today's university is reaching out to more and more students, in part as a reaction to the demands of the 1960s that college education be made available to the poor and minorities and in part as a response to the dwindling numbers of traditional students. Many professors have deep misgivings about the decline of academic standards that often ac-companies open enrollment, extension programs, and credit for such ambiguous accomplishments as "life experience." Although this is a serious problem, it is not an entirely new one. The founders of the American university in the late nineteenth century carried the university to the public through an incredible variety of extension programs. One wonders, for instance, about the quality of instruction in the corre-spondence division of Harper's university. The literature on the exten-sion movement of the 1890s is replete with references to the problems of providing education to workers who lacked adequate preparation.

It is worth recalling also that many of today's respectable university programs began as experiments in in-service education. The extension program for social workers at the University of Chicago, which eventu-ally spawned the Graduate School of Social Service Administration, and New York's Kitchen Garden Association, which culminated in Teachers College of Columbia University, are just two examples.

The upheavals of recent years have hardly touched the intimate relationship between universities, public services, and policy forged in the progressive era. Schools, social welfare agencies, criminal justice in-stitutions, and other government bureaucracies still require functionaries trained by universities. If anything, our large institutions are demanding people with ever more specialized skills. Furthermore, university faculties remain a major source of talent and expertise for political leaders, government agencies, foundations, and corporations. The demand for university expertise is surely not diminishing, as for example, the large number of academicians holding high appointive office in government today illustrates.

In the past, the American university has balanced these various practical and public service activities and the pursuit of knowledge for its own sake. Public service brought material support and prestige to the university, but only part of the university's faculty ever engaged in service activities or taught in vocationally oriented departments or programs. The practical work of some left others relatively free to pursue their scholarly interests. A real danger exists today that our universities, in their search for students and resources, will sacrifice scholarship for its own sake at the altar of public service and vocational training. One hopes, however, the American university will retain its historic capacity to balance practical and purely scholarly activities.

Although university education and expertise remain essential for policy and service delivery, the bureaucracies and expert systems of decision making forged in part by the activist professors of the progressive era are now under vigorous attack. Bureaucracies are now considered the problem. Our faith in the highly trained teacher, guidance counselor, probation officer, caseworker, budget analyst, lawyer, or public administrator has been badly shaken. More and more, we tend to distrust all claims of expertise. Thus far, there have been few serious alternatives proposed to our highly specialized and bureaucratized social order. Perhaps there are none.

This is the crisis of our times. We are increasingly unhappy with the results of liberal solutions that have relied upon an activist and centralized government fortified by expert knowledge and educated bureaucracies. Yet we have no clear vision of an alternative. It is also the real crisis of our universities. The expert credentials dispensed by them remain essential prerequisites for employment and mobility in an ever larger segment of economic life. Yet we are increasingly suspicious of all expertise and doubtful that the pursuit of knowledge ultimately contributes to a better civilization. In such an era of self-doubt and low morale, it is hard to avoid at least a little nostalgia for the optimistic days of William Rainey Harper, Charles R. Henderson, George Herbert Mead, Sophonisba P. Breckinridge, Charles E. Merriam, and their colleagues, who shared the conviction of James Hayden Tufts: "We are in the mere beginning of possible control over human association of politics, and of economic life."

APPENDIXES

Appendix 1

REFORM LEADERS OF CHICAGO, 1892–1919[1]

MEN

Aldis, Arthur Taylor
Allinson, Thomas William
Angell, James Rowland*
Baird, Wyllys Warner
Baker, Alfred Landon
Baker, William T.
Bancroft, Edgar Addison
Barnes, Clifford W.
Bartlett, Adolphus C.**
Billings, Frank
Blaustein, David
Bodine, William Lester
Bond, William Scott
Brown, Edward Osgood
Butler, Edward Burgess
Butler, Nathaniel*
Butler, Rush Clark
Carmen, George Noble
Carpenter, Newton Henry
Catherwood, Robert
Chandler, Henry P.
Churchill, Frank Spooner

Clapp, Clement Long
Cole, George E.
Cowles, Alfred L.
Crane, Charles Richard
Crane, Richard Teller, Jr.
Crowell, Henry P.
Cutting, Charles Sidney
Dau, J. J.
Davis, Abel
Deknatal, Frederick H.
Delano, Frederic A.**
Dixon, George William
Dobyns, Fletcher
Donnelley, Thomas E.**
Dummer, William F.
Eaton, Marquis
Eckhart, Bernard Albert
Elting, Howard
Elting, Victor
Errant, Joseph Washington
Evans, William Augustus*
Farwell, Granger

---

1. People who held leadership positions in three or more of the reform agencies listed in appendix 2 between 1892 and 1919.

Note: * denotes professor; ** denotes University of Chicago trustee.

Favill, Henry Baird
Fisher, Walter L.
Flexner, Bernard
Folds, Charles Weston
Forgan, David R.
Freund, Ernst*
Fyffe, Colin Campbell
Gault, Robert Harvey*
Glessner, John Jacob
Grant, Luke
Graves, William C.
Gray, John Henry*
Greeley, Frederick
Gregory, Stephen Strong
Hale, William Browne
Hall, George C.
Hamill, Ernest Alfred
Harper, William Rainey*
Harris, Abram Winegardner*
Heckman, Wallace**
Henderson, Charles R.*
Higbie, Nathan B.
Hilton, Henry Hoyt
Hirsch, Emil Gustav*
Hoben, Allan*
Hooker, George Ellsworth
Hotchkiss, Willard Eugene*
Howard, Earl Dean*
Hulburd, Charles H.
Hull, Morton Denison
Hurley, Timothy David
Hutchinson, Charles L.**
Ickes, Harold LaClair
Jensen, Jens
Johnson, Frank Seward
Jones, Jenkin Lloyd
Jones, Walter Clyde
Jordan, Edwin O.*
Judson, Harry Pratt*
Kent, William
Kingsley, Sherman Colver
Kohlsaat, Herman Henry**
Kraus, Adolph
Larned, Sherwood Johnson

Lawson, Victor
Lies, Eugene Theodore
Loesch, Frank Joseph
Lyon, F. Emory
MacChesney, Nathan William
McCormick, Alexander Agnew
McCormick, Cyrus H.
McCormick, Joseph Medill
McCormick, Robert Rutherford
McGoorty, John P.
McMurdy, Robert
McVeagh, Franklin**
Mack, Julian W.
Manierra, Francis Edgerton
Mark, Clayton
Marsh, Charles Allen
Mason, Arthur J.
Mathews, Shailer*
Maynard, A. Kenyon
Mead, George Herbert*
Merriam, Charles Edward*
Moderwell, Charles McClennan
Mullenbach, James
Nathan, Adolph
Noel, Joseph R.
Noyes, LaVerne W.
O'Callaghan, Peter Joseph
Otis, Joseph Edward
Palmer, Honroe
Parker, Francis W.
Pellet, Clarence S.
Pick, George
Pinckney, Merritt W.
Pond, Allen Bartlit
Post, Louis F.
Reynolds, Wilfred S.
Riley, Harrison Barnett
Robins, Raymond
Rogers, Henry Wade*
Rosenthal, Lessing
Rosenwald, Julius**
Rosenwald, Morris S.
Schofield, Henry
Scott, Erastus Howard

Scott, Frank H.
Shedd, John Graves
Shurtleff, Wilford C.
Sikes, George C.
Sims, Edwin W.
Singleton, Shelby Magoffin
Skinner, Edward M.
Small, Albion W.*
Sonsteby, John J.
Sprague, Albert A.
Sprague, Albert A. II
Starr, Merritt
Stepina, James F.
Stern, Julius
Stirling, William R.
Stolz, Joseph
Sumner, Walter T.
Sunny, Bernard E.
Sutherland, Douglas

Taylor, Graham
Thurston, Henry Winfred
Tolman, Edgar Bronson
Tufts, James Hayden*
Wacker, Charles H.
Webster, George Washington
Webster, Towner K.
Wentworth, Edward C.
Wheeler, Harry A.
White, R. A.
Whitman, John L.
Wigmore, John Henry*
Wilson, John P.
Wilson, Walter H.
Wing, Frank E.
Wright, Edwin R.
Zeisler, Sigmund
Zueblin, Charles*

WOMEN

Abbott, Edith*
Abbott, Grace
Addams, Jane
Aldis, Mary (Mrs. Arthur T.)
Allinson, Alice Dow (Mrs. Thomas
    William)
Bartelme, Mary Margaret
Bass, Elizabeth (Mrs. George)
Blackwelder, Gertrude (Mrs. I. S.)
Blaine, Anita McCormick
    (Mrs. Emmons)
Bley, Caroline A. (Mrs. John C.)
Bowen, Louise deKoven
    (Mrs. Joseph T.)
Breckinridge, Sophonisba Preston*
Bryant, Ella Swartley
    (Mrs. Arthur W.)
Carpenter, Lula Boone
    (Mrs. George B.)
Dauchy, Marion (Mrs. Samuel)
Dummer, Ethel F. (Mrs. William F.)

Hefferan, Helen Maley
    (Mrs. William S.)
Henrotin, Ellen M. (Mrs. Charles)
Houghteling, Mrs. James L.
Johnson, Annie W. (Mrs. Frank
    Asbury)
Lathrop, Julia C.
Low, Minnie F.
McCormick, Ruth Hanna
    (Mrs. Medill)
McCulloch, Catherine Waugh
    (Mrs. Frank)
McDowell, Mary E.
Merriam, Elizabeth (Mrs. Charles E.)
Nicholas, Anne E.
Pelham, Laura Dainty
Purvin, Jennie Franklin
    (Mrs. Moses L.)
Reider, Edith S.
Robins, Margaret Dreier
    (Mrs. Raymond)

Sears, Amelia
Shears, Jesse E. (Mrs. George F.)
Smith, Mrs. Dunlap
Smith, Mary Rozet
Solomon, Hannah Greenbaum
 (Mrs. Henry)
Stevenson, Sarah Hackett
Thomas, Harriet Park (Mrs. W. I.)
Tracy, Mrs. Frederick K.

Vander Vaart, Mrs. Harriet
Vittum, Harriet E.
Watkins, Minnie A. Edison
 (Mrs. George)
Wilmarth, Mrs. Mary Hawes
 (Mrs. Henry M.)
Wooley, Celia Parker (Mrs. J. H.)
Wyatt, Edith Franklin
Young, Ella Flagg

Appendix 2

REFORM ORGANIZATIONS OF CHICAGO, 1892–1919

"GOOD-GOVERNMENT" AND STRUCTURAL REFORM

Bureau of Public Efficiency, Chicago (founded after Alderman Merriam's revelations of graft and corruption in city government to monitor public expenditures)
Citizens' Association of Chicago
Civil Service Reform Association of Chicago
Constitutional Convention League of Illinois
Initiative and Referendum League of Illinois
Legislative Voters' League of Illinois
Municipal Voters' League of Chicago
New Charter Convention, Chicago (convention of twenty-three organizations to inaugurate a movement for a new city charter for Chicago, 1902)
Short Ballot Association of Illinois
Universities Committee on the State Constitution

PARKS AND PLANNING

Citizens' League to Conserve Chicago's Parks
City Plan Commission, Chicago (private organization founded to press for implementation of Daniel Burnham's *Plan for Chicago*)
Outdoor Improvement Association, Illinois

SETTLEMENT HOUSES

Abraham Lincoln Center
Chicago Commons
Hull House
Maxwell Street Settlement

Northwestern University Settlement
University of Chicago Settlement
Wendell Phillips Settlement

CHARITIES AND SOCIAL SERVICE AGENCIES: GENERAL

Associated Jewish Charities of Chicago
Bureau of Charities, Chicago (merged into United Charities in 1908)
Central Council of Social Agencies, Chicago
Relief and Aid Society, Chicago (merged into United Charities in 1908)
United Charities of Chicago

CHILDREN

Child Welfare Exhibit, Chicago, 1911
Children's Home and Aid Society, Illinois
Consumers' League of Illinois (organized to fight for child labor restriction)
Infant Welfare Society
Joint Committee on Vocational Training of Girls
Juvenile Protective Association
Juvenile Psychopathic Institute
Visitation and Aid Society

WOMEN: SOCIAL SERVICE

Travelers' Aid Society of Chicago and Illinois
Woman's Protective Association ("to follow cases of women offenders in
Municipal Courts and to give protection, and friendly counsel")

WOMAN SUFFRAGE

Committee for the Extension of Municipal Suffrage to Chicago Women
Equal Suffrage Association, Illinois
Political Equality League

SOCIAL HYGIENE AND ANTI-VICE

Committee of Fifteen (anti-prostitution)
Society for Social Hygiene, Chicago and Illinois

IMMIGRANTS AND BLACKS

Immigrants' Protective League
National Association for the Advancement of Colored People, Chicago chapter
Urban League, Chicago chapter

PUBLIC HEALTH AND HOUSING

Committee of Fifty, Illinois (care of epileptics)
Housing Association, Chicago
National Housing Association, Chicago directors
Tuberculosis Institute, Chicago

LABOR AND SOCIAL INSURANCE

Citizens' Committee on the Garment Workers' Strike, 1910
Committee on Social Legislation, Illinois
Illinois Association for Labor Legislation
Industrial Exhibit, Chicago, 1907 (public exhibit on the social impact of
    industrialization)
Women's Trade Union League of Chicago

EDUCATION

Council for Library and Museum Extension
Public Education Association of Chicago
School Extension Committee
Society for University Extension, Chicago

CRIMINAL JUSTICE

American Institute of Criminal Law and Criminology, Illinois branch
Anti-Capital Punishment League of Illinois
Legal Aid Society, Chicago

SOCIAL AND CIVIC CLUBS

(In the case of social clubs, only members of their civic committees were
    included in the tabulation of the reform elite.)
City Club of Chicago
Commercial Club, Civic Service Committees
Merchants' Club of Chicago, Civic Service Committees
Union League Club, Political Action Committee
Woman's Club, Chicago
Woman's City Club of Chicago

OTHER

Association of Commerce, Chicago (members of its housing, education, and
    subscriptions investigation committees only)
Civic Federation of Chicago

General Educational Committee on Chicago Philanthropy (to educate the
   public about philanthropy and charity)
Progressive Party Committee, Cook County
School of Civics and Philanthropy

Appendix 3

BIOGRAPHICAL DATA ON CHICAGO
REFORM LEADERS, 1892–1919

TABLE I. OCCUPATIONS OF 181 MEN AND WORKING WOMEN REFORMERS[a]

	Men		Women		Total	
Occupation	Number	Percentage	Number	Percentage	Number	Percentage
Business	53	33.1	—	—	53	29.3
Law	34	21.3	2	9.5	36	19.9
Judges	5	3.1	—	—	5	2.8
Publishing and newspapers	10	6.3	—	—	10	5.5
University professors	23	14.4	2	9.5	25	13.8
Physicians	8	5.0	1	4.8	9	5.0
Clergymen	6	3.8	—	—	6	3.3
Social work	13	8.1	14	66.7	27	14.9
Other professions	8	5.0	2	9.5	10	5.5

[a]Data were obtained for 160 of the 169 men (94.7 percent). Of the 46 women re-formers, the 21 who could be identified as professionals are included here (45.7 percent of the total). Of the remaining 25 women, 15 definitely did not work, and there were no data for the other 10.

TABLE 2. LEVEL OF HIGHER EDUCATION OF 179 REFORMERS [a]

Level of education	Men		Women		Total	
	Number	Percentage	Number	Percentage	Number	Percentage
No higher education	33	21.2	10	43.5	43	24.0
Undergraduate only	32	20.5	5	21.7	37	20.7
Professional college only	18	11.5	3	13.0	21	11.7
Undergraduate *and* professional college	41	26.3	1	4.3	42	23.5
Undergraduate *and* graduate study [b]	32	20.5	4	17.4	36	20.1

[a]Data were obtained for 179 of the 215 reform leaders, or 83.3 percent. This includes 156 of the 169 men (92.3 percent) and 23 of the 46 women (50.0 percent).

[b]Those who attended undergraduate college, graduate school, *and* professional school are included in this group.

TABLE 3. BIRTHPLACES OF 184 REFORM LEADERS [a]

Place	Men Number	Men Percentage	Women Number	Women Percentage	Total Number	Total Percentage
Chicago	21	13.4	9	33.3	30	16.3
Illinois excluding Chicago	14	8.9	3	11.1	17	9.2
New England[b]	29	18.5	3	11.1	32	17.4
Middle Atlantic States[c]	33	21.0	4	14.8	37	20.1
Midwest[d]	31	19.7	7	25.9	38	20.7
South[e]	9	5.7	1	3.7	10	5.4
West Coast[f]	2	1.3	—	—	2	1.1
Foreign-born	18	11.5	—	—	18	9.8

[a] Data were obtained for 184 of the 215 reform leaders, or 85.6 percent. This includes 157 of the 169 men (92.9 percent) and 27 of the 46 women (58.7 percent).
[b] Maine, Connecticut, Vermont, New Hampshire, Massachusetts.
[c] New York, New Jersey, Pennsylvania.
[d] Ohio, Indiana, Michigan, Missouri, Wisconsin, Minnesota, Iowa, Nebraska.
[e] Virginia, Alabama, Kentucky, North Carolina, Texas, District of Columbia.
[f] California.

TABLE 4. YEARS OF BIRTH OF 169 REFORMERS [a]

Years	Men Number	Men Percentage	Women Number	Women Percentage	Total Number	Total Percentage
1831–40	3	2.0	—	—	3	1.8
1841–50	20	13.2	3	17.6	23	13.6
1851–60	49	32.2	6	35.3	55	32.5
1861–70	51	33.6	2	11.8	53	31.4
1871–80	27	17.8	6	35.3	33	19.5
1881–90	2	1.3	—	—	2	1.2

[a] Data were obtained for 169 of the 215 reform leaders, or 78.6 percent. This includes 152 of the 169 men (89.9 percent) and 17 of the 46 women (37 percent).

Appendix 4

CHICAGO AND NORTHWESTERN UNIVERSITY PROFESSORS INVOLVED IN REFORM, 1892–1919, BY ACADEMIC DEPARTMENT

TABLE 5. FACULTY AT UNIVERSITY OF CHICAGO FIVE YEARS OR MORE INVOLVED IN LOCAL REFORM[a]

Department[b]	Total Number	Number in Reform	Percentage of Total
Anatomy	17	1	5.9
Art History	3	1	33.3
Astronomy	16	1	6.3
Bacteriology	5	2	40.0
Botany	13	2	15.4
Chemistry	13	0	—
Comparative Philology	4	0	—
Comparative Religion	3	0	—
Divinity School	16	3	18.8
Education[c]	25	7	28.0
English	28	5	17.9
General Literature	4	3	75.0
Geography	4	1	25.0
Geology	13	1	7.7
Germanic Languages	12	1	8.3
Greek	8	1	12.5
History	17	5	29.4
Household Administration	3	3	100.0

TABLE 5, continued

Department[b]	Total Number	Number in Reform	Percentage of Total
Latin	9	1	11.1
Law School	8	6	75.0
Math	11	1	9.1
New Testament	5	0	—
Oriental Languages	11	3	27.3
Paleontology	1	0	—
Pathology	6	0	—
Philosophy	6	5	83.3
Physical Culture	2	2	100.0
Physics	9	1	11.1
Physiology	13	1	7.7
Political Economy	12	8	66.7
Political Science	3	3	100.0
Psychology	7	2	28.6
Public Speaking	1	0	—
Rabbinical Language	1	1	100.0
Romance Languages	13	1	7.7
Sociology and Anthropology	15	11	73.3
Zoology	12	0	—
Total	349	83	23.8

[a]This tabulation was obtained from the listings of faculty in vol. 2, 1st ser., *Decennial Publications of the University* (1904): *Publications of the Members of the University*, and *Publications of the Members of the University, 1902−1916* (1916). Where necessary, and for the years 1917−19, these sources were supplemented with the yearly *Annual Register* of the university.

[b]Many faculty were members of more than one department; their main listing in the 1916 list of publications was used here.

[c]Includes both the Department of Education and the School of Education.

TABLE 6. FACULTY AT NORTHWESTERN UNIVERSITY, COLLEGE OF LIBERAL ARTS,
FIVE OR MORE YEARS INVOLVED IN LOCAL REFORM, 1892–1919[a]

Department[b]	Total Number	Number in Reform	Percentage of Total
Astronomy	2	0	—
Biblical Literature	3	1	33.3
Botany	2	0	—
Chemistry	6	0	—
Classical Languages	10	1	10.0
Economics, Finance, and Administration	7	5	71.4
Education	3	0	—
English	15	1	6.7
Geology	7	0	—
Germanic Languages and Literature	10	1	10.0
History	7	2	28.6
Mathematics	9	0	—
Music	1	0	—
Philosophy	5	2	40.0
Physical Training and Hygiene	2	0	—
Physics	6	1	16.7
Political Science	3	1	33.3
Psychology	2	1	50.0
Public Speaking	4	0	—
Romance Languages and Literature	6	1	16.7
Zoology	5	0	—
Totals	115	17	14.8

ᵃThe list of Liberal Arts faculty at Northwestern five years or more during this period was obtained from the university's *Catalogue* for the years 1892 to 1919. The professional schools are not included in this tabulation because they were heavily staffed with part-time faculty who were not primarily professors. The involvement of practicing attorneys who taught part-time at the Law School, or of practicing physicians who also taught at the Medical School in civic affairs more properly belongs in a discussion of the role of lawyers or physicians in civic affairs. Some full-time professors in law, medicine, and pharmacy were active in civic work, and their activities are described in the text. In the case of the School of Commerce, almost all of the full-time academicians on the faculty also held positions in the economics department of the Liberal Arts College, so they are included in these figures, whereas the practicing businessmen who taught part-time are not.

ᵇThe arrangement of departments changed many times during this period. Professors are divided here along the lines of the departmental arrangement in effect in 1919, but some of the people included in these figures actually taught in departments with different names.

Appendix 5

BIOGRAPHICAL DATA ON UNIVERSITY OF CHICAGO TRUSTEES

TABLE 7. OCCUPATIONS OF 45 UNIVERSITY OF CHICAGO TRUSTEES [a]

Occupation	Number	Percentage of Total
Business	20	44.4
Law	8	17.8
Judges	3	6.7
Publishing and newspapers	5	11.1
Physicians	1	2.2
Clergymen	4	8.9
Other professions [b]	4	8.9

[a] Data were obtained for 45 of the 50 trustees between 1892 and 1919 (90 percent).
[b] This includes 3 engineers and 1 accountant.

TABLE 8. LEVEL OF HIGHER EDUCATION OF 44 UNIVERSITY OF
CHICAGO TRUSTEES[a]

Level of Education	Number	Percentage of Total
No higher education	11	25.0
Undergraduate only	14	31.8
Professional college only	3	6.8
Undergraduate *and* professional college	10	22.7
Undergraduate *and* graduate study	6	13.6

[a]Data were obtained for 44 of the 50 trustees between 1892 and 1919 (88 percent).

TABLE 9. YEARS OF BIRTH OF 42 UNIVERSITY OF CHICAGO TRUSTEES[a]

Years	Number	Percentage of Total
1811–20	1	2.4
1821–30	1	2.4
1831–40	6	14.3
1841–50	10	23.8
1851–60	11	26.2
1861–70	6	14.3
1871–80	5	11.9
1881–90	2	4.8

[a]Data were obtained for 42 of the 50 trustees between 1892 and 1919 (84 percent).

TABLE 10. BIRTHPLACES OF 43 UNIVERSITY OF CHICAGO TRUSTEES [a]

Birthplace	Number	Percentage of Total
Chicago	10	23.3
Illinois, excluding Chicago	5	11.6
New England	8	18.6
Middle Atlantic States	8	18.6
Midwest	5	11.6
Foreign-born	7	16.3

[a] Data were obtained for 43 of the 50 trustees between 1892 and 1919 (86 percent).

Appendix 6

BIOGRAPHICAL DATA ON NORTHWESTERN
UNIVERSITY TRUSTEES

TABLE II. OCCUPATIONS OF 98 NORTHWESTERN UNIVERSITY TRUSTEES[a]

Occupation	Number	Percentage of Total
Business	35	35.7
Law	10	10.2
Judges	2	2.0
Physicians	7	7.1
Clergymen	41	41.8
Other professions[b]	3	3.1

[a]Data were obtained for 98 of the 139 trustees between 1892 and 1919 (70.5 percent).

[b]This includes 2 elected governmental officials and 1 professor.

TABLE 12. LEVEL OF HIGHER EDUCATION OF 72 NORTHWESTERN UNIVERSITY TRUSTEES[a]

Level of Education	Number	Percentage of Total
No higher education	24	33.3
Undergraduate only	12	16.7
Professional college only	2	2.8
Undergraduate *and* professional college	30	41.7
Undergraduate *and* graduate study	4	5.6

[a]Data were obtained for 72 of the 139 trustees between 1892 and 1919 (51.8 percent).

TABLE 13. YEARS OF BIRTH OF 66 NORTHWESTERN UNIVERSITY TRUSTEES[a]

Years	Number	Percentage of Total
1821–30	3	4.5
1831–40	7	10.6
1841–50	12	18.2
1851–60	16	24.2
1861–70	21	31.8
1871–80	5	7.6
1881–90	1	1.5
1891–1900	1	1.5

[a]Data were obtained for 66 of the 139 trustees between 1892 and 1919 (47.5 percent).

TABLE 14. BIRTHPLACES OF 68 NORTHWESTERN UNIVERSITY TRUSTEES[a]

Birthplace	Number	Percentage of Total
Chicago	13	19.1
Illinois, excluding Chicago	9	13.2
New England	14	20.6
Middle Atlantic States	10	14.7
Midwest	17	25.0
Foreign-born	5	7.4

[a]Data were obtained for 68 of the 139 trustees between 1892 and 1919 (48.9 percent).

Notes

CHAPTER 1

1. The most important works that interpret this period in terms of bureaucratic rationalization and the development of an organizational society are Robert H. Wiebe, *The Search for Order, 1877–1920*; Samuel P. Hays, "The Politics of Reform in Municipal Government in the Progressive Era"; Roy Lubove, *Twentieth-Century Pittsburgh*; Jerry Israel, ed., *Building the Organizational Society*; and Rowland P. Berthoff, *An Unsettled People*.

2. There is a massive literature on the history of American colleges and universities. The definitive study of American universities is Laurence R. Veysey, *The Emergence of the American University*. Richard Hofstadter's *Academic Freedom in the Age of the College* proved especially useful for this study.

3. The extensive literature on the sociology of professions deals in detail with the characteristics of professions. See especially Talcott Parsons, "Professions"; *The Professions in America*, ed. Kenneth S. Lynn and the editors of *Daedalus*; *Professions and Professionalization*, ed. J. A. Jackson; Wilbert E. Moore and Gerald Rosenblum, *The Professions*; Philip R. Elliott, *The Sociology of the Professions*; Alexander M. Carr-Saunders and Paul A. Wilson, *The Professions*; Robert K. Merton, *Some Thoughts on the Professions in American Society*; and Magoli S. Larson, *The Rise of Professionalism*. The organizational histories cited in n. 1 deal extensively with the rise of modern professions. The best historical study of the emergence of a profession in this period is Roy Lubove, *The Professional Altruist*.

4. On the professionalization of the academic disciplines in the United States, see Mary O. Furner, *Advocacy and Objectivity*; Joseph Ben-David, *The Scientist's Role in Society*, especially chap. 8; Thomas L. Haskell, *The Emergence of Professional Social Science*; Veysey, *Emergence of the American University*; Burton J. Bledstein, *The Culture of Professionalism*; and Daniel J. Kevles, *The Physicists*.

5. Hofstadter, *Academic Freedom*, p. 226.
6. Merle Curti, *American Scholarship in the Twentieth Century*, p. 19.

CHAPTER 2

1. Hugh Hawkins, *Pioneer*, p. 23.
2. Ibid.; John C. French, *A History of the University Founded by Johns Hopkins*, pp. 92, 177, 227–33; Lloyd C. Taylor, Jr., *The Medical Profession and Social Reform, 1885–1945*, pp. 1–14. For Gilman's own account of the university's public services, see his retirement address in Johns Hopkins University, *Johns Hopkins University Celebration of the Twenty-Fifth Anniversary of the University*, pp. 30–32.
3. Dorothy Ross, *G. Stanley Hall*, chaps. 11 and 12.
4. Richard J. Storr, *Harper's University*, pp. 3–5.
5. Ibid., pp. 4–34; Thomas W. Goodspeed, *A History of the University of Chicago*, pp. 1–68.
6. Storr, *Harper's University*, pp. 35–40; Goodspeed, *History*, pp. 69–97.
7. Storr, *Harper's University*, pp. 40–52.
8. Joseph E. Gould, *The Chautauqua Movement*, p. 13.
9. Thomas W. Goodspeed, *William Rainey Harper*, pp. 1–66; Gould, *Chautauqua*, pp. 13–20.
10. Gould, *Chautauqua*, pp. 12–14; Theodore Morrison, *Chautauqua*, pp. 73–78.
11. Gould, *Chautauqua*, pp. 1–12.
12. Ibid., pp. 25–38; Goodspeed, *Harper*, pp. 67–81.
13. Storr, *Harper's University*, pp. 41–55.
14. University of Chicago, *Official Bulletin, No. 1*.
15. Harper to Jane Addams, November 6, 1902, Harper Papers, box 6, folder 20; Harold McCormick to Harper, May 20, 1904, Presidents of the University of Chicago Papers, box 47, folder 23.
16. H. N. Higenbothan to Harper, May 20, 1902, Harper Papers, box 6, folder 15; Robert McCormick to Harper, February 12, 1900, Presidents Papers, box 14, folder 22.
17. *Chicago Tribune*, June 27, 1899.
18. Bledstein provides brief biographical sketches of these men and some other university presidents of that period in *The Culture of Professionalism*, pp. 335–43.
19. Harper to Swift, [1896], Harper Papers, box 2, folder 27; Harper to H. H. Kohlsaat, September 28, 1895, ibid., folder 18; Harper to R. H. Furguson, March 12, 1897, ibid., box 3, folder 11.
20. William Rainey Harper, *The Trend in Higher Education*, p. 44.
21. Ibid., p. 1.
22. Storr, *Harper's University*, pp. 369–70.
23. James Weber Lynn, "A Fighter for the Right."

24. Harry P. Judson, "Is Our Republic a Failure?"; Harry P. Judson, "Municipal Government."

25. Harry P. Judson, "The New Nationalism"; Judson to Jesse Baldwin, April 12, 1917, Presidents Papers, box 64, folder 19; Judson to Ella S. Stewart, December 19, 1908, ibid., box 42, folder 15; Harry P. Judson, "Mr. Roosevelt and the Third Term."

26. Judson to William Ayer McKinney, March 9, 1909, Presidents Papers, box 44, folder 1; Judson to M. W. Alexander, November 5, 1907, ibid., box 42, folder 14; Judson to William Robinson, February 11, 1909, ibid., box 44, folder 23; Judson to Clyde Jones, November 4, 1907, ibid., box 44, folder 1; Judson to Shelby M. Cullon, June 6, 1910, ibid., box 43, folder 3; Anita Blaine to Judson, March 30, 1909, ibid., box 8, folder 30; Judson to Jones, April 2, 1909 and May 12, 1909, ibid., box 44, folder 1; Deneen to Judson, May 8, 1910, ibid.

27. Harper, *Trends in Higher Education*, p. 159.

28. Judson to Sihler, November 20, 1911, Presidents Papers, box 43, folder 4.

29. Nicholas Murray Butler, *The Rise of a University*, 2:84; John W. Burgess, "The Founding of the School of Political Science," p. 363; Herbert Baxter Adams, *The College of William and Mary*, pp. 66–67.

30. French, *Johns Hopkins*, pp. 92–93; Herbert Baxter Adams wrote several lengthy articles on extension education. See especially *Public Educational Work in Baltimore*, and "Summer Schools and University Extension," in *Monographs on Education in the United States*, ed. Nicholas Murray Butler. The latter contains a bibliography that lists all of Adams's writings on the subject as of 1899.

31. Nicholas Murray Butler, *Across the Busy Years*, pp. 176–81; Franklin T. Baker, "Teachers College," in *A History of Columbia University, 1754–1904*, p. 116; Lawrence A. Cremin, David A. Shannon, and Mary E. Townsend, *A History of Teachers College, Columbia University*, pp. 10–40.

32. American Society for Extension of University Teaching, *University Extension*, pp. 3–4

33. Floyd W. Reeves, *University Extension Services*, p. 24.

34. "Memorandum of Regulations to Be Adopted by the School Board in Relation to the Free Lecture System" [1897?], Presidents Papers, box 9, folder 3.

35. Harper to R. R. Hammond, December 31, 1904, Harper Papers, box 7, folder 16; Harper to S. Felton, January 10, 1905, ibid., folder 17; J. N. Faithorn to Harper, April 24, 1905, ibid., box 8, folder 1; Harper to W. H. McDoel and Marvin Hughitt, January 10, 1905, Presidents Papers, box 40, folder 11.

36. "The American Institute of Sacred Literature," undated pamphlet, Mathews Papers, box 12, folder 9.

37. For a more detailed discussion of these programs and their impact through their graduates, see Steven J. Diner, "A City and Its University," pp. 72–84. On the service orientation of Chicago's sociology department, see Steven J. Diner, "Department and Discipline."

38. Estelle F. Ward, *The Story of Northwestern University*, pp. 3–16; Harold F. Williamson and Payson S. Wild, *Northwestern University: A History*, pp. 1–42.

39. Northwestern University, *Catalogue*, 1890.

40. "A New Era for Northwestern—President Rogers," *The Northwestern* 10 (1890): 225–26; "Henry Wade Rogers, A.M., LL.D."; Williamson and Wild, *Northwestern*, pp. 71–72.

41. Ward, *Story of Northwestern*, pp. 213–15; Williamson and Wild, pp. 74–81.

42. Rogers to Wigmore, March 14, 1899, Wigmore Papers.

43. Mary O. Furner, *Advocacy and Objectivity*, pp. 51, 67–68; Richard A. Swanson, "Edmund J. James, 1885–1925."

44. Memorandum, "The Needs of Northwestern University," April 1902, Northwestern University Archives, James box; *The Northwestern* 25 (December 11 and 14, 1903, January 6, 1904), 26 (October 23, 1905), 27 (January 10, 1908); *The Daily Northwestern* 34 (April 29, 1914).

45. "Report to the Board of Trustees of the Special Committee on the Nomination of a President," [1906], Northwestern Archives, Harris folder.

46. Ernest Reckitt, *Reminiscences of Early Days of the Accounting Profession in Illinois*, pp. 121–31; Northwestern University, *A Report Submitted to the Original Guarantors of the Northwestern University School of Commerce*; "University Training in Characteristic Methods and Broader Principles of Business," *Chicago Commerce* 4 (September 11, 1908), p. 13; Ward, *Story of Northwestern*, pp. 328–30; Michael Sedlack, "The Emergence and Development of Collegiate Business Education in the United States, 1881–1974."

47. Ward, *Story of Northwestern*, pp. 327–29.

48. *The Northwestern* 27 (November 18, 1906); "Preliminary Report of the Proposed Merger by the Administration Committee of the Board of Graduate Studies," Northwestern Archives, Graduate School box.

49. Ward, *Story of Northwestern*, p. 233.

50. John Tracy Ellis, *American Catholicism*, pp. 116–88; Robert Cross, *The Emergence of Liberal Catholicism in America*, pp. 146–61.

51. The archives of Loyola University—St. Ignatius College are practically nonexistent, except for a few published reports and the annual catalogue. The archives of De Paul are even more limited than those of Loyola. There is however an unpublished manuscript by Father Patrick Mullens on the history of the university, available at the archives, DePaul University, Chicago, Illinois.

52. DePaul University, *Bulletin of DePaul University*.

53. Frederic Siedenburg, "Report of Courses of Instruction in Social Work Given at Loyola University in 1913–1914"; L. Frederick Happel, "Rev. Frederic Siedenburg, S.J."; "The Loyola School of Sociology," *The Catholic Charities Review* 1 (October 1917), p. 245. See also *Loyola University Magazine* 14 (1915): 54; 15 (1916): 285–86; 16 (1916–17): 47, 123; and 17 (1919–20): 61, 297, 378–81.

54. Laurence R. Veysey, *The Emergence of the American University*, chap. 4.

55. Thorstein Veblen, *The Higher Learning in America*, p. 15.

56. Ibid., p. 140.

57. Ibid., p. 121.

58. Thorstein Veblen, *The Place of Science in Modern Civilization and Other Essays*, pp. 3–4.

59. Albion W. Small, "The New Humanity," pp. 7, 25, and "The Present Outlook of Social Sciences," p. 469.

60. James Hayden Tufts, "The Present Significance of Scholarship," p. 11.

61. Willard Hotchkiss, *Higher Education and Business Standards*, p. 49; Charles E. Merriam, "Outlook for Social Politics in the United States," p. 685.

62. Albion W. Small, "The Civic Federation of Chicago," pp. 101–2.

63. Ernst Freund, "The Problem of Intelligent Legislation." p. 79.

64. Edwin O. Jordan, "Municipal Hygiene," p. 135.

65. Charles R. Henderson, "Business Men and Social Theorists," pp. 389–90.

66. James Hayden Tufts, "The University and the Advance of Justice," p. 197.

67. George Herbert Mead, "Madison," p. 351.

68. Albion W. Small, "Scholarship and Social Agitation," p. 564.

69. Tufts, "Present Significance of Scholarship," p. 12.

70. Henderson, "Business Men and Social Theorists," p. 395.

71. John M. Coulter to Marion Talbot, October 21, 1898, Talbot Papers, box 2.

72. These themes are most elaborately developed in Furner, *Advocacy and Objectivity*. See also Thomas L. Haskell, *The Emergence of Professional Social Science*, and Robert L. Church, "Economists as Experts."

73. On Small, see Vernon K. Dibble, The Legacy of Albion Small; Harry Elmer Barnes, ed., *An Introduction to the History of Sociology*, chap. 18; Charles H. Page, *Class and American Sociology*, chap. 4; Edward C. Hayes, "Albion Woodbury Small"; and George Christakes, *Albion W. Small*.

74. Charles R. Henderson, "The Ministry of Today—Its New Equipment," p. 281; Luther L. Bernard, "William Isaac Thomas," unpublished manuscript in Bernard Papers, pp. 1–2.

75. "Henderson, Charles Richmond," *The Encyclopedia of Social Work*; *Chicago Tribune*, March 30, 1915; *Chicago Daily News*, March 29, 1915; *Survey* 34 (April 10, 1915): 55–56. On the Chicago sociology department in this period, see Diner, "Department and Discipline," pp. 514–53.

76. R. Gordon Hoxie, *A History of the Faculty of Political Science, Columbia University*, pp. 11–13; John W. Burgess, Reminiscences of an American Scholar, pp. 198–99; Albert Somit and Joseph Tanenhaus, *The Development of American Political Science*, pp. 45–48.

77. Barry D. Karl, *Charles E. Merriam and the Study of Politics*, pp. 18–60.

78. Ibid., p. 51.

79. Ibid., pp. 61–168.

80. Burgess, *Reminiscences*, p. 186.

81. There is a considerable scholarly literature on Dewey and pragmatism. On the Chicago department, see especially Darnell Rucker, *The Chicago Pragmatists*.

82. On Dewey's school and his work in education at Chicago, see Katherine Mayhew and Anna Edwards, *The Dewey School*, and Arthur G. Wirth, *John Dewey as Educator*.

83. Rucker, *Pragmatists*, pp. 20–21.

84. George Herbert Mead, "The Working Hypothesis in Social Reform," p. 369. Robert M. Barry analyzes the relationship between Mead's Chicago activities and his social psychology. See Barry, "A Man and a City," pp. 173–93. For Mead's lasting influence on social psychology, see Anselm Strauss, ed., *George Herbert Mead on Social Psychology*, pp. vii–xxv; Rucker, *Pragmatists*, pp. 20–22.

85. Rucker, *Pragmatists*, pp. 22–23.

86. Oscar Kraines, *The World and Ideas of Ernst Freund*; Francis A. Allen, "Ernst Freund and the New Age of Legislation," pp. vii–xlvi.

87. Felix Frankfurter, *Some Observations on Supreme Court Litigation and Legal Education*, p. 4.

88. On the history of early social work education in Chicago, see Louise C. Wade, *Graham Taylor*, chap. 6; Steven J. Diner, "Scholarship in the Quest for Social Welfare," pp. 2–8; and Werner P. Harder, *The Emergence of a Profession*.

89. Helen R. Wright, "Three against Time," p. 41.

90. Wade, *Taylor*, pp. 172–85; Diner, "Scholarship in the Quest for Social Welfare," pp. 2–34; Harder, "Emergence of a Profession," pp. 13–20.

91. Storr, *Harper's University*, pp. 49–51.

92. Ibid., pp. 83–85; Harper's motives in the Bemis case have remained a subject of controversy even until the present. For a thorough discussion of the various views, see Harold E. Berquist, Jr., "The Edward Bemis Controversy at the University of Chicago," pp. 384–93.

93. Walter P. Metzger, *Academic Freedom in the Age of the University*, pp. 153–54.

94. Ibid., pp. 146–77.

95. John Henry Gray, "Harvard Fifty Year Class Book of 1887," autobiographical manuscript in Northwestern Archives, Gray folder. The minutes of the Board of Trustees of Northwestern University are not open to scholars, except to writers of authorized histories of the university. Therefore, it was impossible to verify the accuracy of Gray's recollections. Edward P. Cheyney, *A History of the University of Pennsylvania, 1740–1940*, pp. 293–94.

96. Furner, *Advocacy and Objectivity*, pp. 163–204.

97. Judson to Zueblin, March 7, 1908, Presidents Papers, box 71, folder

13; see also Zueblin to Judson, November 23, 1907, and Judson to Zueblin, November 27, 1907, ibid., box 71, folder 13.

98. Morris Janowitz, ed., *W. I. Thomas on Social Organization and Social Personality*, pp. xiv–xv.

99. Harper to Mrs. Potter Palmer, March 16, 1901, Presidents Papers, box 52, folder 2.

100. Church, "Economists as Experts," pp. 580–83; On Laughlin's career in general, see Alfred Bornemann, *J. Laurence Laughlin*.

CHAPTER 3

1. U.S. Census Bureau, *Statistics of the Population of the United States at the Tenth Census*, p. 448; U.S. Census Bureau, *Fourteenth Census of the United States*, 1:76; Homer Hoyt, *One Hundred Years of Land Values in Chicago*, p. 284.

2. Edith Abbott, *The Tenements of Chicago, 1908–1935*, pp. 11–14, and Michael P. McCarthy, "Chicago, the Annexation Movement, and Progressive Reform," pp. 43–54.

3. *Fourteenth Census*, 1:51.

4. *Hull House Maps and Papers*, p. 143.

5. Ibid., p. 41.

6. Ibid., p. 75.

7. John C. Kennedy, *Wages and Family Budgets in the Chicago Stockyards District*, pp. 48–53, 80.

8. Josiah Flint, "In the World of Graft," p. 328.

9. George Kimble Turner, "The City of Chicago," p. 575.

10. William T. Stead, *If Christ Came to Chicago*, p. 309.

11. Lloyd Wendt and Herman Kogen, *Bosses in Lusty Chicago*, pp. 79, 91, 102, 170.

12. Claudius O. Johnson, *Carter Henry Harrison I*; Carter Henry Harrison II, *Stormy Years* and *Growing Up with Chicago*; for interpretations of the political success of both Harrisons, see Kenneth Fox, *Better City Government*, pp. 18–20, and Martin J. Schiesl, *The Politics of Efficiency*, pp. 47–49, 70–72.

13. Lloyd Wendt and Herman Kogen, *Big Bill of Chicago*; George C. Hoffman, "Big Bill Thompson, His Mayoral Campaign and Voting Strength"; John M. Allswang, *Bosses, Machines, and Urban Voters*, pp. 91–105.

14. On the history of Chicago architecture and planning, see Carl W. Condit, *The Chicago School of Architecture*, and Mark L. Peisch, *The Chicago School of Architecture*.

15. Lincoln Steffens, "Chicago," p. 504.

16. The names of the officers, directors, and members of committees of the leading reform organizations and agencies were compared in order to arrive at these 215 reform leaders. The names were taken from published reports of these

groups, if available, and letterhead stationery if no published reports could be located. For some groups, names for only one or two years could be found. For names of the 215 reform leaders, see app. 1; for list of organizations used to draw up this list, see app. 2.

The biographical data used here were obtained primarily from the 1917 edition of *The Book of Chicagoans*. Some reformers had either left Chicago or died by 1917; their biographies were found in the 1911 or the 1905 edition. For those not in these directories, obituaries in newspapers and other biographical sources were used.

17. Besides the *Book of Chicagoans*, the following are useful references for information on the McCormick family: "First Families of Chicago by the Genealogist," and Frank C. Waldrop, *McCormick of Chicago*.

18. Data were based on addresses listed in the 1917 edition of *Book of Chicagoans*, supplemented by the *Lakeside Directory of Chicago* for 1917. If a 1917 address could not be found, the next closest year for which an address was available was used. Fifteen people were excluded because they lived in social settlements and six because their addresses could not be found.

19. The club's *Annual Reports* were used to determine membership for those not listed as members in *The Book of Chicagoans*.

20. See table 1, app. 3.

21. See table 2, app. 3.

22. *American Jewish Yearbook*, 1918–19, p. 49.

23. See table 3, app. 3. For a collective biography of Chicago's business elite, see Jocelyn M. Ghent and Frederic C. Jaher, "The Chicago Business Elite."

24. On changes in the structure of large corporations, see Alfred D. Chandler, Jr., *Strategy and Structure* and *The Visible Hand*. On the history of the legal profession, see Roscoe Pound, *The Lawyer from Antiquity to Modern Times*; Edson R. Sunderland, *A History of the American Bar Association*; Charles Warren, *A History of the American Bar*; and Herbert L. Packer and Thomas Ehrlich, *New Directions in Legal Education*, chap. 1. On social work, see Roy Lubove, *The Professional Altruist*.

25. Samuel Haber, *Efficiency and Uplift*.

26. Abraham Flexner, *Medical Education*; William Rothstein, *American Physicians in the Nineteenth Century*; and James G. Burrow, *Organized Medicine in the Progressive Era*.

27. Henry B. Favill, "The Responsibility of the Medical Profession," in *Henry Baird Favill, 1860–1916*, ed. John Favill, pp. 314–15.

28. *Chicago Commerce* 5 (May 28, 1909).

29. Louis D. Brandeis, *Business*, pp. 1–2, 12.

30. See app. 5.

31. See n. 18.

32. Hugh Hawkins, *Pioneer*, pp. 4–5; Horace Coon, *Columbia, Colossus on the Hudson*, p. 26; R. Gordon Hoxie, *A History of the Faculty of Political Science, Columbia University*, pp. 4–5, 52.

33. See app. 6.
34. Richard J. Storr, *Harper's University*, pp. 42–44.
35. Richard H. Thomas, "Jenkin Lloyd Jones."
36. On the history of women's clubs, see Jane C. Croly, *The History of the Woman's Club Movement in America*; Mary I. Wood, *History of the General Federation of Women's Clubs*; and Sophonisba P. Breckinridge, *Women in the Twentieth Century*, pp. 11–41.
37. Louise deKoven Bowen, *Growing Up with a City*, p. 102.
38. Ethel S. Dummer, *Why I Think So*. There is no biography or autobiography for Anita Blaine, although she left extensive papers, now located at the Wisconsin State Historical Society in Madison.
39. *Hull House Maps and Papers*, p. 14.
40. M. R. Werner, *Julius Rosenwald*, pp. 93–94.
41. Helen L. Horowitz examines in detail the group of Chicago businessmen responsible for the city's cultural renaissance in *Culture and the City*. She lists a cultural elite of 34 men who were active in at least two cultural institutions in these years. Significantly, 11 of these men also appear in my list of 215 reform leaders, presented in app. 1.
42. Samuel P. Hays, "The Politics of Reform in Municipal Government in the Progressive Era."
43. Commercial Club, *Plan of Chicago*.
44. Douglas Sutherland, *Fifty Years on the Civic Front*; and Lloyd Lewis and Henry Justin Smith, *Chicago*, pp. 235–39; Daniel Levine, *Varieties of Reform Thought*, chap. 3.
45. Minutes of the Illinois Society for Social Legislation, in Tufts Papers. Illinois Society for Social Legislation, *Report*, 1917.
46. Alexis de Tocqueville, *Democracy in America*, p. 117.
47. Louis Wirth, "Urbanism as a Way of Life," p. 22.
48. These figures are based on the number of members listed in the annual report of the City Club for 1916, the Woman's City Club for 1915, the Chicago Woman's Club for 1916–17, and the membership lists in Commercial Club of Chicago's *The Commercial Club of Chicago*, pp. 189–98.
49. *Chicago Record Herald*, March 1, 1911, p. 1.
50. Hoyt King, *Citizen Cole of Chicago*; Sidney J. Roberts, "The Municipal Voters' League and Chicago's Boodlers."
51. Charles H. Dennis, *Victor Lawson*; Waldrop, *McCormick*.
52. On Lathrop, see Jane Addams, *My Friend, Julia Lathrop*.
53. Ray Ginger, *Altgeld's America*, p. 1.
54. Ibid., pp. 1–14.
55. Marion Talbot, *More than Lore*, p. 5.
56. Ginger, *Altgeld's America*, p. 19.
57. *New Republic*, December 18, 1915, p. 158.
58. *University of Chicago Weekly* 3 (July 18, 1895): 431.
59. Quoted in Lewis and Smith, *Chicago*, p. 299.

60. *The World To-Day* 8 (February 1905): 117–18.
61. Thomas F. Holgate, "Why the Great Western Schools Excel Those of the East."
62. "Address of William Rainey Harper at Inauguration of President Edmund James," typescript in Northwestern Archives, James box.
63. Henry L. Mencken, "Civilized Chicago," p. 4.
64. Carl Sandburg, "Chicago," *Chicago Poems*, pp. 3–4.

CHAPTER 4

1. Albion W. Small, "The Dynamics of Social Progress," pp. 134, 137. For Small's views on education, see James Ansbro, "Albion Woodbury Small and Education."
2. William Rainey Harper, "Are School Teachers Underpaid?" p. 942.
3. George Herbert Mead, "The Larger Educational Bearings of Vocational Guidance," in U.S. Bureau of Education, *Vocational Guidance*, p. 17.
4. John C. French, *A History of the University Founded by Johns Hopkins*, p. 92; Edward P. Cheyney, *A History of the University of Pennsylvania, 1740–1940*, pp. 345–46.
5. Lawrence A. Cremin, David A. Shannon, and Mary E. Townsend, *A History of Teachers College, Columbia University*, pp. 10–40; James E. Russell, *Founding Teachers College*.
6. Robert L. McCaul, "Dewey's Chicago"; Ida C. Hefron, *Frances Wayland Parker*, pp. 27–37; Jack K. Campbell, *Colonel Francis W. Parker*, pp. 113–230.
7. "A Proposition to Organize College Work at a Central Point in the City," Presidents Papers, box 8, folder 21; Harper to Anita Blaine, February 8, 1898 and November 3, 1900, Blaine Papers, William R. Harper folder.
8. Arthur G. Powell, "The Education of Educators at Harvard, 1891–1919," in *Social Sciences at Harvard*, ed. Paul Buck, pp. 264–67.
9. French, *Johns Hopkins*, p. 152.
10. Cooley to Harper, August 6 and October 14, 1903, Presidents Papers, box 9, folder 5; W. D. McClintock to Harper, October 24, 1903 and January 7, 1904, ibid., box 20, folder 8.
11. Richard Whittemore, *Nicholas Murray Butler and Public Education, 1862–1911*, pp. 64–75; Nicholas Murray Butler, *Across the Busy Years*, pp. 16–18; and Sol Cohen, *Progressives and Urban School Reform*, pp. 3–42.
12. James B. Crooks, *Politics and Progress*, pp. 93–94; Charles Hirshfield, *Baltimore, 1870–1900*, p. 131.
13. On Eliot's activities, see especially Hugh Hawkins, *Between Harvard and America*, chap. 8.
14. The close ties between university and public school administrators are spelled out most thoroughly by David B. Tyack in *The One Best System*, pp. 133–39.

15. George S. Counts, *School and Society in Chicago*, pp. 35–37; Jean E. Farr, "The History of Public Education in the City of Chicago, 1894–1914," pp. 2–19; and Cherry W. Collins, "Schoolmen, Schoolma'ams, and School Boards."

16. Nightingale to Harper, September 27, 1892, Presidents Papers, box 9, folder 3.

17. Charles S. Thornton to Harper, April 7, 1894, and Edward Bemis to Harper, May 4, 1894, ibid.

18. D. G. Hamilton to Harper, March 13, 1896, and Andrew McLeish to Harper, April 15, 1896, ibid.

19. Harper to McLeish, April 4, 1896, and Nightingale to Harper, April 17, 1896, Harper Papers, box 2, folder 24.

20. Harper to Nightingale, April 18, 1896, ibid.

21. Harper to Lewis Jones, May 20, 1897, ibid., folder 14; W. A. S. Graham to Harper, November 5, 1897, ibid., box 3, folder 19; Harper to Graham, May 25, 1897, Presidents Papers, box 9, folder 4.

22. *Chicago Journal*, June 23, 1898.

23. "Report to the Central Council of the Civic Federation," Presidents Papers, box 27, folder 18.

24. Chicago Educational Commission, *Report of the Educational Commission of the City of Chicago*, pp. vii–viii.

25. Harrison to Harper, [1897], Presidents Papers, box 9, folder 4.

26. Tyack, *One Best System*, p. 127.

27. Theodore Reller, *The Development of the City Superintendency of Schools in the United States*, chap. 8.

28. Chicago Educational Commission, *Report of Educational Commission*; Mary J. Herrick, *The Chicago Schools*, pp. 83–86.

29. Harrison to Harper, February 15, 1899, Presidents Papers, box 9, folder 5.

30. Harper to I. J. McPhersen, December 15, 1898, Harper Papers, box 4, folder 18; McPhersen to Harper, December 20, 1898, Presidents Papers, box 9, folder 5; Herrick, *Chicago Schools*, pp. 103–4; Autobiography of Margaret Haley, Haley Papers, p. 217; Nicholas Murray Butler, "Editorial: The Chicago School Report," p. 306.

31. Harper to Francis Parker, November 15, 1904, Harper Papers, box 7, folder 14; Corbell to Harper, February 6, 1905, Presidents Papers, box 9, folder 5.

32. Counts, *School and Society*, pp. 38–42, 107–30.

33. Harrison to Harper, July 8, 1898, Harper Papers, box 4, folder 9.

34. *Chicago World*, December 4, 1899.

35. *City Club Bulletin* 10 (March 27, 1917): 99.

36. "Thomas F. Holgate, Ph.D.," *Northwestern University Alumni Journal* (1919): 12.

37. Illinois Education Commission, *Final Report of the Education Commission to the Forty-Sixth General Assembly of the State of Illinois*.

38. Ibid.; Illinois Education Commission, *Bulletins Nos. 1–9.*

39. Counts, *School and Society*, pp. 40–41; Walter F. and Sue H. Dodd, *Government in Illinois*, pp. 282–89.

40. Herrick, *Chicago Schools*, pp. 137–39; John T. McManis, *Ella Flagg Young and a Half Century of the Chicago Public Schools*, pp. 156–99.

41. *City Club Bulletin* 7 (December 6, 1915): 164–66 (hereafter cited as CCB).

42. Ibid. 11 (July 17, 1916): 131–32.

43. Ibid. 10 (March 27, 1917): 99.

44. Ibid.

45. Ibid., p. 106.

46. Ibid., p. 108.

47. Mead to Irene Tufts Mead, January 28, 1917, Mead Papers, box 1, folder 14; CCB 10 (March 27, 1917): 97–107; Public Education Association of Chicago, *Bulletins*, nos. 1–3.

48. Herrick, *Chicago Schools*, pp. 132–33.

49. Ibid., pp. 131–35; Dodd and Dodd, *Government in Illinois*, pp. 282–89; Counts, *School and Society*, pp. 40–41.

50. Herrick, *Chicago Schools*, pp. 137–39.

51. School Extension Committee, *Report of the Chicago Permanent School Extension Committee, 1909/1910*, pp. 7–8.

52. Chicago Board of Education, *Report of Social Centers in the Chicago Public Schools.*

53. CCB 10 (May 5 and December 10, 1917): 151, 299–300; Mead to Russell Tyson, February 28, 1916, Aldis Papers, folder 9.

54. CCB 2 (April 21 and 28, 1908): 381–88, 479–83.

55. Advisory Commission on the Chicago Public Library, *A Report Submitted to the Board of Directors of the Chicago Public Library by the Advisory Commission*, pp. 27–28.

56. Carleton B. Joeckel and Leon Carnovsky, *A Metropolitan Library in Action*, pp. 38–44. See also Helen L. Horowitz, *Culture and the City*, pp. 215–16. On the history of urban library reform generally, see Rosemary R. DuMont, *Reform and Reaction.*

57. Lawrence A. Cremin, *The Transformation of the School*, pp. 34–41, 50–51.

58. George Herbert Mead, "Editorial Notes," p. 405. See also "Industrial Education, the Workingman, and the School."

59. Mead to Blaine, February 6, 1912, Blaine Papers, box 494.

60. George Herbert Mead, Ernest A. Wreidt, and William J. Bogan, *Report on Vocational Training in Chicago and in Other Cities*, pp. 2–27; Martin Campbell to Judson, March 8, 1910, Presidents Papers, box 32, folder 10; Mead to Henry Mead, May 6, 1910, Mead Papers, box 1, folder 6; CCB 4 (July 5, 1911): 149–50; 5 (January 31, 1912): 9; 5 (September 28, 1912): 257; *National Municipal Review* 1 (1912): 457–58.

61. *CCB* 5 (December 4, 1912): 373–86.

62. Chicago Association of Commerce, *Industrial and Commercial Education in Relation to the Conditions in the City of Chicago*, pp. 3–8; Chicago Association of Commerce, *Annual Report*, 1909, p. 62.

63. Edwin Cooley, *Vocational Education in Europe*; Chicago Association of Commerce, *Annual Report*, 1910, pp. 45–46, 1911, pp. 56–58, and 1912, pp. 55–57.

64. *CCB* 5 (December 4, 1912): 374–76.

65. Ibid., 8 (May 18, 1915): 105–6; John Dewey, "Some Dangers in the Present Movement for Industrial Education."

66. Counts, *School and Society*, pp. 166–67.

67. Butler to Elmer H. Adams (copy), December 31, 1912, Presidents Papers, box 67, folder 15. See also Counts, *School and Society*, pp. 136–39; Commercial Club of Chicago, *Vocational Education for Illinois*.

68. *CCB* 6 (June 28, 1913): 22; Butler to Judson, January 8, 1913, Presidents Papers, box 67, folder 15.

69. Minutes, Meeting of Committee Appointed by President B. F. Harris of the Illinois Bankers Association to Draft a Model Vocational Education Bill, August 14 and November 9, 1912; Frank Leavitt to Edmund James, September 23, 1912, James Papers, box 38; Nathan William MacChesney to James, October 28 and November 9, 1912, ibid.; Cooley to James, December 12, 1912, ibid.

70. *CCB* 6 (June 28, 1913): 200; *CCB* 7 (May 13, 1914): 141; *CCB* 9 (May 5, 1916): 87; Chicago Association of Commerce, *Annual Report*, 1912, pp. 55–57, 1913, pp. 61–63, 1914, pp. 60–62, 1915, pp. 64–67, 1916, pp. 62–66, 1917, pp. 43–47; Commercial Club of Chicago, *Yearbook*, 1913/14, pp. 198–201, 1914/15, pp. 195–206, 274–76.

71. Charles S. Bilderback, "Fifteen Years of the Smith-Hughes Law in Illinois, 1917–1932," pp. 4–11.

72. Herrick, *Chicago Schools*, pp. 229–30.

73. John M. Brewer, *A History of Vocational Guidance*, pp. 57–61. Arthur Mann, *Yankee Reformers in the Urban Age*, p. 130; Paul H. Hanus, *Adventuring in Education*, pp. 203–5.

74. Breckinridge to Blaine, August 26, 1916, Blaine Papers, box 101.

75. Joint Committee on Vocational Training for Girls, *Vocational Training for Girls: Some Statements in Regard to Its Work*, undated pamphlet in Rosenwald Papers, box 41, folder 9; Chicago School of Civics and Philanthropy, *Finding Employment for Children Who Leave the Grade Schools to Go to Work*; Chicago Association of Commerce, *Annual Report*, 1912, pp. 55–58, 1913, pp. 61–63.

76. Breckinridge to William Graves, November 8 and 21, 1912, Rosenwald Papers, box 41, folder 9; "Report on the Establishment of a Co-Operative Employment Supervision Bureau in Chicago, September 19, 1912," Rosenwald Papers, box 151, folder 9.

CHAPTER 5

1. August Vollmer, "Police Progress in the Past Twenty-Five Years," p. 161.
2. Charles L. Chute, "The Progress of Probation and Social Treatment in the Courts," p. 60.
3. Herman Adler, "Psychiatry as Applied to Criminology in the United States," p. 50.
4. William Healy, "The Prevention of Delinquency and Criminality," p. 75.
5. John Henry Wigmore, "Retrospect," p. 4.
6. On the history of criminology in the nineteenth century see Arthur E. Fink, *Causes of Crime*; Hermann Mannheim, ed., *Pioneers in Criminology*; Mark H. Haller, *Eugenics*; Harry Elmer Barnes and Negley K. Teeters, *New Horizons in Criminology*; and Seymour Halleck, "American Psychiatry and the Criminal." On the relationship of crime theory to urban crime reform, see Mark H. Haller, "Theories of Criminal Violence and Their Impact on the Criminal Justice System."
7. James W. Garner, "Plan for the Journal," p. 6.
8. William Healy, "The Outlook for the Science of Criminalistics," p. 540.
9. Ibid., p. 543.
10. Robert H. Gault, "Adult Probation in Cook County, Illinois," pp. 162–63.
11. On the history of juvenile justice, see Steven L. Schlossman, *Love and the American Delinquent*. On the juvenile court, see Joseph M. Hawes, *Children in Urban Society*, chap. 10; Anthony Platt, *The Child Savers*; and Frank T. Flynn, "Judge Merritt W. Pinckney and the Early Days of the Juvenile Court in Chicago."
12. Louise deKoven Bowen, *Growing Up with a City*, chap. 7.
13. Juvenile Protective Association of Chicago, *Annual Report*, 1912, pp. 31–32.
14. Ibid., 1910, pp. 35–36, 1911, pp. 37–39, 1912, pp. 29–32, 1913, pp. 27–31; Minutes, June 3, 1910 to November 7, 1913, Juvenile Protective Association Papers.
15. Minutes, December 6, 1916, Juvenile Protective Association Papers.
16. Minutes, November 7, 1913, January 5, March 2, and April 6, 1917, ibid.
17. Hyde Park Center, *Bulletin*, 1910–17.
18. "Probation and Politics," *Survey* 28 (March 30, 1912); 2003–14; Hotchkiss to Anita Blaine, March 7, 1912, Blaine Papers, box 307; Hotchkiss to Blaine, January 29, 1913, ibid., box 538.
19. Committee to Investigate Operation of the Juvenile Court of Cook County, *The Juvenile Court of Cook County, Illinois*. See also Willard Hotchkiss, "Child Welfare Problem."
20. Henderson to Directors of the Chicago Society for Social Hygiene, November 30, 1907, Robins Papers, box 3.

21. *The Social Evil: With Special Reference to Conditions Existing in the City of New York.*

22. Morris Janowitz, ed., *W. I. Thomas on Social Organization and Social Personality*, p. xiv; Charles R. Henderson, "Education against Venereal Disease—A Need of the State" (Chicago Society for Social Hygiene [1907?]), in Taylor Papers, Henderson folder; Charles R. Henderson, *Education with Reference to Sex.*

23. Vice Commission of Chicago, *The Social Evil in Chicago*, pp. 27–37.

24. The most complete study of the vice crusade in Chicago in this period is Eric Anderson, "Prostitution and Social Justice." See also Mark M. Haller, "Urban Crime and Criminal Justice"; Walter C. Reckless, *Vice in Chicago*, pp. 1–31; and Walter Lippmann, *A Preface to Politics*, pp. 122–58. On vice reform during the progressive era generally, see Egal Feldman, "Prostitution, the Alien Woman, and the Progressive Imagination," and Roy Lubove, "The Progressive and the Prostitute."

25. Henderson to Deneen, December 16, 1911, Chicago School of Civics and Philanthropy Papers, box 1, folder 2; Breckinridge to Blaine, December 18, 1911, Blaine Papers, box 101; Henderson to Addams, July 22, 1912, Addams Papers.

26. Andrew A. Bruce, "One Hundred Years of Criminological Development in Illinois," pp. 39–41.

27. Charles R. Henderson, "The Parole System," p. 847.

28. Civic Federation of Chicago, *Biennial Meeting and Report of the Executive Committee*, pp. 5–7.

29. Civic Federation of Chicago, *Bulletin No. 11: Annual Report, 1913– 14*, pp. 3–5.

30. Civic Federation of Chicago, *Bulletin No. 8: Biennial Report of the Executive Committee*, (1912–13).

31. Haller, "Urban Crime and Criminal Jutice," pp. 620, 635, and "Civic Reformers and Police Leadership."

32. William J. Bopp and Donald O. Schultz, *A Short History of American Law Enforcement*, pp. 84–85. For surveys of twentieth-century police and reform, see Robert M. Fogelson, *Big-City Police*, and Samuel Walker, *A Critical History of Police Reform.*

33. H. M. Campbell et al., "The Chicago Police—Report of the Civil Service Commission," pp. 81, 84.

34. Chicago City Council, *Report of the City Council Committee on Crime.*

35. Henry Barrett Chamberlin, "The Chicago Crime Commission—How the Business Men of Chicago Are Fighting Crime," pp. 386–97; Chicago Association of Commerce, *Annual Report*, 1919, p. 12.

36. Robert H. Gault, "On the School for Police," pp. 645–46; see also "Proposed Instruction for Police in Northwestern University," *JCLC* 6 (January 1916): 794–96; "Legal Training for Policemen," *Northwestern Alumni Journal*, November 26, 1915, pp. 18–19. On Vollmer and the movement for univer-

sity police science generally, see Alfred Parker, *Crime Fighter*; and Gene E. Carte and Elaine H. Carte, *Police Reform in the United States*.

37. "The Criminologic Laboratory," *JCLC* 20 (August, 1929): 166; "Northwestern University Crime Detection Laboratory," ibid. 23 (July–August, 1932): 309; "Crime Detection School," ibid. 23 (March–April, 1933): 1048.

38. James W. Garner, "The American Institute of Criminal Law and Criminology," pp. 2–5; Gault to Blaine, June 30, 1919, Blaine Papers, box 15.

39. Chicago City Council, *Report of Council Committee on Crime*.

40. Ibid., pp. 42–45, 58–59.

41. Edith Abbott, *The One Hundred and One County Jails of Illinois and Why They Ought to be Abolished*, and *The Real Jail Problem*.

42. Chicago City Council, *Report of Council Committee on Crime*, pp. 91–95.

43. Ibid., p. 95.

44. Ibid., pp. 96–98, 106–13; Gault to Merriam, October 27, 1914, Merriam Papers, box 16, folder 14.

45. Chicago City Council, *Report of Council Committee on Crime*, pp. 149–50.

46. Charles Merriam, "Chicago: An Intimate View," unpublished autobiography, 1920, chap. 6, p. 4, Merriam Papers.

47. Ibid., p. 95.

48. Legal Aid Society of Chicago, *Annual Report*, 1912, 1916; Joel D. Hunter, "The Legal Clinic of Northwestern University School of Law," pp. 272–74; United Charities of Chicago, *The Legal Aid Bureau's Service—The Poor Man's Law Office*, p. 3.

CHAPTER 6

1. Roy Lubove, *The Professional Altruist*, pp. 1–54.

2. Charles Hirshfeld, *Baltimore, 1870–1900*, pp. 138–55; Fabian Franklin, *The Life of Daniel Coit Gilman*, pp. 267–75; Daniel C. Gilman, "Special Training for Philanthropic Work," in *The Launching of a University and Other Papers*, pp. 343–66; Edward T. Devine, *When Social Work Was Young*, pp. 21–28, 132–33; R. Gordon Hoxie, *A History of the Faculty of Political Science, Columbia University*, pp. 78–79; Jergen Herbst, "Francis Greenwood Peabody," pp. 45–69; James E. Mooney, *John Graham Brooks*, p. 27.

3. Minutes, Chicago Bureau of Charities, February 1, 1895, December 14, 1896, March 17, 1897, January 22 and May 31, 1899, United Charities of Chicago Papers.

4. Ibid., January 18, March 14 and April 4, 1910.

5. Ibid., February 26, 1915.

6. Breckinridge to Blaine, July 28, August 9 and 29, 1911, Blaine Papers, box 101; Chicago Association of Commerce, *Classified List of Local Philanthropic and Charitable Organizations*, and *Annual Report*, 1911, p. 95.

7. National Conference of Catholic Charities, *Proceedings*, 1914, pp. 48–50; Donald P. Gavin, *The National Conference of Catholic Charities*, pp. 36–37.

8. Charles Zueblin, "The Chicago Ghetto," *Hull House Maps and Papers*, pp. 91–111; Russell Ballard, "The Years at Hull House," pp. 432–34; see also "Memorandum for Miss Addams, Suggesting a Plan to Be Proposed by the Relief Committee for the Care of Tramps Who Asked for Food at Hull House," undated, Breckinridge Papers, container 1.

9. "Circular No. 1: The Northwestern University Settlement Association," [1892], and "Northwestern University Settlement," [1900], undated pamphlets in Northwestern Archives, Northwestern University Settlement folder. *The Northwestern* throughout this period contains numerous articles on the settlement's activities.

10. Richard J. Storr, *Harper's University*, pp. 186–87; University of Chicago Settlement, *The University of Chicago Settlement*, pp. 5–10; Settlement Minutes, October 12, 1899 and January 15, 1900, McDowell Papers.

11. Settlement Minutes, December 8, 1909, McDowell Papers.

12. University of Chicago Settlement, *A Study of Chicago's Stockyards Community*.

13. Mead to Blaine, December 24, 1909, Blaine Papers, box 495.

14. Settlement Minutes, October 12, 1910, McDowell Papers.

15. Ibid., July 31, 1910.

16. Mead to Henderson, July 7, 1912, copy, McDowell Papers, folder 15a.

17. Settlement Minutes, November 11 and 15, December 9, 1912, February 17, March 11, and May 12, 1913, McDowell Papers. Ethel S. Dummer, *Why I Think So*, p. 40.

18. Mead to Blaine, June 14, 1912, Blaine Papers, box 494. Ernest Wreidt, "A Bureau of Social Research in Chicago," mimeographed, June 1913, Rosenwald Papers, box 4, folder 20.

19. Minutes of Meeting of the Special Committee at the City Club, January 23, 1913, Rosenwald Papers, box 4, folder 20.

20. Charles Merriam, "The Need of a Survey as the First Step in Community Welfare," p. 163.

21. Breckinridge to Anita Blaine, November 28, 1914, Blaine Papers, box 101.

22. Charles Merriam, "Chicago: An Intimate View," unpublished autobiography, 1920, chap. 8, pp. 14–18, Merriam Papers, box 94.

23. On the growth of social science involvement in the United States Census Bureau and other federal agencies in this period, see David M. Grossman, "Professors and Public Service, 1885–1925," pp. 23–72.

24. Robert L. Buroker, "From Voluntary Association to the Welfare State"; Grace Abbott to Breckinridge, 1912, Breckinridge Papers, container 1; Freund letter to members of Immigrants' Protective League, December 12, 1921, Immigrants' Protective League Papers, folder 47.

25. Illinois Immigrants' Protective League, *Annual Reports*, 1909–10, pp.

37–38, 1912–13, p. 7; "Suggestions for Increasing Federal Activities for the Protection of Immigrants," "Considerations Bearing on the Creation of a Federal Immigrant Protective Bureau," and "Federal Bureau of Information and for the Protection of Immigrants in Chicago," undated memos in Freund Papers.

26. Breckinridge to Camden, July 24 and August 24, 1914, Breckinridge Papers, container 1; Camden to Breckinridge, August 19, 1914, ibid.

27. Breckinridge to Blaine, February 9, 1916, Blaine Papers, box 101.

28. Freund to Edgar A. Bancroft, December 18, 1918, Freund Papers; Freund to Blaine, July 4, 1920, Blaine Papers, box 264.

29. Buroker, "From Voluntary Association to Welfare State," pp. 656–60.

30. Wendell Phillips Settlement folder, box 30, folder 16, Rosenwald Papers; Breckinridge to Blaine, July 16, 1915, March 7 and 26, April 11, 1918, Blaine Papers, box 101; and Breckinridge to Katherine Pierce, December 2, 1918, ibid.

31. Thomas W. Allinson to Talbot, January 9, 1915, Talbot Papers, box 20; Talbot to Young, January 8, 1915, ibid.; Young to Talbot, January 11, 1915, ibid.; *Chicago Herald*, January 10, 1915.

32. Arvarh E. Strickland, *History of the Chicago Urban League*, pp. 26–30; Chicago Urban League, *Annual Reports*, 1916–19; William Graves to Park, Breckinridge, et al., January 23, 1917, Rosenwald Papers, box 9, folder 13; T. Arnold Hill to Graves, July 6, 1917, ibid.; Graves to Rosenwald, November 23, 1917, ibid.; "Public meetings," appended to letter by T. Arnold Hill to Arthur Aldis, July 5, 1917, Aldis Papers, folder 6.

33. Arthur I. Waskow, *From Race Riot to Sit-In*, chap. 5; Minutes, Race Commission, March 12, 1920, Rosenwald Papers, box 6, folder 4; Minutes, Executive Committee of Race Commission, March 18, 1920, ibid. (Hereafter cited as Minutes, Executive Committee and Minutes, Commission, respectively.)

34. Minutes, Executive Committee, September 15, 1920; Minutes, Commission, January 23 and March 12, 1920.

35. Horace Coon, *Columbia, Colossus on the Hudson*, pp. 156–61; John C. French, *A History of the University Founded by Johns Hopkins*, pp. 150, 177; James B. Crooks, *Politics and Progress*, pp. 165–66.

36. Bessie L. Pierce, *A History of Chicago*, 3:309–13; Edwin O. Jordan, "The Chicago Drainage Canal."

37. Edwin O. Jordan, "A Report on Certain Species of Bacteria Observed in Sewage," pp. 188–89; William Burrows, "Biographical Memoir of Edwin Oakes Jordan, 1866–1936," p. 200–203. Jordan to Harper, September 26, 1896, Presidents Papers, box 15, folder 11.

38. Isham Randolph to Harper, January 7, 1899, Presidents Papers, box 15, folder 11; Jordan to Harper, September 26, 1896 and January 11, 1899, ibid.

39. Edwin O. Jordan, "Report of the University of Chicago," in Sanitary District of Chicago, *Report of Streams Examination, Chemic and Bacteriologic*, pp. 21–42.

40. S. B. Grubbs, *Public Health Administration in Illinois*, pp. 1480–81.

41. John Harper Long, "Chemical and Bacteriological Examination of the Waters of the Illinois River and Its Principal Tributaries," in Illinois State Board of Health, *Report of the Sanitary Investigations of the Illinois River and Its Tributaries*, pp. 76–77; see also Robert F. Zeit and Gustave Futterer, "Chemical and Bacteriological Examinations of the Waters of the Illinois River and Its Tributaries," in ibid., pp. 78–93; John H. Long, "Chemical Investigations of the Water Supplies of Illinois, 1888–89," in Illinois State Board of Health, *Preliminary Report to the Illinois State Board of Health*. John H. Long, "Chemical and Bacteriological Examinations of the Waters of the Illinois, Missouri, and Mississippi Rivers," in Illinois State Board of Health, *Report of the Sanitary Investigations of the Illinois, Mississippi, and Missouri Rivers with Relation to the Effect of the Sewage of the City of Chicago, and the Sanitary Conditions of the Water Supplies of the Cities of Chicago and St. Louis*, pp. 1–15; and F. Robert Zeit, "Identification of Pathogenic and Sewage Bacteria Found in the Illinois, Mississippi, and Missouri Rivers," in ibid., pp. 1–21.

42. Burrows, "Jordan," p. 207.

43. Jordan, J. H. Long, and F. R. Zeit to Joseph Downey, October 1, 1902, Jordan Papers.

44. Breckinridge to Evans, February 11, 1910, Breckinridge Papers, container 1; Evans to Breckinridge, February 14, 1910, ibid.

45. *CCB* 4 (July 5, 1911): 160.

46. Ibid. 4 (July 5, 1911): 149–50; ibid. 6 (June 28, 1913): 200–201; ibid. 7 (May 13, 1914): 140; Civic Federation of Chicago, *Bulletin No. 8* (1913), pp. 9–10.

47. "Report of Committee on Regulations for the Pasteurization of Milk," p. 975; Edwin O. Jordan, "Municipal Regulation of the Milk Supply," pp. 2286–91; Edwin O. Jordan, "The Campaign for Pure Milk," pp. 485–87.

48. Minutes, Committee on Housing Conditions, City Club, November 25, 1908, Tufts Papers, box 2, folder 13; *CCB* 3 (February 16, 1910): 190–91; ibid. 4 (July 5, 1911): 145–46.

49. *CCB* 5 (September 28, 1912): 260–64; E. M. Henderson to Tufts, February 13, 1911, Tufts Papers, box 2, folder 12; E. C. Jensen to Tufts, May 7, 1912, ibid.

50. Robert F. Steadman, *Public Health Organization in the Chicago Region*, pp. 165–66.

51. Edith Abbott, *The Tenements of Chicago, 1908–1935*, p. ix.

52. Roy Lubove, *The Struggle for Social Security, 1900–1935*, pp. 52–53.

53. National Conference of Charities and Correction, *Proceedings* (1906), pp. 252–56.

54. Minutes of the Illinois Industrial Commission, January 31 to October 27, 1906.

55. Illinois Industrial Insurance Commission, *Report to the Governor*; Earl R. Beckner, *A History of Labor Legislation in Illinois*, pp. 434–37.

56. Lubove, *Struggle for Social Security*, p. 53; Beckner, *Labor Legisla-*

tion, pp. 64–65, 437–82; Joseph L. Castrovinci, "Prelude to Welfare Capitalism," pp. 80–102.

57. Beckner, *Labor Legislation*, pp. 272–82; Illinois Commission on Occupational Diseases, *Report of the Commission on Occupational Diseases*, pp. 5–20.

58. Minutes, Illinois Committee for Social Legislation, February 19, 23, 1913 and June 11, 1914, Tufts Papers, box 3, folders 2 and 4; *CCB* 10 (January 15, 1917): 21–23.

59. Tufts to Mary Aldis, October 10, 1916, Tufts Papers, box 3, folder 5; Tufts to Victor Olander, Agnes Nestor, and Lies, November 8, 1916, ibid.; Tufts to W. L. Noble, November 15, 1916, ibid.; Tufts to George B. Andrews, December 7, 1916, ibid.; Lies to Tufts, September 26, 1916, ibid.; Lies to Tufts, November 15, 1916, ibid.; George B. Andrews to Tufts, December 7, 1916, ibid.; Olander to Tufts, November 15, 1916, ibid.; Lucius Teter to Tufts, October 14, 1916, ibid.; Andrews to Tufts, May 23, 1917, ibid.; Tufts to Andrews, May 31, 1917, ibid.; Tufts to Andrews, January 3, 1917, ibid., box 1, folder 9.

60. Beckner, *Labor Legislation*, pp. 484–86; Illinois Health Insurance Commission, *Report of the Health Insurance Commission of the State of Illinois*; Harry A. Millis, *Sickness and Insurance*, pp. 118–21. On the health insurance movement generally, see Maurice B. Hammevitch, "History of the Movement for Compulsory Health Insurance in the United States," pp. 281–99; Ronald L. Numbers, *Almost Persuaded*; and James G. Burrow, *Organized Medicine in the Progressive Era*, pp. 133–53.

61. Lubove, *Struggle for Social Security*, pp. 149–58; Beckner, *Labor Legislation*, p. 397.

62. *CCB* 4 (July 5, 1911): 160; *Northwestern University Bulletin* (Alumni Journal Number) 18 (March 2, 1918): 17; *Northwestern University Alumni Journal* 19 (May 3, 1919): 19; Beckner, *Labor Legislation*, pp. 422–24.

63. Beckner, *Labor Legislation*, p. 398; *CCB* 4 (July 5, 1911): 159–61; Illinois Immigrants' Protective League, *Annual Report*, 1909–10, pp. 37–38.

64. Mayor's Commission on Unemployment, *Report of the Mayor's Commission on Unemployment*, pp. 5–14; Beckner, *Labor Legislation*, pp. 407–10; Charles R. Henderson, "How Chicago Met the Unemployment Problem of 1915," pp. 721–22.

65. Henderson, "Unemployment Problem," pp. 721–22; Beckner, *Labor Legislation*, pp. 411–18; Graham Taylor, "Charles Richmond Henderson," *Survey* (April 10, 1915), pp. 55–56; "Charles Richmond Henderson," *University of Chicago Magazine* 7 (1915), pp. 168–71; Daniel Nelson, *Unemployment Insurance*, pp. 10–21.

66. Beckner, *Labor Legislation*, pp. 183–86.

67. Freund to Fitch, December 16, 1911, February 3, 1912, and May 1, 1912, Freund Papers; Fitch to Freund, December 18, 1911, and February 6, 1912, ibid.

68. Andrews to Freund, January 19, 1912, and January 17, 1913, Freund Papers; Freund to Andrews, January 25, 1913, ibid.

69. Freund to Edward C. Curtis, February 11, 1913, Freund Papers; Curtis to Freund, February 17, 1913, ibid; "Secretary's Report," Illinois Committee for Social Legislation, June 22, 1915, Tufts Papers, box 3, folder 3.

70. American Association for Labor Legislation, *Proceedings of Second Annual Meeting*, p. 21, *Proceedings of Third Annual Meeting* (1910), pp. 24–27; *CCB* 5 (May 27, 1912): 220–21.

71. Tufts to Dunne, April 9, 1913, Tufts Papers, box 3, folder 4; Luke Grant and Deibler to Dunne, [1913], ibid.; Freund to Efficiency and Economy Committee, July 3, 1914, Freund Papers.

72. Lafayette G. Harter, Jr., *John R. Commons*, pp. 89–129; Hoxie, *Faculty of Political Science*, p. 186; Herbert Heaton, *A Scholar in Action*, p. 88; Edward T. Devine, *Report on the Desirability of Establishing an Employment Bureau in the City of New York*.

73. Citizens' Committee on the Garment Workers' Strike, *Concerning the Garment Workers' Strike: Report of the Subcommittee to the Citizens' Committee*.

74. Ibid.

75. Ibid.

76. Chicago Joint Board, Amalgamated Clothing Workers of America, *The Clothing Workers of Chicago, 1910–1922*, pp. 17–71; Earl D. Howard, *The Hart Schaffner and Marx Labor Agreement*; Howard and Hillman to Tufts, December 31, 1918, and undated and untitled memo on Tufts, Hart Schaffner and Marx Labor Arbitration Agreement Papers, box 1, folder 1 (hereafter cited as HS&M Papers); Hoxie, *Faculty of Political Science*, p. 186.

77. Text of resolution, in Mead Papers, box 9, folder 22.

78. Earl Dean Howard, "Rectification of Industrial Relations: Statement of Principle," June 10, 1920, HS&M Papers, box 2, folder 15.

79. This argument is spelled out in detail in Buroker, "From Voluntary Association to Welfare State," pp. 643–60.

80. Edith Abbott, *Social Welfare and Professional Education*, p. 11.

81. Charles R. Henderson, "The Direction of Social Advance," p. 16.

CHAPTER 7

1. Rosenwald to H. A. Lipsky, March 31, 1911, Rosenwald Papers, box 25, folder 11.

2. Samuel P. Hays, "The Politics of Reform in Municipal Government in the Progressive Era," pp. 162–63.

3. George H. Norton, "The Scholar and Social Reform," *The Northwestern* 18 (May 7, 1898): 13–14; Gray, "Harvard 50 Year Class Book Autobiography," p. 2, Northwestern Archives; on Lorimer and Yerkes, see Joel Arthur Tarr, *A Study in Boss Politics*, pp. 75–88.

4. Charles E. Merriam, "Home Rule in Chicago's New Charter," pp. 30–31; Benjamin Park DeWitt, *The Progressive Movement*, pp. 278–79.

5. John H. Gray, "Home Rule for Chicago," pp. 32–33, 39.

6. Kenneth Fox, *Better City Government*, pp. 51–62.

7. Civic Federation of Chicago, Report on Reform Legislation, *Civic Federation Papers*, no. 16, p. 6; "New Charter for Chicago," *The Northwestern* 15 (February 28, 1895): 3.

8. Chicago New Charter Convention, *Proceedings of the New Charter Convention*; Chicago New Charter Campaign Committee, *The Chicago New Charter Movement*; CCB 2 (May 19, 1909): 451–52.

9. Augustus R. Hatton, ed., *Digest of City Charters*, p. vii; Hatton to Judson, August 22, 1906, Presidents Papers, box 47, folder 11.

10. Freund obituary, *Chicago Tribune*, October 21, 1932; *Chicago Charter Convention Proceedings*, Friday, March 1, 1907, p. 1198; Merritt Starr to Freund, January 12. 1907, Freund Papers.

11. Charles Merriam, *Report on the Municipal Revenues of Chicago*, pp. v–vi.

12. Ibid., pp. 71–76, 141–42.

13. Chicago New Charter Convention, *Proceedings*, October 3, 1906, pp. 5–9; CCB 1 (June 26, 1907): 157–63.

14. Merriam, "Home Rule," pp. 24–31; CCB 1 (June 19, 1907): 148–52; ibid. (October 30, 1907): 212–20; and ibid. 2 (May 19, 1909): 451–52.

15. Edmund James to Abram W. Harris, April 17, 1913, James Papers, box 32; James to Wigmore, October 24, 1913, Wigmore to James, October 30, 1913, ibid., box 42; Wigmore to James, October 23, 1913, Wigmore Papers.

16. Minutes, Universities Committee on the State Constitution, March 7 to December 5, 1914, Presidents Papers, box 61, folder 28; CCB 9 (February 3, 1915): 52–55.

17. Citizens' Association of Chicago, *Bulletin No. 37* (1917); S. M. Singleton to Merriam, February 18, 1915, Merriam Papers, box 12, folder 8; Merriam to Grace Wilbur Trout, February 22, 1915, ibid., box 23, folder 7; George Cole to Merriam, March 9, 1915, ibid., box 15, folder 6; Cole to Merriam, August 18, 1916, ibid.; Merriam to Lowden, December 21, 1916, ibid., box 19, folder 2.

18. Merriam to James Garner, June 7, 1917, Merriam Papers, box 16, folder 12; Merriam to Mrs. Herman Landauer, July 3, 1917, ibid., box 18, folder 15; Merriam to Trout, July 7 and September 16, 1917, ibid., box 23, folder 7; Trout to Merriam, September 3, 1917, ibid.

19. Walter F. and Sue H. Dodd, *Government in Illinois*, pp. 46–50.

20. James B. Crooks, *Politics and Progress*, p. 103; Nicholas Murray Butler, *Across the Busy Years*, pp. 369–70; Albert Bushnell Hart, "Government," in *The Development of Harvard University since the Inauguration of President Eliot, 1869–1929*, ed. Samuel E. Morison, p. 186; Harvey Eagleson, *William Bennett Munroe*, p. 25.

21. Benjamin G. Rader, *The Academic Mind and Reform*, p. 84; John C. French, *A History of the University Founded by Johns Hopkins*, p. 197; Robert

M. Haig, *Some Probable Effects of the Exemption of Improvements from Taxation in the City of New York*.

22. DeWitt, *Progressive Movement*, pp. 319–20.

23. Municipal Museum Scrapbook, 1904–05; Vincent to Anita Blaine, October 20 [1905?] and January 23, 1906, Blaine Papers, box 713.

24. Crooks, *Politics and Progress*, pp. 101–2.

25. Merriam to Garner, February 19, March 10 and 13, June 1 and 11, July 10, October 15, 1908, Merriam Papers, box 12, folder 17; Garner to Merriam, March 11, June 8, July 15, 1908, ibid.; Garner to Clyde Jones, June 2, 1908, ibid.; Charles McCarthy to Merriam, May 25, June 29, 1908, ibid., folder 21; Merriam to McCarthy, May 26, 1908, ibid.; *CCB* 2 (December 9, 1908): 195–96; Dodd and Dodd, *Government in Illinois*, p. 159.

26. *CCB* 2 (July 8, 1908): 165–67; ibid. 4 (July 6, 1911): 165; ibid. 5 (September 28, 1912): 270; *National Municipal Review* 1 (1912): 740–41.

27. "Address of Charles E. Merriam, City Planning Conference, Kansas City, May 9, 1917," typescript, Merriam Papers, box 71, folder 9; Carl W. Condit, *Chicago, 1910–1929*, pp. 59–85.

28. *CCB* 2 (March 4, 1908): 1–3; *The Commons* 5 (September 1900): 18; ibid. 6 (September 1901): 5; Charles Zueblin, "Municipal Playgrounds in Chicago"; Charles Merriam, "Chicago: An Intimate View," unpublished autobiography, 1920, chap. 7, p. 4, Merriam Papers (hereafter cited as Merriam, "Chicago"). On the playground movement in Chicago generally, see Benjamin McArthur, "The Chicago Playground Movement."

29. Illinois State Park Commission, *Report*; Vernon R. Loucks, *James Alton James*, pp. 103–7.

30. Chicago Harbor Commission, *Report to the Mayor and Aldermen of the City of Chicago by the Chicago Harbor Commission*, p. 3; Lloyd Lewis and Henry Justin Smith, *Chicago*, pp. 403–46.

31. Merriam to Goode, March 2 and 16, 1908, Merriam Papers, box 12, folder 18.

32. Chicago Harbor Commission, *Report*, p. 149.

33. Ibid., pp. 55–58, 159–61.

34. Chicago Harbor Commission, *Harbor Commission Report*; Minutes, Chicago Harbor Commission; Lewis and Smith, *Chicago*, pp. 403–6.

35. Merriam to Lee, July 3 and 13, August 16, 1911, February 1 and December 19, 1912, January 11 and 29, 1913, Merriam Papers, box 18, folder 18; Lee to Merriam, August 12 and 26, 1911, July 21 and December 14, 1912, January 25, 1913, ibid.; Dodd and Dodd, *Government in Illinois*, pp. 73–74.

36. Judson to Males, March 15 and April 7, 1913, Presidents Papers, box 44, folder 1; City Club of Chicago, *The Short Ballot in Illinois*; Dodd and Dodd, *Government in Illinois*, pp. 74–75.

37. Merriam to Mrs. J. T. Mason, April 6, 1917, Merriam Papers, box 19, folder 16; Merriam to Frank Scott, April 9, 1917, ibid., box 22, folder 6; Merriam to H. O. Edmunds, April 9 and May 16, 1917, ibid., box 14, folder 10;

Merriam to Trout, May 8, 1917, ibid., box 23, folder 7; Merriam to Gotthard A. Gahlberg, May 24, 1917, ibid., box 16, folder 12; *CCB* 6 (November 29, 1913): 304–6; Judson to Lowden, November 16, 1917, Presidents Papers, box 47, folder 22.

38. See Aileen S. Kraditor, *The Ideas of the Woman Suffrage Movement, 1890–1920*, especially chap. 5; Andrew Sinclair, *The Emancipation of the American Woman*, p. 324; "Woman Suffrage Hearing, April 15, 1909," pamphlet, in Talbot Papers, addenda, box 2; and "Suffrage Hearing at Springfield, April 14, 1909," penciled text in ibid.

39. Edith Abbott and Sophonisba P. Breckinridge, *The Wage-Earning Woman and the State*.

40. Dodd and Dodd, *Government in Illinois*, pp. 75–76; Catherine McColloch to Merriam, December 18, 1912, Merriam Papers, box 19, folder 8; Merriam to McColloch, December 21, 1912, ibid.; Elizabeth Booth to Merriam, December 24, 1912 and January 27, 1913, ibid., box 14, folder 3.

41. Woman's City Club, *The Woman's City Club: Its Book*, pp. 44–47, 51–52.

42. Edith Abbott, "Are Women a Force for Good Government?" pp. 437–45; Abbott, "Statistics in Chicago Suffrage," p. 151; and Abbott, "The Woman Voter and the Spoils System in Chicago," pp. 460–65.

43. Barry D. Karl, *Charles E. Merriam and the Study of Politics*, pp. 1–41.

44. Merriam, "Chicago," chap. 5, pp. 1–7; undated memo on Merriam Commission, Merriam Papers, box 80, folder 1; *CCB* 3 (June 8, 1910): 315–17; ibid. 4 (August 16, 1911): 195–208; Martin J. Schiesl, *The Politics of Efficiency*, pp. 100–108, 123–24.

45. Jane S. Dahlberg, *The New York Bureau of Municipal Research*, pp. 3–27.

46. Merriam, "Chicago," chap. 7, pp. 2–4.

47. Karl, *Merriam*, pp. 65–68.

48. Merriam, "Chicago," chap. 3, pp. 20–21; Campaign pamphlet, Merriam Papers, box 74, folder 4.

49. Rosenwald to H. A. Lipsky, March 31, 1911, Rosenwald Papers, box 25, folder 11.

50. Karl, *Merriam*, pp. 68–72; Harold Ickes, *The Autobiography of a Curmudgeon*, pp. 115–44.

51. Address of Charles E. Merriam, temporary chairman, State Convention, Progressive party, August 3, 1912, Merriam Papers, box 73, folder 3; Merriam to Roosevelt, November 19, 1912, ibid., box 22, folder 1; Karl, *Merriam*, pp. 72–77.

52. Merriam, "Chicago," chap. 5, pp. 8–11.

53. Merriam, "Address of Charles E. Merriam, City Planning Conference, May 9, 1917," pp. 5–6, Merriam Papers, box 71, folder 9; Merriam, "Chicago," chap. 7, pp. 4–7; George Hooker to Merriam, March 9, 1917,

Merriam Papers, box 15, folder 2; Richard W. Wolf to Merriam, March 9, 1917, ibid., box 24, folder 8; Dwight Akers to Merriam, March 22, 1917, ibid., box 13, folder 13.

54. Merriam, "Chicago," chap. 7, p. 8; Max Loeb to Merriam, May 12, 1916, Merriam Papers, box 19, folder 1; Lies to Merriam, June 1, 1916, ibid., box 18, folder 20; Merriam to Lies, June 5, 1916, ibid.

55. Merriam, "Chicago," chap. 7, pp. 9–10; "Address at City Planning Conference," pp. 3–4. Chicago Association of Commerce, *Electrification of Railway Terminals and Elimination of Smoke in Chicago*; *Chicago Examiner*, *Chicago Daily News*, and *Chicago American*, September 23, 1910.

56. Merriam, "Chicago," chap. 7, pp. 4–5; Harry Herwitz to Harriet Vittum, February 1, 1917, Merriam Papers, box 23, folder 12.

57. Merriam, "Chicago," chap. 8, pp. 14–17.

58. Ibid., chap. 6, pp. 1–3.

59. Chicago City Council, *Report of the City Council Committee on Crime*, pp. 9–16; Merriam, "Chicago," chap. 8, pp. 3–8.

60. Harry Olson to Merriam, September 27, 1915, Merriam Papers, box 20, folder 13; Minnie Low to Merriam, December 13, 1915, ibid., box 19, folder 2; Edith Abbott to Merriam, January 12, 1916, ibid., box 13, folder 10; Merriam to Charles Thompson, January 19, 1916, ibid., folder 4.

61. Karl, *Merriam*, pp. 79–83.

62. McDowell, Addams, and Blaine Endorsements, Merriam Papers, box 75, folder 5.

63. Karl, *Merriam*, pp. 96–99.

64. Victor Elting, *Recollections of a Grandfather*, p. 193.

CHAPTER 8

1. In *Mars and Minerva*, Carol S. Gruber demonstrates perceptively how American professors used the crisis of World War I to strengthen their reputation for usefulness.

2. Gene M. Lyons, *The Uneasy Partnership*, pp. 38–40; Jane S. Dahlberg, *The New York Bureau of Municipal Research*, pp. 81–92.

3. Barry D. Karl, *Executive Reorganization and Reform in the New Deal*; Lyons, *Uneasy Partnership*, p. 17.

4. Barry D. Karl, "Presidential Planning and Social Science Research."

5. Mel Scott, *American City Planning since 1890*, pp. 300–311, 343–46.

6. Edwin E. Witte to Edith Abbott, October 18, 1939, Abbott Papers, box 54, folder 5. Grace Abbott's role in shaping the Social Security Act is detailed in Winifred Walsh, "Grace Abbott and Social Action, 1934–1939."

7. See Roy Lubove, *The Struggle for Social Security, 1900–1935*, and Clarke A. Chambers, *Seedtime of Reform*.

8. Interview with Martin Bickham, 1971, and Martin H. Bickham, "Con-

densed Outline of Career and Various Activities of Dr. Martin Hayes Bickham," pp. 2–3.

9. Arthur Millspaugh, *Crime Control by the National Government*, pp. 50–51.

10. National Commission on Law Observance and Enforcement, vol. 14, *Report on Police* and vol. 10, *Report on Crime and the Foreign-Born*.

11. National Commission on Law Observance and Enforcement, Vol. 3, *Report on Criminal Statistics*, p. 8; International Association of Chiefs of Police, *Uniform Crime Reporting*; U.S. Federal Bureau of Investigation, "Ten Years of Uniform Crime Reporting, 1930–1939," pp. 1–2.

12. U.S. Federal Bureau of Investigation, *A History of the FBI Laboratory*, p. 2.

13. National Advisory Committee on Education, *Federal Relations to Education*; National Advisory Committee on Education, *Report of the Committee, February 1938*; Frank J. Munger and Richard F. Fenno, Jr., *National Politics and Federal Aid to Education*, pp. 3–8.

14. Clark Kerr, *The Uses of the University*, pp. vi–vii.

15. Clark Kerr, "What We Might Learn from the Climacteric," p. 1.

Bibliography

MANUSCRIPTS

Champaign, Illinois
University of Illinois Libraries
    Edmund J. James Papers

Chicago, Illinois
Chicago Historical Society
    Margaret Haley Papers
    Mary McDowell and the University of Chicago Settlement Papers
    United Charities of Chicago Papers
Newberry Library
    Graham Taylor Papers
Northwestern University Law School Library
    John Henry Wigmore Papers
University of Chicago Libraries
    Grace and Edith Abbott Papers
    Jane Addams Correspondence (microfilm)
    Chicago Harbor Commission Minutes
    Chicago Municipal Museum Scrapbook
    Chicago School of Civics and Philanthropy Papers
    Ernst Freund Papers
    William Rainey Harper Papers
    Hart Schaffner and Marx Labor Arbitration Agreement Papers
    Illinois Industrial Commission Minutes
    Edwin O. Jordan Papers
    Shailer Mathews and the Divinity School Papers
    George Herbert Mead Papers

Charles E. Merriam Papers
Municipal Museum Scrapbook, 1904–1905
Presidents of the University of Chicago Papers
Julius Rosenwald Papers
Marion Talbot Papers
James H. Tufts Papers
University of Illinois at Chicago Circle Libraries
Arthur Aldis Papers
Immigrants' Protective League of Illinois Papers
Juvenile Protective Association Papers

Evanston, Illinois
Northwestern University Libraries
Northwestern University Archives

Madison, Wisconsin
Wisconsin State Historical Society
Anita McCormick Blaine Papers
Raymond Robins Papers

University Park, Pennsylvania
Pennsylvania State University
Luther L. Bernard Papers

Washington, D.C.
Library of Congress
Sophonisba P. Breckinridge Papers

OTHER PRIMARY SOURCES

Abbott, Edith. "Are Women a Force for Good Government?" *National Municipal Review* 4 (1915): 437–45.
———. *The One Hundred and One County Jails of Illinois and Why They Ought to Be Abolished*. Chicago: Juvenile Protective Association, 1916.
———. *The Real Jail Problem*. Chicago: Juvenile Protective Association, 1915.
———. *Social Welfare and Professional Education*. Chicago: University of Chicago Press, 1931.
———. "Statistics in Chicago Suffrage." *New Republic* 3 (1915): 151.
———. *The Tenements of Chicago, 1908–1935*. Chicago: University of Chicago Press, 1936.
———. "The Woman Voter and the Spoils System in Chicago." *National Municipal Review* 5 (1916): 460–65.
———, and Breckinridge, Sophonisba P. *The Wage-Earning Woman and the State: A Reply to Miss Minnie Bronson*. Boston: Boston Equal Suffrage Association for Good Government, [1912].
Adams, Herbert Baxter. *The College of William and Mary: A Contribution to*

the History of Higher Education, with Suggestions for Its National Promotion. Washington, D.C.: Government Printing Office, 1887.

———. *Public Educational Work in Baltimore*. Johns Hopkins University Studies in Historical and Political Science, ser. 17, no. 12. Baltimore: Johns Hopkins University Press, 1899.

———. "Summer Schools and University Extension." *Monographs on Education in the United States*. Edited by Nicholas Murray Butler. Albany: J. B. Lyon Company, 1899.

Addams, Jane. *My Friend, Julia Lathrop*. New York: Macmillan, 1935.

———. *Twenty Years at Hull House*. New York: Macmillan, 1910.

Adler, Herman. "Psychiatry as Applied to Criminology in the United States." *Journal of Criminal Law and Criminology* 24 (1933): 50–59.

Advisory Commission on the Chicago Public Library. *A Report Submitted to the Board of Directors of the Chicago Public Library by the Advisory Commission*. Chicago, 1909.

American Association for Labor Legislation. *Proceedings of Annual Meeting*. New York, 1907–9.

American Jewish Yearbook. New York: American Jewish Committee, 1919.

American Society for Extension of University Teaching. *University Extension: Its Definition, History, System of Teaching, and Organization*. Philadelphia, 1891.

Bickham, Martin H. "Condensed Outline and Career and Various Activities of Dr. Martin Hayes Bickham." Unpublished autobiography, January 12, 1966, courtesy of Mrs. Emma Pitcher.

The Book of Chicagoans. Chicago: A. N. Marquis and Company, 1905 (1st ed.); 1911 (2nd ed.); 1917 (3rd ed.).

Bowen, Louise deKoven. *Growing Up with a City*. New York: Macmillan, 1926.

Brandeis, Louis D. *Business: A Profession*. Boston: Small, Maynard and Company, 1914.

Breckinridge, Sophonisba P. *Women in the Twentieth Century: A Study of Their Political, Social and Economic Activities*. New York: McGraw Hill, 1933.

Bruce, Andrew A., "One Hundred Years of Criminological Development in Illinois," *Journal of Criminal Law and Criminology* 24 (1933): 11–49.

Burgess, John W. "The Founding of the School of Political Science," *Columbia University Quarterly* 22 (1930): 351–79.

———. *Reminiscences of an American Scholar: The Beginning of Columbia University*. New York: Columbia University Press, 1934.

Butler, Nicholas Murray, *Across the Busy Years: Recollections and Reflections*. New York and London: Charles Scribner's Sons, 1939.

———. "Editorial: The Chicago School Report." *Educational Review* 17 (1899): 306–8.

———. *The Rise of a University*. Vol. 2, *The University in Action*. New York: Columbia University Press, 1937.

Campbell, H. M., Flynn, John J., and Elton, Louis. "The Chicago Police: Report of the Civil Service Commission," *Journal of the American Institute of Criminal Law and Criminology* 3 (1912): 62–84.

Catholic Charities Review. Washington, D.C., 1917–19.

Chamberlin, Henry Barrett. "The Chicago Crime Commission: How the Business Men of Chicago Are Fighting Crime." *Journal of Criminal Law and Criminology* 11 (1920): 386–97.

Chicago Association of Commerce. *Annual Reports.* Chicago, 1905–19.

———. *Classified List of Local Philanthropic and Charitable Organizations.* Chicago, 1913–19.

———. *Electrification of Railway Terminals and Elimination of Smoke in Chicago: Report of a Committee of the Chicago Association of Commerce.* Chicago, 1910.

———. *Industrial and Commercial Education in Relation to the Conditions in the City of Chicago.* Chicago, 1909.

Chicago Board of Education. *Report of Social Centers in the Chicago Public Schools.* Chicago, 1912–17.

Chicago Charter Convention. *Proceedings of the Chicago Charter Convention.* Chicago, 1907.

Chicago City Council. *Report of the City Council Committee on Crime.* Chicago, 1915.

Chicago Commerce, 1904–19.

Chicago Educational Commission. *Report of the Educational Commission of the City of Chicago.* Chicago, 1899.

Chicago Harbor Commission. *Report to the Mayor and Aldermen of the City of Chicago by the Chicago Harbor Commission.* Chicago, 1909.

Chicago Joint Board, Amalgamated Clothing Workers of America. *The Clothing Workers of Chicago, 1910–1922.* Chicago, 1922.

Chicago New Charter Campaign Committee. *The Chicago New Charter Movement: Why the Pending Constitutional Amendment Should be Approved.* Chicago, 1904.

Chicago New Charter Convention. *Proceedings of the New Charter Convention.* Chicago, [1902].

Chicago School of Civics and Philanthropy, *Finding Employment for Children Who Leave the Grade Schools to Go to Work.* Chicago, 1911.

Chicago Urban League. *Annual Reports.* Chicago, 1916–19.

Chicago Woman's Club. *Annual Announcement.* Chicago, 1892–1919.

Chute, Charles L. "The Progress of Probation and Social Treatment in the Courts." *Journal of Criminal Law and Criminology* 24 (1933): 60–73.

Citizens' Association of Chicago, *Bulletin.* Chicago, 1901–20.

Citizens' Committee on the Garment Workers' Strike. *Concerning the Garment Workers' Strike: Report of the Subcommittee to the Citizens' Committee.* Chicago, 1910.

City Club Bulletin. Chicago, 1907–19.

City Club of Chicago. *The Short Ballot in Illinois: Report of the Short Ballot Committee*. Chicago, 1912.

———. *Yearbook, 1904–16*.

Civic Federation of Chicago. *Biennial Meeting and Report of the Executive Committee*. Chicago, 1909.

———. *Bulletin, 1910–19*.

———. *Report on Reform Legislation*. Civic Federation Papers, no. 16. Chicago: R. R. Donnelley, 1899.

Commercial Club of Chicago. *The Commercial Club of Chicago: Its Beginnings and Something of Its Work*. Chicago, 1910.

———. *The Plan of Chicago*. Chicago, 1909.

———. *Vocational Education for Illinois*. Chicago, [1915].

———. *Yearbook*. Chicago: 1908–19.

Committee to Investigate the Operation of the Juvenile Court of Cook County. *The Juvenile Court of Cook County, Illinois: Report of a Committee Appointed under Resolution of the Board of Commissioners of Cook County*. Chicago, 1912.

The Commons, 1896–1905.

Cooley, Edwin. *Vocational Education in Europe: Report to the Commercial Club of Chicago*. Chicago: Commercial Club, 1912.

Croley, Jane C. *The History of the Woman's Club Movement in America*. New York: H. G. Allen, 1898.

The Daily Northwestern, 1905–19.

DePaul University. *Bulletin of DePaul University: First Annual Report of the President*. Chicago, 1909.

Devine, Edward T. *Report on the Desirability of Establishing an Employment Bureau in the City of New York*. New York: Charities Publication Committee, 1909.

———. *When Social Work Was Young*. New York: Macmillan, 1939.

Dewey, John. "Some Dangers in the Present Movement for Industrial Education." *Child Labor Bulletin* 1 (1913): 69–74.

DeWitt, Benjamin Park. *The Progressive Movement: A Non-Partisan Comprehensive Discussion of Current Tendencies in American Politics*. New York: Macmillan, 1915.

Dummer, Ethel S. *Why I Think So: The Autobiography of an Hypothesis*. Chicago: Clarke-McElroy, 1937.

Elementary School Teacher, 1901–14.

Elting, Victor. *Recollections of a Grandfather*. Chicago: A. Kroch, 1940.

Favill, John, ed. *Henry Baird Favill, 1860–1916: A Memorial Volume*. Chicago: Privately printed, 1917.

Flint, Josiah. "In the World of Graft." *McClure's* 16 (1901): 327–34.

Freund, Ernst. "The Problem of Intelligent Legislation." In *Proceedings of the American Political Science Association at Its Fourth Annual Meeting*, pp. 69–79. Baltimore: Waverly Press, 1908.

Garner, James W. "The American Institute of Criminal Law and Criminology." *Journal of the American Institute of Criminal Law and Criminology* 1 (1910): 2–5.

———. "Plan for the Journal." *Journal of the American Institute of Criminal Law and Criminology* 1 (1910): 5–6.

Gault, Robert H. "Adult Probation in Cook County, Illinois." *Journal of the American Institute of Criminal Law and Criminology* 6 (1915): 162–63.

———. "On the School for Police," *Journal of the American Institute of Criminal Law and Criminology* 7 (January, 1917): 644–48.

Gilman, Daniel C. *The Launching of a University and Other Papers: A Sheaf of Remembrances.* New York: Dodd, Mead, 1906.

Gray, John Henry. "Home Rule for Chicago." *The Voter: A Monthly Magazine of Politics* (1905): 32–33, 39.

Grubbs, S. B. *Public Health Administration in Illinois.* U.S. Public Health Service, Public Health Reports, Reprint no. 275. Washington, D.C.: Government Printing Office, 1915.

Haig, Robert M. *Some Probable Effects of the Exemption of Improvements from Taxation in the City of New York: A Report Prepared for the Committee on Taxation of the City of New York.* New York: C. S. Nathan, 1915.

Hanus, Paul H. *Adventuring in Education.* Cambridge, Mass.: Harvard University Press, 1937.

Happel, L. Frederick. "Rev. Frederic Siedenburg, S.J." *Loyola University Magazine* 8 (1914): 111–15.

Harper, William Rainey. "Are School Teachers Underpaid?" *The World To-day* 7 (1904): 941–43.

———. *The Trend in Higher Education.* Chicago: University of Chicago Press, 1905.

Harrison, Carter Henry, II. *Growing Up with Chicago: Sequel to "Stormy Years."* Chicago: Ralph Fletcher Seymour, 1944.

———. *Stormy Years: The Autobiography of Carter H. Harrison.* Indianapolis and New York: Bobbs-Merrill, 1935.

Hatton, Augustus R., ed. *Digest of City Charters.* Chicago: Charter Convention, 1906.

Healy, William. "The Outlook for the Science of Criminalistics," *Journal of the American Institute of Criminal Law and Criminology* 5 (1914): 540–43.

———. "The Prevention of Delinquency and Criminality." *Journal of Criminal Law and Criminology* 24 (1933): 74–87.

Henderson, Charles R. "Business Men and Social Theorists." *American Journal of Sociology* 1 (1896): 385–97.

———. "The Direction of Social Advance." *Calcutta Review* 271 (1913): 16–24.

———. *Education with Reference to Sex.* Eighth Yearbook of the National Society for the Scientific Study of Education. Chicago: University of Chicago Press, 1909.

———. "How Chicago Met the Unemployment Problem of 1915." *American Journal of Sociology* 20 (1915): 721–30.

———. "The Ministry of Today—Its New Equipment." *University of Chicago Record* 3 (1899): 279–81.

———. "The Parole System." *Journal of the American Institute of Criminal Law and Criminology* 1 (1911): 847–48.

"Henry Wade Rogers, A.M., LL.D." *Syllabus* (1891): 112–14.

A History of Columbia University, 1754–1904. New York: Columbia University Press, 1904.

Holgate, Thomas F. "Why the Great Western Schools Excel Those of the East." *Inter-Ocean*, July 17, 1904, p. 4.

Hotchkiss, Willard. "Child Welfare Problem." *Institution Quarterly* 4 (1913): 214–16.

———. *Higher Education and Business Standards*. Boston and New York: Houghton Mifflin, 1918.

Howard, Earl D. *The Hart Schaffner and Marx Labor Agreement: Industrial Law in the Clothing Industry*. Chicago: University of Chicago Press, 1920.

Hull House Maps and Papers. New York: Thomas Y. Crowell, 1895.

Hunter, Joel D. "The Legal Clinic of Northwestern University School of Law." *Journal of Criminal Law and Criminology* 32 (1941): 272–74.

Hyde Park Center. *Bulletin*. Chicago, 1910–17.

Ickes, Harold. *The Autobiography of a Curmudgeon*. New York: Reynal and Hitchcock, 1943.

Illinois Commission on Occupational Diseases. *Report of Commission on Occupational Diseases*. Chicago: Warner Printing Company, 1911.

Illinois Education Commission. *Bulletins*, nos. 1–9. Springfield, 1908–9.

———. *Final Report of the Education Commission to the Forty-Sixth General Assembly of the State of Illinois*. Springfield, 1909.

Illinois Health Insurance Commission. *Report of the Health Insurance Commission of the State of Illinois*. Springfield, 1919.

Illinois Immigrants' Protective League. *Annual Report*. Chicago, 1909–17.

Illinois Industrial Insurance Commission. *Report to the Governor*. Springfield, 1907.

Illinois Society for Social Legislation. *Report*. Chicago, 1917.

Illinois State Board of Health. *Preliminary Report to the Illinois State Board of Health: Water Supplies of Illinois and the Pollution of Its Streams*. Springfield: State Printers, 1889.

———. *Report of the Sanitary Investigations of the Illinois, Mississippi, and Missouri Rivers with Relation to the Effect of the Sewage of the City of Chicago, and the Sanitary Conditions of the Water Supplies of the Cities of Chicago and St. Louis*. Springfield: State Printers, 1903.

———. *Report of the Sanitary Investigations of the Illinois River and Its Tributaries, with Special Reference to the Effect of the Sewage of Chicago*. Springfield: Phillips Brothers, State Printers, 1901.

Illinois State Park Commission. *Report*. Springfield, 1911.

International Association of Chiefs of Police. *Uniform Crime Reporting: A Complete Manual for Police.* New York, 1929.

Johns Hopkins University. *Johns Hopkins University: Celebration of the Twenty-Fifth Anniversary of the University.* Baltimore: Johns Hopkins University Press, 1902.

Joint Committee on Vocational Guidance for Girls. *Vocational Training for Girls: Some Statements in Regard to Its Work.* Chicago, n.d.

Jordan, Edwin O. "The Campaign for Pure Milk." *Christendom* 1 (1903): 485–87.

———. "The Chicago Drainage Canal." *American Monthly Review of Reviews* 11 (1899): 56–58.

———. "Municipal Hygiene." *Popular Science Monthly* 63 (1903): 132–40.

———. "Municipal Regulation of the Milk Supply." *Journal of the American Medical Association* 61 (1914): 2286–91.

———. "A Report on Certain Species of Bacteria Observed in Sewage." *Massachusetts State Board of Health Report for 1888/1889.* Pt. 2: *Water Supply and Sewage.* Boston: Wright and Potter Publishing Company, 1889.

Journal of Criminal Law and Criminology (originally *Journal of the American Institute of Criminal Law and Criminology*), 1910–35.

Judson, Harry P. "Is Our Republic a Failure?" *American Journal of Sociology* 1 (1895): 28–40.

———. "Mr. Roosevelt and the Third Term." *Independent* 72 (1912): 653–55.

———. "Municipal Government." *Yearbook of the Sunset Club* (1892/93): 143–48.

———. "The New Nationalism." *Outlook* 96 (1910): 876–78.

Juvenile Protective Association of Chicago. *Annual Report.* Chicago, 1907–20.

Lakeside Directory of Chicago. Chicago: Lakeside Directory Company, 1917.

Legal Aid Society of Chicago. *Annual Report.* Chicago, 1905–18.

Lynn, James Weber. "A Fighter for the Right." *University of Chicago Magazine* 19 (1927): 270–71.

Mayor's Commission on Unemployment. *Report of the Mayor's Commission on Unemployment.* Chicago: Cameron, Amberg and Company, 1914.

Mead, George Herbert. "Editorial Notes." *Elementary School Teacher* 8 (1908): 402–6.

———. "Industrial Education, the Workingman, and the School." *Elementary School Teacher* 9 (1909): 369–83.

———. "Madison—The Passage of the University of Wisconsin through the State Political Agitation of 1914." *Survey* 35 (1915): 349–51, 354–61.

———. "The Working Hypothesis in Social Reform." *American Journal of Sociology* 5 (1899): 367–71.

———; Wreidt, Ernest A.; and Hogan, William J. *Report on Vocational Training in Chicago and in Other Cities.* Chicago: City Club, 1912.

Mencken, Henry L. "Civilized Chicago." *Chicago Sunday Tribune,* October 28, 1917.

Merriam, Charles E. "Home Rule in Chicago's New Charter." *The Voter: A Monthly Magazine of Politics* 51 (1907): 24–31.

———. "The Need of a Survey as the First Step in Community Welfare." *Institution Quarterly* 5 (1914): 161–65.

———. *Report on the Municipal Revenues of Chicago.* Chicago: City Club, 1906.

Millis, Harry A. *Sickness and Insurance: A Study of the Sickness Problem and Health Insurance.* Chicago: University of Chicago Press, 1937.

National Advisory Committee on Education. *Federal Relations to Education: Report of the National Advisory Committee on Education.* Washington, D.C.: Government Printing Office, 1931.

———. *Report of the Committee, February 1938.* Washington, D.C.: Government Printing Office, 1938.

National Commission on Law Observance and Enforcement. *Report.* 6 vols. Washington, D.C.: Government Printing Office, 1931.

National Conference of Catholic Charities. *Proceedings.* Washington, D.C., 1910–19.

National Conference of Social Work (originally National Conference of Charities and Correction). *Proceedings.* New York, 1892–1919.

National Municipal Review, 1912–19.

New Republic, 1914–19.

The Northwestern, 1894–98.

Northwestern University. *Catalogue,* 1890–1919.

———. *A Report Submitted to the Original Guarantors of the Northwestern University School of Commerce.* Evanston: Northwestern University, 1923.

Northwestern University Alumni Journal, 1915–19.

Norton, George H. "The Scholar and Social Reform." *The Northwestern* 18 (May 7, 1898): 13–14.

O'Connor, M. A. "Catholic Schools of Sociology." *Loyola University Magazine* 16 (1916): 2–7.

Public Education Association of Chicago. *Bulletins,* nos. 1–3. Chicago: 1916–17.

Reckitt, Ernest. *Reminiscences of Early Days of the Accounting Profession in Illinois.* Chicago: Illinois Society of Certified Public Accountants, 1953.

"Report of Committee on Regulations for the Pasteurization of Milk." *Journal of the American Medical Association* 57 (1911): 975.

Russell, James E. *Founding Teachers College: Reminiscences of the Dean Emeritus.* New York: Teachers College Press, 1937.

Sandburg, Carl. *Chicago Poems.* New York: Henry Holt, 1916.

Sanitary District of Chicago. *Report of Streams Examination, Chemic and Bacteriologic.* Chicago: Blakeley Printing Company, 1902.

School Extension Committee. *Report of the Chicago Permanent School Extension Committee, 1909/1910.* Chicago, 1910.

———. *School Extension Committee.* Chicago, 1901.

Siedenburg, Frederic. "Report of Courses of Instruction in Social Work Given at Loyola University in 1913–1914." *Proceedings of the National Conference of Catholic Charities* (1914): 61–62.

Small, Albion W. "The Civic Federation of Chicago: A Study in Social Dynamics." *American Journal of Sociology* 1 (1895): 79–103.

———. "The Dynamics of Social Progress." *Proceedings of the American Institute of Instruction* 60 (1889): 122–37.

———. "The New Humanity." *University Extension World* 4 (1894): 7–34.

———. "The Present Outlook of Social Science." *American Journal of Sociology* 18 (1913): 433–69.

———. "Scholarship and Social Agitation." *American Journal of Sociology* 1 (1896): 564–82.

The Social Evil: With Special Reference to Conditions Existing in the City of New York. New York and London: G. P. Putnam Sons, 1902.

Stead, William T. *If Christ Came to Chicago*. London: Review of Reviews, 1894.

Steffens, Lincoln. "Chicago: Half Free and Fighting on." *McClure's* 21 (1903): 563–77.

Survey (formerly *Charities and the Commons*), 1904–19.

Talbot, Marion. *More than Lore*. Chicago: University of Chicago Press, 1936.

Taylor, Graham. "Charles Richmond Henderson." *Survey* 35 (1915): 55–56.

Tufts, James Hayden. "The Present Significance of Scholarship." *Washington University Record* 10 (1914): 1–12.

———. "The University and the Advance of Justice." *University of Chicago Magazine* 5 (1913): 168–98.

Turner, George Kimble. "The City of Chicago: A Study of Great Immoralities." *McClure's* 28 (1907): 575.

United Charities of Chicago. *The Legal Aid Bureau's Service—The Poor Man's Law Office*. Chicago, 1927.

U.S. Bureau of Education. *Vocational Guidance: Papers Presented at the Organizational Meeting of the Vocational Guidance Association, 1913*. Bulletin No. 14. Washington, D.C.: Government Printing Office, 1914.

U.S. Census Bureau. *Fourteenth Census of the United States Taken in the Year 1920*. 11 vols. Washington, D.C.: Government Printing Office, 1921.

———. *Statistics of the Population of the United States at the Tenth Census*. Washington, D.C.: Government Printing Office, 1883.

U.S. Federal Bureau of Investigation. *A History of the FBI Laboratory*. Washington, D.C.: Government Printing Office, 1974.

———. "Ten Years of Uniform Crime Reporting, 1930–1939." Mimeographed report, copy in Library of Congress. Washington, D.C.: Federal Bureau of Investigation, 1939.

University of Chicago. *Official Bulletin*. No. 1. Chicago, 1890.

University of Chicago Magazine. Chicago, 1908–19.

University of Chicago Settlement. *A Study of Chicago's Stockyards Community*.

3 vols. Vol. 1, *Opportunities in School and Industry for Children of the Stockyards District*, by Ernest L. Talbert. Vol. 2, *The American Girl in the Stockyards District*, by Louise Montgomery. Vol. 3, *Wages and Family Budgets in the Chicago Stockyards District*, by John C. Kennedy. Chicago: University of Chicago Press, 1912–14.

———. *The University of Chicago Settlement*. Chicago, 1901.

University of Chicago Weekly. Chicago, 1892–1902.

Veblen, Thorstein. *The Higher Learning in America: A Memorandum on the Conduct of Universities by Business Men*. New York: Hill and Wang, 1957.

———. *The Place of Science in Modern Civilization and Other Essays*. New York: B. W. Huebsch, 1919.

Vice Commission of Chicago. *The Social Evil in Chicago: A Study of Existing Conditions with Recommendations*. Chicago, 1911.

Vollmer, August. "Police Progress in the Past Twenty-Five Years." *Journal of Criminal Law and Criminology* 24 (1933): 74–87.

Wigmore, John Henry. "Retrospect." *Journal of Criminal Law and Criminology* 23 (1932): 3–5.

Woman's City Club. *The Woman's City Club: Its Book*. Chicago, 1915.

———. *Yearbook*. Chicago, 1910–15.

The World To-Day. 1901–12.

Zueblin, Charles. "Municipal Playgrounds in Chicago." *American Journal of Sociology* 4 (1898): 145–58.

SECONDARY SOURCES

Allen, Francis A. "Ernst Freund and the New Age of Legislation." Preface to 1965 edition of *Standards of American Legislation* by Ernst Freund. Chicago and London: University of Chicago Press, 1965.

Allswang, John M. *Bosses, Machines, and Urban Voters: An American Symbiosis*. Port Washington, N.Y.: Kennikat Press, 1977.

Anderson, Eric. "Prostitution and Social Justice: Chicago, 1910–1915." *Social Service Review* 48 (1974): 203–28.

Ansbro, James. "Albion Woodbury Small and Education." Ph.D. dissertation, Loyola University of Chicago, 1978.

Ballard, Russell. "The Years at Hull House." *Social Service Review* 22 (1948): 432–34.

Barnes, Harry Elmer, ed. *An Introduction to the History of Sociology*. Chicago and London: University of Chicago Press, 1948.

———, and Teeters, Negley K. *New Horizons in Criminology*. 3d ed. Englewood Cliffs, N.J.: Prentice-Hall, 1959.

Barry, Robert M. "A Man and a City: George Herbert Mead in Chicago." In *American Philosophy and the Future*, edited by Michael Novak. New York: Scribners, 1968.

Beckner, Earl R. *A History of Labor Legislation in Illinois*. Chicago: University of Chicago Press, 1929.

Ben-David, Joseph. *The Scientist's Role in Society: A Comparative Study*. Englewood Cliffs, N.J.: Prentice-Hall, 1971.

Berquist, Harold E., Jr. "The Edward Bemis Controversy at the University of Chicago." *AAUP Bulletin* 54 (1972): 384–93.

Berthoff, Rowland T. *An Unsettled People: Social Order and Disorder in American History*. New York: Harper and Row, 1971.

Bilderback, Charles S. "Fifteen Years of the Smith-Hughes Law in Illinois, 1917–1932." Master's thesis, University of Chicago, 1932.

Bledstein, Burton J. *The Culture of Professionalism: The Middle Class and the Development of Higher Education in America*. New York: W. W. Norton, 1976.

Bopp, William J., and Schultz, Donald O. *A Short History of American Law Enforcement*. Springfield, Ill.: Charles C. Thomas, 1972.

Bornemann, Alfred. *J. Laurence Laughlin: Chapters in the Career of an Economist*. Washington, D.C.: American Council on Public Affairs, 1940.

Brewer, John M. *A History of Vocational Guidance*. New York: Harper Bros., 1942.

Buck, Paul, ed. *Social Sciences at Harvard*. Cambridge: Harvard University Press, 1965.

Buroker, Robert L. "From Voluntary Association to the Welfare State: The Illinois Immigrants' Protective League, 1908–1926." *Journal of American History* 58 (1971): 643–60.

Burrow, James G. *Organized Medicine in the Progressive Era: The Move toward Monopoly*. Baltimore: Johns Hopkins University Press, 1977.

Burrows, William. "Biographical Memoir of Edwin Oakes Jordan, 1866–1936." *National Academy Biographical Memoirs*. Washington, D.C.: National Academy of Sciences, 1939.

Campbell, Jack K. *Colonel Francis W. Parker: The Children's Crusader*. New York: Teachers College Press, 1967.

Carr-Saunders, Alexander M., and Wilson, Paul A. *The Professions*. London: Frank Cass, 1964.

Carte, Gene E.; and Carte, Elaine H. *Police Reform in the United States: The Era of August Vollmer, 1905–1932*. Berkeley and Los Angeles: University of California Press, 1975.

Castrovinci, Joseph L. "Prelude to Welfare Capitalism: The Role of Business in Enactment of Workmen's Compensation Legislation in Illinois, 1905–1912." *Social Service Review* 50 (1976): 80–102.

Chambers, Clarke A. *Seedtime of Reform: American Social Service and Social Action, 1918–1933*. Minneapolis: University of Minnesota Press, 1963.

Chandler, Alfred D., Jr. *Strategy and Structure: Chapters in the History of the Industrial Enterprise*. Cambridge and London: M.I.T. Press, 1962.

———. *The Visible Hand: The Managerial Revolution in American Business*. Cambridge: Harvard University Press, 1977.

Cheyney, Edward P. *A History of the University of Pennsylvania, 1740–1940.* Philadelphia: University of Pennsylvania Press, 1940.

Christakes, George. *Albion W. Small.* Boston: Twayne Publishers, 1978.

Church, Robert L. "Economists as Experts: The Rise of an Academic Profession in the United States, 1879–1920." *The University in Society,* vol. 2, edited by Lawrence Stone. Princeton, N.J.: Princeton University Press, 1974.

Cohen, Sol. *Progressives and Urban School Reform: The Public Education Association of New York City, 1895–1954.* New York: Teachers College Press, 1964.

Collins, Cherry W. "Schoolmen, Schoolma'ams, and School Boards: The Struggle for Power in Urban School Systems in the Progressive Era." Ed.D. dissertation, Harvard University, 1976.

Condit, Carl W. *Chicago, 1910–1929: Building, Planning, and Urban Technology.* Chicago and London: University of Chicago Press, 1973.

———. *The Chicago School of Architecture: A History of Commercial and Public Building in the Chicago Area, 1875–1925.* Chicago and London: University of Chicago Press, 1964.

Coon, Horace. *Columbia, Colossus on the Hudson.* New York: E. P. Dutton and Company, 1947.

Counts, George S. *School and Society in Chicago.* New York: Harcourt, Brace, 1928.

Cremin, Lawrence A. *The Transformation of the School: Progressivism in American Education, 1876–1957.* New York: Vintage, 1964.

———; Shannon, David A.; and Townsend, Mary E. *A History of Teachers College, Columbia University.* New York: Columbia University Press, 1954.

Crooks, James B. *Politics and Progress: The Rise of Urban Progressivism in Baltimore, 1895–1911.* Baton Rouge: Louisiana State University Press, 1968.

Cross, Robert. *The Emergence of Liberal Catholicism in America.* Cambridge: Harvard University Press, 1958.

Curti, Merle. *American Scholarship in the Twentieth Century.* Cambridge: Harvard University Press, 1953.

Dahlberg, Jane S. *The New York Bureau of Municipal Research: Pioneer in Government Administration.* New York: New York University Press, 1966.

Dennis, Charles H. *Victor Lawson: His Time and His Work.* Chicago: University of Chicago Press, 1935.

Dibble, Vernon K. *The Legacy of Albion Small.* Chicago and London: University of Chicago Press, 1975.

Diner, Steven J. "A City and Its University: University of Chicago Professors and Elite Reform, 1892–1919." Ph.D. dissertation, University of Chicago, 1972.

———. "Department and Discipline: The Department of Sociology at the University of Chicago, 1892–1920." *Minerva* 8 (1975): 514–53.

———. "Scholarship in the Quest for Social Welfare: A Fifty-Year History of the *Social Service Review.*" *Social Service Review* 51 (1977): 1–68.

Dodd, Walter F., and Dodd, Sue H. *Government in Illinois.* Chicago: University of Chicago Press, 1923.

DuMont, Rosemary R. *Reform and Reaction: The Big-City Public Library in American Life.* Westport, Conn.: Greenwood Press, 1977.

Eagleson, Harvey. *William Bennett Munroe, 1875–1957: A Memoir.* Pasadena: Privately printed, 1959.

Elliott, Philip R. *The Sociology of the Professions.* New York: Herder and Herder, 1972.

Ellis, John Tracy. *American Catholicism.* Chicago and London: University of Chicago Press, 1956.

Farr, Jean E. "The History of Public Education in the City of Chicago, 1894–1914." Masters thesis, University of Chicago, 1939.

Feldman, Egal. "Prostitution, the Alien Woman, and the Progressive Imagination: 1910–1915." *American Quarterly* 19 (1967): 192–206.

Fink, Arthur E. *Causes of Crime: Biological Theories in the United States, 1800–1915.* Philadelphia: University of Pennsylvania Press, 1938.

"First Families of Chicago by the Genealogist." *Chicago Herald Examiner,* November 27, 1932.

Flexner, Abraham. *Medical Education: A Comparative Study.* New York: Macmillan Company, 1925.

Flynn, Frank T. "Judge Merritt W. Pinckney and the Early Days of the Juvenile Court in Chicago." *Social Service Review* 28 (1954): 20–30.

Fogelson, Robert M. *Big-City Police.* Cambridge and London: Harvard University Press, 1977.

Fox, Kenneth. *Better City Government: Innovation in American Urban Politics, 1850–1937.* Philadelphia: Temple University Press, 1977.

Frankfurter, Felix. *Some Observations on Supreme Court Litigation and Legal Education.* Chicago: University of Chicago Law School, 1954.

Franklin, Fabian. *The Life of Daniel Coit Gilman.* New York: Dodd, Mead, 1910.

French, John C. *A History of the University Founded by Johns Hopkins.* Baltimore: Johns Hopkins University Press, 1946.

Furner, Mary O. *Advocacy and Objectivity: A Crisis in the Professionalization of American Social Science, 1865–1905.* Lexington: University of Kentucky Press, 1975.

Gavin, Donald P. *The National Conference of Catholic Charities: 1910–1960.* Milwaukee: Catholic Life Publications, 1962.

Ghent, Jocelyn M., and Jaher, Frederic C. "The Chicago Business Elite: A Collective Biography." *Business History Review* 50 (1976): 288–328.

Ginger, Ray. *Altgeld's America: The Lincoln Ideal versus Changing Realities.* New York: Funk and Wagnalls, 1958.

Goodspeed, Thomas W. *A History of the University of Chicago: The First Quarter Century.* Chicago: University of Chicago Press, 1916.

————. *William Rainey Harper: First President of the University of Chicago.* Chicago: University of Chicago Press, 1928.

Gould, Joseph E. *The Chautauqua Movement: An Episode in the Continuing American Revolution.* Albany: State University of New York Press, 1961.

Grossman, David M. "Professors and Public Service, 1885–1925: A Chapter in the Professionalization of the Social Sciences." Ph.D. dissertation, Washington University, 1973.

Gruber, Carol S. *Mars and Minerva: World War I and the Uses of the Higher Learning in America.* Baton Rouge: Louisiana State University Press, 1975.

Haber, Samuel. *Efficiency and Uplift: Scientific Management in the Progressive Era, 1890–1920.* Chicago and London: University of Chicago Press, 1964.

Halleck, Seymour. "American Psychiatry and the Criminal: A Historical Review." *American Journal of Psychiatry* 121 (1965): i–xxi.

Haller, Mark H. "Civic Reformers and Police Leadership: Chicago, 1905–1935." In *Police in Urban Society*, edited by Harlan Hahn. Beverly Hills and London: Sage Publications, 1971.

————. *Eugenics: Hereditarian Attitudes in American Thought.* New Brunswick, N.J.: Rutgers University Press, 1963.

————. "Theories of Criminal Violence and Their Impact on the Criminal Justice System." In *Crimes of Violence: A Staff Report Submitted to the National Commission on the Causes and Prevention of Violence.* Vol. 13. Washington, D.C.: Government Printing Office, 1969.

————. "Urban Crime and Criminal Justice: The Chicago Case." *Journal of American History* 57 (1970): 619–35.

Hammevitch, Maurice B. "History of the Movement for Compulsory Health Insurance in the United States." *Social Service Review* 27 (1953): 281–99.

Harder, Werner Paul. *The Emergence of a Profession: Social Work Education in Chicago, 1903–1920.* Chicago: University of Chicago School of Social Service Administration, 1976.

Harter, Lafayette G., Jr. *John R. Commons: His Assault on Laissez-Faire.* Corvallis: Oregon State University Press, 1962.

Haskell, Thomas L. *The Emergence of Professional Social Science: The American Social Science Association and the Nineteenth-Century Crisis of Authority.* Urbana: University of Illinois Press, 1977.

Hawes, Joseph M. *Children in Urban Society: Juvenile Delinquency in Nineteenth-Century America.* New York: Oxford University Press, 1971.

Hawkins, Hugh. *Between Harvard and America: The Educational Leadership of Charles W. Eliot.* New York: Oxford University Press, 1972.

————. *Pioneer: A History of the Johns Hopkins University, 1874–1889.* Ithaca, N.Y.: Cornell University Press, 1960.

Hayes, Edward C. "Albion Woodbury Small." In *American Masters of Social Science*, edited by Howard W. Odum. New York: Henry Holt, 1927.

Hays, Samuel P. "The Politics of Reform in Municipal Government in the Progressive Era." *Pacific Northwest Quarterly* 55 (1964): 157–69.

Heaton, Herbert. *A Scholar in Action: Edwin F. Gay.* Cambridge: Harvard University Press, 1952.

Heffron, Ida C. *Francis Wayland Parker: An Interpretive Biography.* Los Angeles: Ivan Deach, Jr., 1934.

"Henderson, Charles Richmond." *The Encyclopedia of Social Work.* 16th issue. New York: National Association of Social Work, 1971. 1:579–81.

Herbst, Jergen. "Francis Greenwood Peabody: Harvard's Theologian of the Social Gospel." *Harvard Theological Review* 54 (1961): 45–69.

Herrick, Mary J. *The Chicago Schools: A Social and Political History.* Beverly Hills and London: Sage Publications, 1971.

Hirshfeld, Charles. *Baltimore, 1870–1900: Studies in Social History.* Baltimore: Johns Hopkins University Press, 1941.

Hoffman, George C. "Big Bill Thompson, His Mayoral Campaigns and Voting Strength." Ph.D. dissertation, University of Chicago, 1956.

Hofstadter, Richard. *Academic Freedom in the Age of the College.* New York: Columbia University Press, 1961.

Horowitz, Helen L. *Culture and the City: Cultural Philanthropy in Chicago from the 1880s to 1917.* Lexington: University of Kentucky Press, 1976.

Hoxie, R. Gordon. *A History of the Faculty of Political Science, Columbia University.* New York: Columbia University Press, 1955.

Hoyt, Homer. *One Hundred Years of Land Values in Chicago: The Relationship of the Growth of Chicago to the Rise in Its Land Values, 1830–1933.* Chicago: University of Chicago Press, 1933.

Israel, Jerry, ed. *Building the Organizational Society: Essays on Associational Activities in Modern America.* New York: Free Press, 1972.

Jackson, J. A., ed. *Professions and Professionalization.* Cambridge: Cambridge University Press, 1970.

Janowitz, Morris, ed. *W. I. Thomas on Social Organization and Social Personality.* Chicago and London: University of Chicago Press, 1966.

Joeckel, Carleton B., and Carnovsky, Leon. *A Metropolitan Library in Action: A Survey of the Chicago Public Library.* Chicago: University of Chicago Press, 1940.

Johnson, Claudius O. *Carter Henry Harrison I.* Chicago: University of Chicago Press, 1928.

Karl, Barry D. *Charles E. Merriam and the Study of Politics.* Chicago and London: University of Chicago Press, 1974.

———. *Executive Reorganization and Reform in the New Deal: The Genesis of Administrative Management, 1900–1919.* Cambridge: Harvard University Press, 1963.

———. "Presidential Planning and Social Science Research: Mr. Hoover's Experts." *Perspectives in American History* 3 (1969): 347–409.

Kerr, Clark. *The Uses of the University.* Cambridge: Harvard University Press, 1964.

———. "What We Might Learn from the Climacteric." *Daedalus* 104 (1975): 1–7.

Kevles, Daniel J. *The Physicists: The History of a Scientific Community in Modern America*. New York: Alfred A. Knopf, 1978.

King, Hoyt. *Citizen Cole of Chicago*. Chicago: Horder's, Inc., 1931.

Kraditor, Aileen S. *The Ideas of the Woman Suffrage Movement, 1890–1920*. New York: Columbia University Press, 1965.

Kraines, Oscar. *The World and Ideas of Ernst Freund: The Search for General Principles of Legislation and Administrative Law*. University, Ala.: University of Alabama Press, 1974.

Larson, Magoli S. *The Rise of Professionalism: A Sociological Analysis*. Berkeley and Los Angeles: University of California Press, 1977.

Levine, Daniel. *Varieties of Reform Thought*. Madison: State Historical Society of Wisconsin, 1964.

Lewis, Lloyd, and Smith, Henry Justin. *Chicago: The History of Its Reputation*. New York: Harcourt, Brace, 1929.

Lippmann, Walter. *A Preface to Politics*. New York: Mitchell Kennerley, 1914.

Loucks, Vernon R. *James Alton James: A Short Biography*. Evanston: Northwestern University Press, 1963.

Lubove, Roy. *The Professional Altruist: The Emergence of Social Work as a Career*. New York: Atheneum, 1965.

———. "The Progressive and the Prostitute." *Historian* 24 (1962): 308–30.

———. *The Struggle for Social Security, 1900–1935*. Cambridge, Mass.: Harvard University Press, 1968.

———. *Twentieth-Century Pittsburgh: Government Business and Environmental Change*. New York: John Wiley, 1969.

Lynn, Kenneth S., and the editors of *Daedalus*, eds. *The Professions in America*. Boston: Houghton Mifflin, 1965.

Lyons, Gene M. *The Uneasy Partnership: Social Science and the Federal Government in the Twentieth Century*. New York: Russell Sage Foundation, 1969.

Mann, Arthur. *Yankee Reformers in the Urban Age: Social Reform in Boston, 1880–1900*. Cambridge, Mass.: Harvard University Press, 1954.

Mannheim, Hermann, ed. *Pioneers in Criminology*. 2d ed. Montclair, N.J.: Patterson, Smith, 1972.

Mayhew, Katherine, and Edwards, Anna. *The Dewey School*. New York: D. Appleton-Century Company, 1936.

McArthur, Benjamin. "The Chicago Playground Movement: A Neglected Feature of Social Justice." *Social Service Review* 49 (1975): 376–93.

McCarthy, Michael P. "Chicago, the Annexation Movement, and Progressive Reform." In *The Age of Urban Reform: New Perspectives on the Progressive Era*, edited by Michael H. Ebner and Eugene M. Tobin. Port Washington, N.Y.: Kennikat Press, 1977.

McCaul, Robert L. "Dewey's Chicago." *School Review* 67 (1959): 258–80.

McManis, John T. *Ella Flagg Young and a Half Century of the Chicago Public Schools*. Chicago: A. C. McClurg, 1916.

Merton, Robert K. *Some Thoughts on the Professions in American Society*.

Brown University Papers, no. 37. Providence, R.I.: Brown University, 1960.
Metzger, Walter P. *Academic Freedom in the Age of the University*. New York: Columbia University Press, 1955.
Millspaugh, Arthur. *Crime Control by the National Government*. New York: DaCapo Press, 1972.
Mooney, James E. *John Graham Brooks: Prophet of Social Justice*. Worcester, Mass.: Privately printed, 1968.
Moore, Wilbert E., and Rosenblum, Gerald. *The Professions: Roles and Rules*. New York: Russell Sage Foundation, 1970.
Morison, Samuel E., ed. *The Development of Harvard University since the Inauguration of President Eliot, 1869–1929*. Cambridge, Mass.: Harvard University Press, 1930.
Morrison, Theodore. *Chautauqua: A Center for Education, Religion, and the Arts in America*. Chicago and London: University of Chicago Press, 1974.
Munger, Frank J., and Fenno, Richard F., Jr. *National Politics and Federal Aid to Education*. Syracuse, N.Y.: Syracuse University Press, 1962.
Nelson, Daniel. *Unemployment Insurance: The American Experience, 1915–1935*. Madison: University of Wisconsin Press, 1969.
Numbers, Ronald L. *Almost Persuaded: American Physicians and Compulsory Health Insurance, 1912–1920*. Baltimore: Johns Hopkins University Press, 1978.
Packer, Herbert L., and Ehrlich, Thomas. *New Directions in Legal Education*. New York: McGraw-Hill, 1972.
Page, Charles H. *Class and American Sociology: From Ward to Ross*. New York: Dial Press, 1940.
Parker, Alfred. *Crime Fighter: August Vollmer*. New York: Macmillan, 1961.
Parsons, Talcott. "Professions." *The International Encyclopedia of the Social Sciences*, 12:536. Edited by David L. Sills. New York: Macmillan, 1968.
Peisch, Mark L. *The Chicago School of Architecture*. New York: Random House, 1964.
Pierce, Bessie L. *A History of Chicago*. 3 vols. New York: Knopf, 1937, 1940, 1957.
Platt, Anthony. *The Child Savers: The Invention of Delinquency*. Chicago and London: University of Chicago Press, 1969.
Pound, Roscoe. *The Lawyer from Antiquity to Modern Times*. St. Paul, Minn.: West Publishing, 1953.
Rader, Benjamin G. *The Academic Mind and Reform: The Influence of Richard T. Ely in American Life*. Lexington: University of Kentucky Press, 1966.
Reckless, Walter C. *Vice in Chicago*. Chicago: University of Chicago Press, 1933.
Reeves, Floyd W. *University Extension Services*. The University of Chicago Survey, vol. 8. Chicago: University of Chicago Press, 1933.
Reller, Theodore. *The Development of the City Superintendency of Schools in the United States*. Philadelphia: Privately printed, 1935.
Roberts, Sidney J. "The Municipal Voters' League and Chicago's Boodlers."

Journal of the Illinois State Historical Society 53 (1960): 117–48.

Ross, Dorothy. *G. Stanley Hall: The Psychologist as Prophet.* Chicago and London: University of Chicago Press, 1972.

Rothstein, William. *American Physicians in the Nineteenth Century.* Baltimore: Johns Hopkins University Press, 1972.

Rucker, Darnell. *The Chicago Pragmatists.* Minneapolis: University of Minnesota Press, 1969.

Schiesl, Martin J. *The Politics of Efficiency: Municipal Administration and Reform in America, 1800–1920.* Berkeley and Los Angeles: University of California Press, 1977.

Schlossman, Steven L. *Love and the American Delinquent: The Theory and Practice of "Progressive" Juvenile Justice, 1825–1920.* Chicago and London: University of Chicago Press, 1977.

Scott, Mel. *American City Planning since 1890.* Berkeley and Los Angeles: University of California Press, 1969.

Sedlack, Michael. "The Emergence and Development of Collegiate Business Education in the United States, 1881–1974: Northwestern University as a Case Study." Ph.D. dissertation, Northwestern University, 1977.

Sinclair, Andrew. *The Emancipation of the American Woman.* New York: Harper and Row, 1966.

Somit, Albert, and Tanenhaus, Joseph. *The Development of American Political Science: From Burgess to Behavioralism.* Boston: Allyn and Bacon, 1967.

Steadman, Robert F. *Public Health Organization in the Chicago Region.* Chicago: University of Chicago Press, 1930.

Storr, Richard J. *Harper's University: The Beginnings.* Chicago and London: University of Chicago Press, 1966.

Strauss, Anselm, ed. *George Herbert Mead on Social Psychology: Selected Papers.* Chicago and London: University of Chicago Press, 1964.

Strickland, Arvarh E. *History of the Chicago Urban League.* Urbana and London: University of Illinois Press, 1966.

Sunderland, Edson R. *A History of the American Bar Association and Its Work,* [Ann Arbor?]: Privately printed, 1953.

Sutherland, Douglas. *Fifty Years on the Civic Front.* Chicago: Civic Federation, 1943.

Swanson, Richard A. "Edmund J. James, 1885–1925." Ph.D. dissertation, University of Illinois, 1966.

Tarr, Joel Arthur. *A Study in Boss Politics: William Lorimer of Chicago.* Urbana: University of Illinois Press, 1971.

Taylor, Lloyd C., Jr. *The Medical Profession and Social Reform, 1885–1945.* New York: Saint Martin's Press, 1974.

Thomas, Richard H. "Jenkin Lloyd Jones: Lincoln's Soldier of Righteousness." Ph.D. dissertation, Rutgers University, 1967.

Tocqueville, Alexis de. *Democracy in America.* Edited by Phillips Bradley. New York: Alfred A. Knopf, 1945.

Tyack, David B. *The One Best System: A History of American Urban Educa-*

tion. Cambridge, Mass.: Harvard University Press, 1974.

Veysey, Laurence R. *The Emergence of the American University*. Chicago: University of Chicago Press, 1965.

Wade, Louise C. *Graham Taylor: Pioneer for Social Justice, 1851–1938*. Chicago and London: University of Chicago Press, 1964.

Waldrop, Frank C. *McCormick of Chicago: An Unconventional Portrait of a Controversial Figure*. Englewood Cliffs, N.J.: Prentice Hall, 1966.

Walker, Samuel. *A Critical History of Police Reform: The Emergence of Professionalism*. Lexington, Mass.: Lexington Books, 1977.

Walsh, Winifred. "Grace Abbott and Social Action, 1934–1939." Ph.D. dissertation, University of Chicago, 1965.

Ward, Estelle F. *The Story of Northwestern University*. New York: Dodd, Mead, 1924.

Warren, Charles. *A History of the American Bar*. Boston: Little, Brown, 1911.

Waskow, Arthur I. *From Race Riot to Sit-In: 1919 and the 1960s*. Garden City, N.Y.: Doubleday, 1966.

Wendt, Lloyd, and Kogen, Herman. *Big Bill of Chicago*. Indianapolis and New York: Bobbs-Merrill, 1953.

———. *Bosses in Lusty Chicago: The Story of Bathhouse John and Hinky Dink*. Bloomington and London: Indiana University Press, 1967.

Werner, M. R. *Julius Rosenwald: The Life of a Practical Humanitarian*. New York and London: Harper, 1939.

Whittemore, Richard. *Nicholas Murray Butler and Public Education, 1862–1911*. New York: Teachers College Press, 1970.

Wiebe, Robert H. *The Search for Order, 1877–1920*. New York: Hill and Wang, 1967.

Williamson, Harold F., and Wild, Payson S. *Northwestern University: A History, 1850–1975*. Evanston, Ill.: Northwestern University, 1976.

Wirth, Arthur G. *John Dewey as Educator: His Design for Work in Education, 1894–1904*. New York: John Wiley and Sons, 1966.

Wirth, Louis. "Urbanism as a Way of Life." *American Journal of Sociology* 44 (1938): 1–24.

Wood, Mary I. *History of the General Federation of Woman's Clubs*. New York: General Federation of Woman's Clubs, [1912].

Wright, Helen R. "Three against Time: Edith and Grace Abbott and Sophonisba P. Breckinridge." *Social Service Review* 28 (1954): 41–53.

Index